Japan at the Summit

Its Role in the Western Alliance and
in Asian Pacific Co-operation

Japan at the Summit

Its Role in the Western Alliance and in Asian Pacific Co-operation

Shiro Saito

R

ROUTLEDGE
London and New York
for
THE ROYAL INSTITUTE OF INTERNATIONAL AFFAIRS
London

First published 1990
by Routledge
11 New Fetter Lane, London EC4P 4EE

Simultaneously published in the USA and Canada
by Routledge
a division of Routledge, Chapman and Hall, Inc.
29 West 35th Street, New York, NY 10001

Phototypeset in 10pt Times by
Mews Photosetting, Beckenham, Kent
Printed and bound in Great Britain by
Biddles Ltd, Guildford and King's Lynn

British Library Cataloguing in Publication Data

Saito, Shiro
    Japan at the Summit : its role in the Western
    Alliance and in Asian Pacific cooperation.
    1. Japan. Foreign relations. Policies of government,
    history
    I. Title
    327.52
    ISBN 0-415-04271-2

Library of Congress Cataloging in Publication Data

Saitō, Shirō, 1929–
        Japan at the summit: Japan's role in the western alliance and
    Asian Pacific cooperation / Shiro Saito.
            p.   cm.
        Bibliography: p.
        Includes index.
        ISBN 0-415-04271-2
        1. Japan – Foreign relations – 1945–   2. World politics – 1945–
    3. Summit meetings. I. Title.
    DS889.5.S25   1990
    327.52–dc20   89–10357
                                                                              CIP

The Royal Institute of International Affairs is an independent body which promotes the rigorous study of international questions and does not express opinions of its own. The opinions expressed in this publication are the responsibility of the author.

Contents

Tables

Preface

Japan is today in the middle of revolutionary changes in terms both of its internal structure and of its external environment. The 'risen yen' symbolizes developments which affect almost the whole fabric of Japanese economic life as well as the world's trade and business transactions. Just as Japan has been the greatest beneficiary of the US-led GATT/Bretton Woods system, it will also be the hardest hit by that system's declining efficacy. In spite of calls for a new framework of Pacific co-operation as an alternative to the weakening Bretton Woods system, the issues of leadership and structure for such a system remain a key stumbling-block.

The shift in the economic balance of power does not result in an automatic transfer of leadership in the political and security spheres. In the Western alliance system, the United States still intends to perform the supreme role in the global strategic context, despite its relative decline in economic strength. Europe tends to assume an independent political leadership, but with no global strategic role in its perception. By contrast, Japan's economic and financial supremacy has hardly been translated into any politico-strategic power.

Japan now needs to redefine its perception of itself, which stems from its geopolitical circumstances, historical experiences, and domestic ruling pattern, in accordance with its changing status in the world order. The hazards of undertaking a study of the basic issues are indeed formidable. Yet it is precisely at this point of transition that the effort should be made. This book is one such endeavour.

Perhaps a few words are needed to explain my title, *Japan at the Summit*. Based on an idea first suggested by Professor Ronald Dore, it was conceived with two implications: first, Japan as an actor in the annual summit meetings of the seven major industrial powers; and, second, Japan as having climbed to the top of the economic ladder of world prestige. Both positions require the Japanese to learn how to attain a proper equilibrium so as to avoid the pitfalls and dangers of a hierarchical relationship not only with the West but also with their Asian neighbours, which is one of the main themes of this book.

Preface

The initial research for the book was undertaken during my assignment as a Visiting Research Fellow at the Royal Institute of International Affairs (Chatham House) in London in 1984–5. That year provided me with the opportunity to attempt to sum up my experiences over the past years, spent mainly in Western Europe and South-east Asia. My appreciation goes, first, to the Director of Chatham House, Sir James Eberle, and the Director of Studies, Dr William Wallace, who took the initiative to conduct this project. I hasten to add my gratitude to Hanabusa Masamichi, Shibusawa Masahide, and Yamamoto Tadashi, who used their good offices in arranging my attachment and who gave me generous support and encouragement. I am indebted to the Japan Foundation and the East-West Seminar, Tokyo, for valuable financial support.

In the course of the research work I was deeply indebted to the research and library staff of Chatham House, and to the members of a study group who met there: Sir Hugh Cortazzi, Mark Elliott, Enkyo Soichi, K. Kesavapany, Dr Michael Leifer, Dr Wolf Mendl, Oba Sadao, Ota Hajime, John Roper, Shigeta Hiroshi, Professor Shiratori Rei, Michael Smith, Professor Arthur Stockwin, Tokinoya Atsushi, Toriihara Masatoshi, Martin Uden, Nicolas Wolfers, HE Yamazaki Toshio, and many others who made valuable comments and criticisms. I owe a special debt to Nicholas Bayne, Professor Ronald Dore, Hasegawa Kazutoshi, Dr Jean-Pierre Lehmann, Motono Moriyuki, Professor Ian Nish, Professor Robert Putnam, and Satoh Yukio, who have given me valuable insights and information at one stage or another. I am very grateful to Professor Louis Allen, Professor Reinhard Drifte, Dr Wolf Mendl, Shibusawa Masahide, and Charles Smith for kindly reading and checking the manuscript. None of those mentioned bears any responsibility for its contents, conclusions, or shortcomings.

This book would never have been completed without the help of Dr Brian Bridges, whose editorial suggestions, as well as the organizational support he provided, were indispensable for the whole exercise. I also wish to express my warm thanks to Lucy MacDermot, Rosamund Howe, Helen Robins, Patricia Louison, and Jean Hodges for their work on the text, and to Pauline Wickham for her attentive advice in preparing the book for publication. My wife, Etsuko, has provided patient support for the whole endeavour, in London as well as in Tokyo; the book is dedicated to her.

Saito Shiro

Note. Throughout this book, Japanese names are given in their original order, with the family name first and the personal name second. However, for bibliographical convenience, the author's name has been westernized on the jacket and title-page.

Chapter one

Introduction

In December 1987 the new Japanese Prime Minister, Takeshita Noboru, made his first overseas visit, to attend a meeting with the leaders of the Association of South-East Asian Nations (ASEAN) in Manila; the following month he visited the United States to meet President Ronald Reagan. By the time he attended the Toronto summit in June 1988, he had also visited South Korea and Western Europe (twice within a month). These visits represented, both symbolically and practically, the two areas traditionally vital to Japan's national interest and international position: Asia and the West. In the Japanese perception, the two terms imply more than a geographical dimension, for they have existed as the basic framework of the historical pattern of the nation's foreign policy throughout the pre-war and post-war periods.

The history of modern Japan's external relations has proved to be a mixture of aloofness from and intervention in the continent of Asia, and both tendencies have coincided with its alignment with the Western powers. A seclusionist Tokugawa was forced by the Western powers to open the nation to the outside world, not by Asians, and Asian wars led Japan to alliances with the West. The Anglo-Japanese alliance (1902), which first truly placed Japan in the international system against the background of the power balance in the Asian theatre, was replaced by the Four-Power Treaty (1921) and the Nine-Power Treaty (1922) during the great-power rivalry over China. The signing of the Anti-Comintern Pact with Germany (1936) marked the beginning of Japan's relations with the Axis powers, and the Tripartite Pact between Germany, Italy, and Japan followed (1940). After the war Japan entered into the alliance with the United States.

Alongside these alliances with the West, Japan's political position in Asia was either interventionist or isolationist. There was no third position based upon a harmonious equal footing. If one compares Japan's Asian involvement before and after World War II, one can see a complete about-face in its conduct, from arrogance to low posture. Partly reinforced by fears of stirring up wartime memories in Asia, and partly as a result of being under the protection of the United States, Japan's self-image as an Asian nation, as well as a member of the Western world, has dictated low-profile policies in every sphere. Nevertheless, given the sharp contrast between political circumspection on the one hand and economic aggressiveness on the other, in both Asia and the West, Japan has been caught in an awkward position. How to overcome this ambiguity will be the most crucial issue for the future of Japan's overall Asia–West relations.

The objectives of this study are, therefore, to discover the relationship and interaction between Japan's policies across Asia and the West in the post-war world, and to look at the possibilities for a coherent strategy for balancing its interests in these broad areas. For Japan will not be able to integrate itself into the international community until it can articulate policy programmes that attempt to unite the various systems of the Asian and Western nations. Perhaps the term 'macro-diplomacy' would serve in this context – a coinage to denote the grasping together of the main forces at work in the various interrelated sectors of the nation's foreign policy. The final target of Japan's macro-diplomacy is twofold; first, to reconcile different overarching geopolitical interests in East Asia and the West; and, second, to assume the political role usually incumbent upon an economic power.

Inevitably, with such a vast theme, the issues have to be dealt with selectively; it is impossible to cover all aspects of Japan–Asia and Japan–West relations. This book therefore focuses on two key areas of the inter-relationship: dialogue with Japan's Asian partners through the vehicle of the annual ministerial meetings of ASEAN, and Japan's involvement in Western affairs through its participation in the seven-power economic and political summits. A futher word on the framework of the study is needed.

The conventional analysis of Asia divides the continent into regions, such as East Asia, with its sub-regions of North-east and South-east on the periphery of continental China, and South Asia, extending to the Indian subcontinent. A current concept of Asia is an open-ended one, identifying sea-oriented countries under the heading the 'Asian Pacific' or 'Pacific Asian' region. In these terms the Soviet Union cannot be ignored. The problem here is that the conventional definitions obscure the evolving realities in regional affairs on the one hand, and also lead to a certain duplication of old constituencies on the other. Moreover, the perceptual focus of the pivotal region has been shifting over the years and differs from country to country. Thus, in the post-war period, Japan's primary concern with Asia has been increasingly the rimland of the western Pacific, whereas pre-war Japan often saw Asia as centred on heartland China. One of the main emphases of this study is to explore Japan's relations with the Western Pacific region, including Australia and New Zealand, which may be assumed to be a viable entity linked by seas rather than by land.

As regards 'the West', there is no difficulty about defining it in terms of international politics and the world economy centred on East–West relations. The Western alliance, including Japan, can be clearly identified as a system by its political, economic, and security ties, and it is in this context that Japan is a member of the Western world. Yet, although Japan's relations with the West have been more stable in the post-war period than they were in the pre-war one, there is not total symmetry in the trilateral relationship between North America, Western Europe, and Japan. From the Japanese perspective, the ties with the United States are predominant, especially in terms of the security relationship. Similarly, there is a certain divergence between the policies of the United States and those of the West European countries towards Japan and Asia. The framework of Japan–West relations should, therefore, be set forth in a plural context, and this study endeavours to draw out in particular how the Euro-Japanese relationship fits into the broader Japan–West–East Asia relationship.

The question of Japan's position, respectively, in Asia and the West, as well as its place between the two, is still a constant preoccupation in domestic and foreign-policy circles. Ever since the appearance of an influential essay 'Quit Asia, enter Europe' in the Meiji era, a basic cleavage within national opinion has remained, between the 'Asianists' and those whose priority is the West. To say that Japan's position in Asia and in relation to the Western industrial world resembles that of Britain towards continental Europe and the United States has become axiomatic: both are part of each, but not fully on either side. Japan's place, however, is more detached than Britain's, because Japan's modernization process differed from that of any other country, whereas Britain was part of the mainstream of the world's industrialization from the beginning. 'The very facts of Japanese development have set this nation apart,' an American scholar has observed, with the result that 'it is, but not fully, in Asia. Its problems, as well as its progress, align it naturally with the advanced West, and particularly with the United States, yet the sense of mutual identification on both sides is significantly weaker than one might presume.'[1]

Apart from such considerations, Japan's cultural proclivities for separateness have worked against its becoming a full member of the international community. As a British writer put it: 'The country of the rising sun does not see itself as one nation-state among a lot of others. They are still acting as part of a separate civilization consciously measuring themselves against the Western world.'[2] Another comment made from a different angle: 'The Japanese still view international as well as interpersonal relations in hierarchical terms, and a relationship of equality is difficult for the Japanese.'[3] The former Chancellor of West Germany, Helmut Schmidt, expressed his views in the following strong terms:

The source of possible future tensions lies in the fact that Japan does not enjoy close relations with her Far East and Southeast Asian regions. Relations with China, with all the ASEAN countries and with Korea and Taiwan are normal, but there is no relationship comparable to the conference of the states within the European Community or between the European states on the one hand and the North American states on the other. . . . The Japanese do not seem to be seeking closer friendship with other nations. This insularity may be part of the historic heritage of the long Tokugawa self-isolation; but it has been pursued also in this century.[4]

Some Japanese themselves also admit to 'self-isolation' and argue that 'the dichotomy between the West and Asia continued to be a problem, and Japan remained a loner, not really part of any international system'.[5] But such a dichotomy does not rule out a positive diplomatic stance aimed at achieving a balance between policies designed for the Asian region and those geared to the Western world. Parallel to the cleavage between the Asianists and the Westernizers, there has been a school of thought persistently advocating an independent position which is capable of initiating compatible policies in both directions. Thus, in an article written in 1964, the Japanese Foreign Minister, Ohira Masayoshi, declared:

Japan is a sea-faring nation as a result of her geographical position northeast of the Asiatic continent. So, she is inseparably bound in friendship to our neighbour nations of the continent and to the countries of Southeast Asia. At the same time, we maintain friendly relations with Britain and other European countries as well as with the United States of America. . . . It can be said that for most countries of Asia, the facts of Japan's existence as a free democracy, and her position in the rank of the world's advanced industrial nations, encourage them to give her their trust and reliance and so increase their sense of security. We are convinced that only by a firm adherence to the free world and by a vigorous pursuance of her present policy in Asia can Japan contribute to the stabilization of the Asian region and promote the cause of true world peace.[6]

As is so well expressed in this statement, the very fact of Japan's ambivalent position makes it imperative that it should find a way of using its economic power in the cause of regional prosperity and stability. As will be shown in subsequent chapters, one of the underlying motivations of Japanese foreign policy has been a 'twin-track' diplomacy: one that combines the two principles of the 'ambivalent state', which is both a nation in Asia and a member of the Western world.

At the end of the occupation, Japan turned away from the continent of Asia and away from China, which had been one of its most important pre-war markets, and looked towards the United States and South-east Asia for its trading partners. This was a natural consequence of the changed Asian situation, in which the United States – in the wake of the victory of communism in China and the outbreak of the Korean war – needed Japan's help in stabilizing the Western Pacific region through increasing trade and commerce. In return, Japan was allowed to join, as a donor nation, the Colombo Plan (1950–1), set up by British Commonwealth countries and joined by the United States in South and South-east Asia. There were at this time strong arguments between the Japanese government (Prime Minister Yoshida Shigeru) and Washington about whether the Japanese and South-east Asian economies were complementary in terms of trade and investment, thus making possible long-range economic integration in the region. Launching the bold idea of a kind of 'Marshall Plan for Asia', the Japanese government invited a funding contribution from Washington, and suggested that the Colombo Plan become the organizational focus for a regional development. Although nothing came of this idea at the time, subsequent developments in the mid-1960s led to the positive pursuit of Japan's economic diplomacy.

These early experiences in successful economic diplomacy determined the emphasis in Japanese external relations on South-east Asia – in order to demonstrate Japan's importance as a nation in Asia. Just about all post-war Japanese Prime Ministers (from Yoshida to Takeshita) tried to draw US attention to East and South-east Asia when they visited Washington. They adopted a similar policy for Western Europe, as evidenced by the participation in the Colombo Plan through extending development assistance, and then the admission to the Organization for Economic Co-operation and Development (OECD) on the premiss of joining the Development Aid Committee (DAC). The blurred dichotomy in a 'macro-diplomacy' rendered obsolete the argument of 'Quit Asia, enter Europe' which had carried weight since the Meiji era. Thus, although the policies pursued for greater interdependence between Japan and the Western industrial nations are closely bound up with those of the Asian states, especially the non-communist countries, Japan's position in the structure is asymmetrical: economically, it belongs much more to the US-led Western industrial world than to Asia, to which it is affiliated geographically and culturally; and, in terms of politico-security, it depends most on the US system in the western Pacific. On all counts, it leans lopsidedly towards the other side of the Pacific.

Being caught in such an asymmetrical structure, Japan should aim to transform its relationship with the United States into a more open one, so as to broaden its relations with the Asian and European countries. Unless it does so, it will hardly be perceived as an independent partner in any dialogue with Europeans and Asians. Only by direct or plural diplomatic channels with other countries, and by easing strains due to the special relationship with the United States, can Japan pursue a coherent foreign policy. It is precisely in this context that the present study examines Japan's position in the now routine annual discussions of the Western summit meetings and the ASEAN dialogue.

The gradual transformation of Japan's foreign relations reached a watershed towards the end of the 1970s and the beginning of the 1980s, when the world political climate changed suddenly with the deterioration in East–West relations which accompanied the crises in Afghanistan, Cambodia, Iran, and Poland as well as in the international economy. Japan's response to these developments brought out the common interests and concerns not only with the United States but also with the West European and South-east Asian nations. Although there has been some divergence of interests between Japanese and West European governments, there has been an intensification of mutual contacts and official consultations covering developments in the Middle East, Africa, Eastern Europe, and the Soviet Union. Through these interactions Japan and Western Europe have become involved for the first time in the post-war period in foreign and security policy co-ordination on a global scale. The crisis in Cambodia, particularly with the refugee problem, has also brought out the common interests of the Japanese, US, West European, and ASEAN governments.

Through the meetings of the Western summits and of ASEAN the Japanese government began to share responsibilities and to assume a role in the solution of international political conflicts. After their inception in 1975 the main focus of discussion at the seven-power Western summits had been on the world economy. However, from the turn of the decade onwards, the summits shifted emphasis from economics to politics, against the backdrop of heightened international tension. The same can be said for the meetings of ASEAN, which was originally intended to be an economic co-operative body. As a regular member of the Western summits, and a leading dialogue partner of ASEAN, Japan could no longer preserve its insularity.

Of course, economic questions have not ceased to be a central item on the agenda of the summits. Japan has taken part actively in discussions on the macro-economic policy co-ordination of the Western industrial democracies, on international monetary matters, on energy problems and, finally, on North–South economic issues. Indeed, in this last subject-area, it has tended to speak on behalf of the developing countries.

Whereas a co-operative relationship has evolved in the dialogue over political and security policy between Japan, the West, and non-communist Asia, a somewhat antagonistic element predominates in their economic relations. The trade imbalances resulting from unfavourable competition with Japan, not only in world markets but also in domestic markets, have often generated a frustration on the part of the West and of Asia. In short, Japan's involvement both in the Western summits and in the ASEAN dialogue has turned out to be most fruitful as regards the broadening of its foreign policy. However, it remains to be seen whether the asymmetry between Japanese relations with the United States and with other partners in the West and Asia, and between its character of economic giant and political dwarf, has been, or will be, duly rectified. Although the Japanese government has stepped into international politics and dealt with security matters on various stages, American influence over Japan's policies still predominates. Moreover, economic friction and trade disputes seem, in some strange way, to reinforce interdependence or mutual reliance between the two countries. And as long as Japan relies upon US leadership in security and political matters, there can be little prospect of an independent foreign-policy stance.

Nevertheless, there is a growing demand for Japan, as the world's largest creditor nation, with a huge balance of payments surplus, to play a more prominent role in international affairs. Some Japanese now argue that the relative decline of US hegemony offers Japan new opportunities in the management of global issues. Yet, for Japan, which has gained a pre-eminent status within a relatively short period, it is still hard to conceive of exerting real international political leadership. Even so, Japan has reached the summit and must behave accordingly.

This study consists of three parts. Part I is an outline of the main trends in Japan's post-war foreign policy, and attempts to pull together the differing approaches of successive Prime Ministers as they tried to reconcile the dichotomy of Japanese diplomacy towards Asian neighbours and Western allies. Part II examines aspects of the transformation of the interdependent trilateral relationship of the countries of North America, Western Europe, and Japan. Particular attention is paid to Japan's role in the Western summits; the survey focuses on the period since 1979, when the summits took on a broader political dimension. The final section, Part III, concentrates on the so-called 'ASEAN dialogues', which have been conducted by the ASEAN nations with such external partners as the United States, Japan, Canada, Australia, New Zealand, and the European Community since the late 1970s. The dialogues are interesting both historically and ideologically: historically, in that the six ASEAN countries are closely associated with both Japan and the West; ideologically, because of their free-enterprise system and also because of their moderating position in international society.

Particular emphasis is given to Pacific co-operation, a topic which has attracted much attention in recent years. A concluding chapter attempts to draw the various threads together and to suggest areas for policy development.

Part I

Japan in the Post-war World

Chapter two

A Departure from the Old Order

Much of the literature on Japan's post-war foreign relations has been about Japan's search for a role, on the assumption that it has lacked one. According to one observer, however, the Japanese are now finding that they have always had a role and have seemed to accept it because they lacked the consensus for an alternative.[1] For years the denial of its existence inhibited Japan's participation in the international community. Now, perhaps, a more positive attitude is about to emerge.

Political abdication and economic resurgence

By the time that Japan returned to its place in international society in 1952, under the terms of the San Francisco peace treaty, the political and economic maps of East Asia and the western Pacific had been completely redrawn. After World War II the old pattern of power in the region had been altered by the cold war, and by fierce struggles between the superpowers for spheres of influence. Politically, Japan, the wartime loser, was excluded from such competition. Economically, its problems were compounded by the failure of its 'co-prosperity policy' for East Asia, and by the loss of its pre-war empire. Devastated by war, only hard work and good fortune could ensure its survival. The emergence of the People's Republic of China in 1949 and the outbreak of the Korean war (1950–3) further bipolarized the East Asian region. With the 1951 San Francisco treaty, it was hoped that the menace from rising Asian communism could be stemmed and US containment policy in Asia implemented. As for Japan, its dependence on American protection and leadership forced its abdication from international politics – a considerable departure from its pre-war status in the world.

Alongside the superpowers' contest in East Asia, another kind of power competition between the old forces of colonial rule and the new forces of national independence resulted in a profound political transformation in South-east Asia – the *nampo* (as the Japanese used to call the 'southern regions'). The new nationalist movements that emerged after World War II demanded, and won, independence from their former colonial masters – Britain, France, and the Netherlands. By the mid-1950s, Europe – like Japan – was no longer present as a power in Asia.

Under these circumstances, Japan's initial position in the post-war period came to be defined as a 'special' relationship with the United States. It was the closest and most intensive relationship in Japan's history, and implied a diminution of its traditional associations both with Asian and with West European countries. Europe's withdrawal from South-east Asia had inevitably led to fewer direct political and security contacts with Japan. Furthermore, Japan's abdication from Asian politics modified Euro-Japanese interactions there. Even so, the long-cultivated nexus between Japan and Asia, as well as earlier Euro-Japanese inter-relations in South-east Asia, could not be completely disregarded when Japan found itself returning to these areas for its economic survival.

Economic and trade relations in East Asia had likewise altered considerably, on the surface, from the pre-war pattern of more or less interconnected commercial and financial transactions to the post-war division into state-controlled or free-market economies. From the view-point of Japan's vital interests, the most serious situation appeared to be the poor prospects for trade with China. The 1949 communist revolution had placed the mainland market behind a bamboo curtain. As Table 1 shows, Japan's trade with China, which continued to be a substantial component of its foreign commerce until the end of the war, was rapidly superseded by trade with the United States immediately after the war, and then by trade with Western Europe after the Chinese communist revolution. Japan's trade access to the Chinese mainland became further complicated by the US embargo policy prohibiting the export of strategic materials to China, whose military intervention in the Korean war had clearly marked it out as an enemy of the West.

Table 1: Japan's main trading partners, 1939–54 (¥ million)

Year	China	Europe	United States
1939	2,462	357	1,644
1942	2,737	81	14
1945	1,226	3	22
1946	553	78	4,988
1949	16,685	19,788	207,544
1952	37,107	60,746	360,943
1954	50,793	65,757	407,268

Note. The figures refer to total trade of exports plus imports; 'Europe' means the UK, France, and Germany.
Source: International Historical Statistics, ed. B.R. Mitchell (Macmillan Press/Hara Shobo, Tokyo, 1984).

The Korean war had a further important effect on the general conditions surrounding Japanese trade. It broke out at the very moment when, as a result of the austerity policy to end post-war inflation, the Japanese economy was beginning to show an upward trend. The additional boost given by large-scale special procurement orders placed with Japan for commodities and supplies needed by the US-led United Nations forces fighting in Korea proved to be a turning-point in the country's economic resurgence.

The Japan–US–South-east Asia nexus

The boom brought about by the Korean war was bound to be temporary. The war could not guarantee a continuous source of dollar earnings, and neither could Japan's attempts at further external economic expansion. In fact the Japanese export trade went into decline soon after the cease-fire in Korea. It was under these circumstances that Japan's economic growth was tied to US economic and military programmes, and its external economic expansion diverted away from continental Asia – from China – towards a triangular integration with the United States and South-east Asia, under the new rubric 'US–Japan economic co-operation'.[2] The concept of economic co-operation was based on the US policy-makers' intention that Japan's industrial capacity and manpower should be mobilized fully to support the free world's military efforts in Asia. In view of the USA's containment policy and the strategic importance of South-east Asia under the threat from Soviet expansionism, the Japanese experience in the *nampo* before and during World War II was now considered a valuable asset which could be utilized by the Americans for the purpose of promoting political stability and economic prosperity in the region.

The revival of Japanese industry as a means of furthering the stability of South-east Asia received encouragement from another quarter as well. The British government regarded Japan's economic revival as essential to prevent domestic political chaos, and a healthy Japanese economy was seen by the Board of Trade and the Colonial Office as being in the interests of consumers in British territories in South-east Asia, since only Japan could satisfy the demand for cotton textiles and other goods at appropriate prices.[3] The Foreign Office, at first, was more cautious, and worried about the threat from Japanese competition to British exporting industries and the risk from Japan's strengthened position in buying raw materials.[4] Nevertheless, it had to accept the fact of a recovery in Japanese trade with South-east Asia, whether it liked it or not, in the interests of Anglo-American co-operation. It was hoped, therefore, that enhanced South-east Asian economic development would act as a deterrent to the spread of communism.[5] Thus Japan's post-war economic rehabilitation and the politico-strategic policy approach of the United States and Britain were an important ingredient in the Japan–US–South-east Asia nexus.

By the mid-1950s Japan's trade with South-east Asia had achieved a strong position, catching up with US and European trade. In both Indonesia and Thailand, Japan became a leading trade partner, while in the Philippines and Malaya the United States and Britain, the former metropolitan countries, continued to maintain their superior positions. These remarkable achievements were the result of vigorous trade promotion during the final phases of the occupation. Meanwhile the Japanese government continued to devote a great deal of its energies to exploring the possibilities of long-range economic integration with the United States and South-east Asia.

The 'US–Japan economic co-operation' scheme and the new bloc economy, however, could not be carried forward without tensions between the two countries.[6] The structure of combined economic and military co-operation was partially formalized under the Mutual Security Assistance (MSA) agreement concluded between Japan and the United States in 1954.[7] This was accompanied by the passing of two 'defence' laws on the Japanese side. But there existed a continuing disagreement about economic and military priorities, which first emerged in 1950–1 with Prime Minister Yoshida's outright opposition to the request of John Foster Dulles, the US envoy, for Japan's rearmament. On the blueprint drawn in Washington, 'economic co-operation' was inseparable from US military policies, and involved more than the two countries themselves, being an endeavour to create an anti-communist capitalist bloc in Asia. At this point Tokyo's sceptical appraisal of American policy grew stronger.

The 1954 MSA agreement exemplified the full symbiosis of US aid, trade, and military policies, for it placed agreement concerning such areas as foreign investment, purchase of US agricultural commodities, and 'triangular trade transactions' under the roof of an aid programme explicitly directed to the expansion of indigenous military forces. As a step in the definition of Japan's global policy, the MSA agreement clarified the Japan–US security relationship in the following three respects: Japan's indefinite dependence upon US grand strategy, Japan's economic as well as military commitment to containment and counter-revolution in Asia, and its commitment to incremental remilitarization. As a step towards the resolution of Japan's economic crisis, however, the new military arrangement was of dubious value, and, in the eyes of Prime Minister Yoshida and those close to him, Japan's place within the San Francisco system remained precarious. MSA was America's military response to Japan's request for economic assistance; the two defence laws were, in turn, Japan's qualified response to US pressure for remilitarization.[8]

It was after the MSA agreement that an ambivalent pattern of co-operation and conflict arose in the management of the San Francisco system. US pressure presented the Yoshida government with a crucial choice of priorities, between a military and an economic arrangement. The US suggestion had been that Japan should accept rearmament as a prior condition to the signing of the peace treaty. However, Japan's acceptance of MSA involved obligations difficult to fulfil, such as an increased defence capability and a limitation on trade with the communist bloc. Certainly, there were sections of government and business circles that responded enthusiastically to the suggested promotion of the defence industry, in that this might represent a welcome additional source of dollar earnings. But Prime Minister Yoshida's group resisted outright the pressures from the United States as well as those from the domestic sector. To invest vast sums of money in armaments, in Yoshida's eyes, would seriously retard Japan's economic recovery. Furthermore, it might well kindle suspicion and antagonism in neighbouring Asian countries. For these reasons, he resolutely opposed rearmament. As to the MSA obligations, he obtained the concession that promotion of a defence industry should rest upon the precondition of economic stability. Ultimately, Yoshida's go-slow policy on rearmament led to Washington's disavowal of his premiership. Yet the legacy survived, and the 'Yoshida doctrine' ensures him a place in history.[9]

Yoshida's 1954 world tour: a prototype

In the summer of 1954, after establishing the groundwork of Japan's new start in the post-war world, the Yoshida government was counting its final days. The Diet sessions were clouded by controversy over the defence and security issues relating to the MSA agreement, the enactment of the Self-defence Forces Law, and the introduction of a new policy system. The opposition, especially the extreme left of the Japan Socialist Party, resorted to violence to avert the passage of the police system legislation. The Conservatives eventually succeeded in passing these Bills, but the confusion in the Diet forced Prime Minister Yoshida to postpone his world tour, originally fixed for June. However, after the dust had settled, he was able to rearrange his itinerary and enjoy foreign travel in several Western countries for nearly eight weeks, from September to November.[10]

The original plan had been to start from North America, move on to Western Europe, and then go on to India, Pakistan, Thailand, and Singapore. The actual sequence was as follows: Canada first, then by sea to Europe – France, West Germany, Italy (including the Vatican), and the United Kingdom – and finally back across the Atlantic to the United States. The trip to the Asian countries was dropped completely.

Interestingly, the six countries which Yoshida visited in the mid-1950s were precisely those that joined together as dialogue partners in the Western economic summits in the mid-1970s.

The journey, the first of its kind since the war, was, for Yoshida, an affirmation that in global affairs Japan was fundamentally a 'Western' nation. He saw the trip as symbolizing strengthened bonds between Japan and the West. However, the journey generated no enthusiasm inside Japan, since Yoshida had by this time lost political and public support. Apparently, the government party simply regarded the tour as a stage in the process of the Premier's retirement, and the Socialists actually denounced it as unpatriotic because of the linkage with US policy in Asia, which appeared to stress military solutions.

In a political move calculated to meet the Japanese public's reservations about US Asian policy, Prime Minister Yoshida did in fact try to criticize the US-style confrontationalist approach to Asian problems. A position paper handed over to the British emphasized the 'Yoshida doctrine' by declaring that, in fighting communism, political and economic strength was as important as military might, if not more so.[11] As will be shown later, this statement was repeatedly stressed by the Yoshida mission, not only in the United States but also in Western Europe. Yoshida hoped that, before arriving in Washington, he might find support in European capitals to soften the rigidity of US policy towards Asia. British policy, for instance, was regarded as more pragmatic than US policy in dealing with Asian problems, especially as regards China. Furthermore, in general terms, Japanese opinion was strongly in favour of developing relations with European countries after the long interruption of war and the US occupation. 'The British and European response to this wish,' an article argued, 'implies no rivalry with America, for Japan's ties with the whole free world will grow stronger as it is brought back into wide international intercourse, instead of depending on a single power.'[12] Obviously, the European part of Yoshida's tour was as important as that on the other side of the Atlantic.

The China issue in Anglo-Japanese talks

In Ottawa, on the first leg of his journey, Yoshida met Malcolm MacDonald, the British Commissioner-General for South-east Asia, to discuss the issues of China and South-east Asia. According to the confidential report addressed to the Foreign Office from Ottawa, Yoshida's main concern was trade with China, which he regarded as vital to Japan's economic health. He believed that the long-term policy of the West should be to detach China from dependence on Russia, and so weaken the link between the two great communist powers. Better trading relations between Japan and China could help in this. The United

States might be opposed to such a policy, but Yoshida recognized that the British government shared his general aims, and he hoped the matter could be discussed further in London.[13]

Before reaching London, however, Yoshida met the leaders of France, West Germany, and Italy, and talked about the economic rehabilitation of post-war Europe as well as domestic and international issues. A common interest between Yoshida and such men as Pierre Mendès-France and Konrad Adenauer was how to deal with the communist world. Yoshida stressed the need for unifying the free world in order to counter the Soviet Union's divisive strategies against the West. He also repeated his pet theory about separating China from the Soviet Union during his talks with each leader. This 'Sino-Russian separation' policy seemed to attract a certain amount of attention from the European leaders, even though it lacked any concrete proposals. Vague as it was, however, Yoshida's cherished doctrine showed the gift of foresight, as history proved in the long run.

The British government had been well informed about the aims of Yoshida's journey and his hopes of the discussions in London. It had seen the MacDonald report, and it also received – from the Japanese ambassador, Matsumoto Shunichi – a copy of a comprehensive position paper entitled 'Japan and the United Kingdom'. The document referred to Japan's admission to the United Nations, general political issues, and security in the Pacific. The importance of Japan's role in the security of the western Pacific formed a central part of the document, and 'economic programmes' were linked with the collective security of Southeast Asia.[14] In the context of Japan's Asian policy, the document argued for social and economic stability as the alternative to a conventional military solution – a concept that could be seen as moving towards a comprehensive approach to security. Of course, the term 'comprehensive security' was not actually used in the 1954 position paper, but it was very much present as an idea, and was even more radical than the concept (to be discussed later) which developed in the late 1970s.

The Anglo-Japanese talks in London, in late October 1954, developed as anticipated. At dinner the two Prime Ministers, Yoshida and Winston Churchill, discussed China, focusing primarily on the likelihood of China being separated from the Soviet Union. Yoshida argued that this might be achieved if China's trade were opened to the West. He said that he would put this viewpoint to the US government when he visited Washington, and he hoped for the British government's support. Churchill expressed sympathy with the general aim.

Before this, China had also been the focus of a conversation with the Foreign Secretary, Anthony Eden, who agreed that it was important to detach China from the communist alliance, and said that he understood the Americans thought so too; but this aim might not be easy to achieve.

On trade questions, Eden said that the British had not found the Chinese at all easy to deal with, and in any case the British did not wish to be out of step with the Americans. There was no specific mention of Japan's role in the western Pacific and South-east Asia by either party. However, perhaps this was taken for granted, for British officials had earlier commented, 'We assure him [Yoshida] that we are aware of the important role that Japan can play in the western Pacific. As regards economic co-operation in South-east Asia, Japan has now become a member of the Colombo Plan.'[15] Although the talk surrounding Japan's proposals on China and South-east Asia could be no more than an exchange of views, it is interesting that the general political problems common to the two countries' interests stemmed from the situation in East and South-east Asia, and as such projected a consultative pattern for future discussions.

At the request of the Japanese, Yoshida met the President of the Board of Trade, Peter Thorneycroft, to discuss general trade problems as well as Japan's accession to the General Agreement on Tariffs and Trade (GATT). Thorneycroft said that although Anglo-Japanese trade was not in itself unsatisfactory, trade relations between the two countries could never be entirely happy unless something were done about unfair trade practices in Japan, such as the copying of designs, export incentives, and the subsidization of shipping. As regards Japan's access to the GATT, the British felt that it was likely to create problems for the major Western trading nations, especially the sterling area in the Asian Pacific, since Japanese industry had in the past shown a capacity for such rapid development in particular manufactures that competing industries in other countries found themselves unable to adjust.[16] The British attitude towards trade with Japan, therefore, can be summarized as a belief in the need for certain safeguards and for vigilance – a view to which Western public opinion continued to adhere. Nevertheless, trade between Japan and the United Kingdom-cum-the Asian Pacific Commonwealth countries expanded considerably during the first half of the 1950s, producing a favourable balance for Japan.

Prime Minister Yoshida wound up his official visit to London by delivering a speech before a group of British MPs of the Inter-Parliamentary Union at the House of Commons. This speech provides an important indication of what post-war Japan conceived to be its initial role as a 'Western' partner in Asia at the outset of its re-entry into international society:

> We have lost our once flourishing China trade. But, fortunately, the neighbouring South-east Asian countries are rich in natural resources and they have launched long-range development projects under the Colombo Plan with financial and technological help extended by the

British and other Commonwealth nations. . . . I am much gratified that Japan has now joined the Colombo Plan as a donor country. Although our capacity is obviously limited, we are prepared to do our utmost to aid these countries by sending experts or training local technicians. . . . A satisfactory development of the region and the resulting higher standard of living of its peoples would serve not only to eliminate the danger of communist infiltration but also to create a new market for the rest of the world.[17]

An Asian Marshall Plan

In his major speech in Washington, at the National Press Club on 8 November, Yoshida developed his ideas further. He urged the United States to set up a development fund to be established as an Asian version of the Marshall Plan under the Organization for European Economic Co-operation (OEEC).[18] Yoshida and his delegation argued the case for this plan as being in line with US–Japanese economic co-operation in that it would create a new market integrating Japan, the United States, and South-east Asia. The backwardness of South-east Asian non-communist economies created problems for Japan, forcing it to extend long-term credit, and their then slow rate of economic growth offered meagre promise of a durable and expanding outlet for Japanese capital goods. Obviously, then, from the Japanese point of view, there was an urgent need to enlarge the flow of capital funds.

There was also a political motivation to Yoshida's proposal. The Japanese, including Yoshida, saw the vulnerability of the South-east Asian region to communism as being the result not of military weakness but of economic stagnation.

Economics represents a vital element in determining the political future of South-east Asia [they claimed]. If China under Communist control makes rapid economic progress, leaving the comparatively slow South-east Asian countries far behind, there will develop a great margin between the Communist and non-Communist areas of Asia, enabling Communist China to place the whole of Southeast Asia under her influence without resorting to arms.[19]

So the Japanese went on to suggest a concrete and ambitious 'counter-offensive' in which their point of reference was explicitly China.

During his courtesy call on President Eisenhower, Prime Minister Yoshida mentioned this idea of a 'peace offensive' against the threat of communism in Asia. In his discussion with Secretary of State Dulles he spoke of the possibility of setting up some sort of 'high command' in Singapore to combat communism. This scheme had already been put to Malcolm MacDonald and to the British government; the high command would be organized into a combined body with French, British, Australian, and Japanese participation, in addition to that of the United States.

How did the United States respond to the Japanese grand scheme for Asia? Both Eisenhower and Dulles were courteously noncommittal. The final statement, jointly issued at the White House on 10 November 1954, referred briefly to the mutual benefit which might arise from Japan's participation with the other free nations of South and South-east Asia in the economic development of the area. But there were no references either to the Colombo Plan or to an OEEC-style organization for economic co-operation in Asia. As to the suggestion for a new Asian Marshall Plan, Dulles disclosed publicly his view that there were great differences between the economic situation in Asia then (the mid-1950s) and that in Europe in 1947. He mentioned the need for planning in Asia, on the one hand, and the limitation upon the capacity of the Asian countries to absorb large quantities of external capital quickly, on the other.

In short, Yoshida's attempts to change US Asian policy came to nothing. He had hoped to secure British support in exerting pressure on the United States to relax the China trade embargo, since British views on trade with China were less rigid than those of the Americans. However, the British were pro-American before being in any way pro-Japanese. Ironically, among the subjects which the State Department lists as having been discussed with Yoshida, there is no mention of Japanese trade with China.[20] Perhaps Yoshida refrained from raising the matter again, because of its cool reception from the Americans and the ambiguous attitude of the British.

In summary, the 1954 Yoshida mission had more significance in focusing international attention on the major areas of Japan's concerns than in attaining any concrete results. The goals of the mission were threefold: intensive economic development of South-east Asia in a trilateral linkage with Japan and the United States (and possibly Britain); relaxation in trade relations with China; and promotion of non-discriminatory trade with the Western countries under the GATT regime. Yoshida's diplomatic journey achieved virtually nothing in any of these areas. Nevertheless, in style and substance it became a model to be repeatedly followed by his successors. Its style was typical of the diplomacy conducted abroad by top leaders since the Meiji era. Its substance remained unchanged in geopolitical terms: the issues would have to be continuously tackled by successive governments, at least in the next decade or so. Moreover, Yoshida himself continued to give considerable diplomatic guidance, though unobtrusively, even after his retirement.[21]

A diplomatic interlude

The themes of the Yoshida era, which sowed the seeds for strengthening the bonds of Japan with Asia and the West, were interrupted for a few years by the governments of Hatoyama Ichiro and Ishibashi Tanzan, and were not revived until 1957 under the government of Kishi Nobosuke.

In December 1954, shortly after his world tour, Yoshida finally stepped down and handed over the premiership to his political enemy, Hatoyama. The Hatoyama government, in which the veteran diplomat Shigemitsu Mamoru received the Foreign Ministry portfolio, strongly criticized the pro-American policy of the Yoshida regime, and drew public attention instead to the readjustment of diplomatic relations with communist countries. With the cease-fire in Korea and the end of the war in Indochina, as well as the change of leadership in the Kremlin, a thaw had set in in the cold war in East Asia and the world as a whole. This offered Japan the opportunity to negotiate an agreement for the restoration of diplomatic relations with the USSR. Prime Minister Hatoyama visited Moscow in October 1956. A joint declaration for the normalization of relations between the two countries was issued, but no peace treaty was signed because of the territorial disputes over the northern islands. The normalization, however, removed one major stumbling-block, namely Moscow's veto on Japan's admission to the United Nations, thereby ending the so-called 'partial peace' settlement. On the day of Japan's admission to the United Nations, 18 December, Foreign Minister Shigemitsu's speech before the General Assembly defined Japan's role as that of mediator between East (Asia) and West.

Japan at this time was certainly not yet ready to play such a role. During his two years in office, Prime Minister Hatoyama never met any leaders of the United States or the other Western nations, except for a courtesy call on British Prime Minister Eden on his way back from Moscow. The only parley with Washington was over security and defence issues, when Foreign Minister Shigemitsu visited the capital in August 1955, and this was a bitter failure. On the Asian scene, the power of post-war Asian nationalism was demonstrated by the First Asian–African Conference, held in Bandung, Indonesia, in April 1955. Shigemitsu missed an important chance to represent Japan at the Bandung conference, and his proxy (Takasaki Tatsunosuke, Secretary of the Economic Planning Agency) was outshone by such distinguished Asian leaders as Sukarno, Zhou Enlai, Nehru, and Nasser. Nevertheless, the first contact between Japan and communist China since the war did occur at this conference – at a breakfast meeting between Zhou Enlai and Takasaki.

Hatoyama was succeeded in December 1956 by Ishibashi, who stayed in office for only two months because of illness. Ishibashi favoured closer co-operation with the United States, while still remaining rather cool towards Washington. On the issue of normalization of relations with the People's Republic of China, he expressed the view that the China question should be settled first in the United Nations, which had denounced Peking as an 'invader' in the Korean war. His short term of office, however, prevented Ishibashi from developing a distinctive foreign policy.

Chapter three

A Twin-track Diplomacy

Japan's post-war foreign policy has been marked by what may be styled a 'twin-track' diplomacy. One track is designed to strengthen the bonds between Japan and the West; the other, to tie together Japan and Asia's Pacific Rim states. The two tracks are closely interwoven: without an assured political and security relationship with the West, especially with the United States, Japan could not safely pursue its economic interests in the Asian Pacific region; without roots in Asia, it would not count for much in the Western world.

In this context, Yoshida's 1954 mission was incomplete, since he had reluctantly had to abandon the Asian part of his tour, even though his meetings with Western leaders had an Asian content. The next two governments, under Hatoyama and Ishibashi, were unable to follow up the high-level contacts initiated by their predecessor. The twin-track diplomacy had to wait for the arrival of the Kishi government at the end of February 1957.

Three basic principles proclaimed

Within weeks of his accession to power, in February 1957, Prime Minister Kishi announced an extensive tour of six countries of South-east and South Asia, to take place in May, immediately before a visit to Washington. The tour was apparently planned in this way, in two legs, in order to strengthen Kishi's bargaining position in Washington by demonstrating a convergence of interests between Japan and the Asian region, which could be usefully combined in a triangular association with the United States.

The tour started in Burma, then went on to India, Pakistan, Ceylon, and Thailand, and ended up in the Republic of China (Taiwan). One of its main aims was to sell to those countries the idea of a 'South-east Asian Development Fund'. The fund could be established with an initial payment of, say, $300 million, to be increased to the level of $3 billion within four or five years. The Americans were expected to be the main

23

contributors, and the financial resources could be channelled through the Colombo Plan organization, which already included Japan and the United States as official members, in addition to the original member countries of the British Commonwealth. Taiwan should also be invited.

The idea had much in common with the 'Asian Marshall Plan' proposed by Yoshida in Washington three years earlier. The two schemes were similar not only in their economic function but also in their political context, in that both were seen as a means of reducing the threat of communism in the region. The theory was, of course, that regional security depended primarily upon economic and social stability, and that a rising standard of living in the free countries of South-east Asia could effectively deter communist penetration. Kishi went further than Yoshida towards committing Japan's interests to the nations of South-east Asia in that he was the first Prime Minister to visit Asian states after the war and to have direct talks with national leaders there. He believed that the strengthening of Japan's position in neighbouring Asia would help to put Japan–US relations on a more equal footing; conversely, he was determined to use Japan's steady relationship with the United States to obtain assistance for the Asian countries.[1]

Kishi's scheme for the development fund, however, met with a cool reaction from Asian countries, particularly from India and Burma. The non-aligned countries were reluctant to become involved in a scheme which might have anti-communist political strings attached to it, and were therefore hesitant about receiving economic assistance from the United States, even through the mediation of a regional organization. For these reasons the idea lost momentum before ever reaching Washington. In the late 1950s it was still premature for Japan to try to mediate between Asia and the West for regional development aid.

Having completed his tour of Asia, Prime Minister Kishi visited Washington the following month to discuss various matters with the Eisenhower administration but mainly matters related to the revision of the 1951 Japan–US security treaty. The resultant joint statement characterized relations between the two countries as 'entering a new era'. One concrete step was the establishment of an intergovernmental committee to study problems arising out of the security treaty, the revision of which was subsequently to provide a continuing source of controversy in the Diet and among the Japanese public.

The joint statement also addressed the subject of economic development in Asia. Kishi said that in his recent tour of Asian countries he had been deeply impressed with the efforts that were being made towards economic development; he felt sure that further economic progress would greatly contribute to the stability of the region. President Eisenhower expressed his full agreement. The two leaders then discussed ways in which free Asian countries might be further assisted in developing their economies. The final statement made no mention of the proposal of a South-east Asian development fund, merely that the views of the Prime Minister would be studied by the United States. If, however, one compares the Japan–US joint statement which was issued on the occasion of the 1954 Yoshida visit with that of the 1957 Kishi visit, there are indications that the US government was beginning to take the idea of an economic development fund seriously. Yet it was not until 1965, when the Asian Development Bank was established, that any joint economic development plans could take shape.

In November 1957 Prime Minister Kishi made a second trip to South-east Asia and Australasia. Starting from South Vietnam, he went on to Cambodia, Laos, Malaya, Singapore, Indonesia, Australia, New Zealand, and finally the Philippines. Although the idea of a regional development fund was still included on the agenda, economic co-operation by means of wartime reparations emerged as the most important topic of the November tour. By that time, the reparation negotiations with Burma and the Philippines were concluded, but the case of Indonesia and South Vietnam remained to be settled. The Indonesia reparation problem, which was the toughest, was solved when Kishi visited Jakarta. The way was then opened for normalization of relations with South-east Asian countries, especially in the field of economic, trade, and development co-operation. The visit to Australia and New Zealand was aimed at easing the anti-Japanese feeling that still lingered from the war in the Pacific.

The most crucial task in Prime Minister Kishi's term of office was to overcome the split in parliamentary and public opinion concerning the revision of the Japan–US security treaty. In the early stages of the Diet debates, both ruling and opposition parties, for different reasons, supported Kishi's attempt to steer negotiations towards more equal terms for defence arrangements. But whereas the government and ruling party sought equal and mutual co-operation within an alignment with the United States, the opposition required autonomy and self-determination for a non-aligned and neutral Japan.

One opposition leader argued that the alignment policy of the Kishi government was so firmly centred on the West that Asian countries could not help but distrust Japan. In answer to this, Kishi said that it was inappropriate to regard the revision of the security treaty as being antagonistic towards Asia because the revised treaty would in fact enable Japan to decide security issues independently, on the basis of equal sovereignty.[2] But his argument had little effect on the opposition. Indeed, his mishandling of the ratification Bill in the Diet in early 1960 virtually put an end to his political career. The 1960 crisis over the security treaty clearly revealed not only domestic political sensitivities but also a certain incompatibility between Japan's external relations with Asia on the one hand and those with the West on the other.

Despite domestic unpopularity and political failure, the diplomatic efforts of the Kishi government should be acknowledged in two areas: the security relationship with the United States and economic access to Asian countries. Through tough bargaining with the Americans, Kishi obtained a number of quite significant concessions which, in effect, placed Japan in a more favourable position than it had enjoyed under the old security treaty.[3] In addition, trade negotiations in 1957 and 1960 allowed Japan the advantage of freer trade with the United States. He was also able, by means of reparations, to heal rifts with South-east Asia and to draw American attention to the area.

Japan's return to international society in the first decade following the war was marked by such major steps as the 1956 entry into the United Nations, the more solid alignment with the West under the new Japan–US security treaty and the normalization of diplomatic relations with the Asian region (apart from mainland China and the Korean peninsula).[4] Against this background, the government proclaimed three basic principles which were to act as guidelines for Japanese external policy: first, it would be 'UN-centred'; second, it would co-operate with the Western free democratic nations; and, third, it would identify closely with the countries of Asia. The three principles derived from a statement made by Foreign Minister (as he then was) Kishi in the Diet, on 4 February 1957; they were later elaborated on in the first volume of the Blue Book which the Foreign Ministry published in September 1957.

The first of the three, UN-centred diplomacy, was eroded within a few years, mainly because of increasing awareness of the UN's limitations as an effective system of collective security. Consequently, references to 'UN centralism' had disappeared from Japan's public foreign-policy documents by 1960.[5] The other two principles, however, continued to serve as the basis of Japan's foreign policy.

The separation of economics from politics

When Prime Minister Ikeda Hayato came to office in July 1960 he faced severe political discord at home and tension in relations with the United States. He met the challenge by adopting different policy stances from his predecessor, both in domestic and in foreign relations. On the domestic front, he turned the nation's gaze away from political confrontation to economic development, by putting forward a programme for 'doubling income in ten years'. As for relations with the United States, he tried to shift the emphasis from mutual co-operation in an exposed anti-communist alignment to a broader security system based on economic collaboration.

The year 1960 saw a change of government in the United States as well. The remaining traces of the occupation period were left behind; the arrival of President John F. Kennedy marked a new phase in Japan–US relations. The Kennedy administration seemed to count Japan as a much more substantial partner than the previous administration had done; and in June 1961, as a result of a meeting between Ikeda and Kennedy, a cabinet-level committee was set up between the two countries to deal with trade and economic affairs. This committee was to assist in achieving the objectives of Article II of the Treaty of Mutual Co-operation and Security.[6] Moreover, by introducing economic factors into the working of the treaty, it led to the *economization* of the alliance.[7]

There remained, however, a certain perception gap between the two countries. From the US viewpoint, strategic and security considerations still prevailed over economic co-operation; Japan's preoccupation, by contrast, lay in promoting economic and trade interests while minimizing political and security risks. This difference in emphasis has continued to overshadow the alliance ever since.

Be that as it may, the committee continued to exist as a key consultative body for Japanese–American economic and trade issues throughout the 1960s and even into the early 1970s. The close contacts and consultations that it afforded provided Japan with greater opportunities for access to the US-led Western free-trade network. It was at the second annual meeting of the committee, in 1962, that the Ikeda government expressed its intention of participating in the 1963–7 Kennedy Round for liberalizing international trade. In the meetings that followed, the United States, for its part, requested Japan to eliminate not only residual import quotas but also restrictions on capital investment. In the event, trade liberalization, which it had been thought would deal a severe blow to Japanese manufacturing industry, actually strengthened its competitive power. So the economization of the alliance, it can be said, was satisfactory beyond all expectations as far as Japan's interests were concerned.

Although the United States never specifically brought political and strategic issues to the trade and economics committee, it did expect from Japan increasing participation in general discussions of Asian problems, especially those relating to communist China and Korea.[8] However, the Americans understood 'participation' to mean agreement with their own views on the containment of communism in Asia. Japan went along with the United States by blocking the representation of the People's Republic of China in the United Nations. The issue of the UN representation and the unification of Korea fell into the same category.

It was under such constraints that Japan had to adopt the principle of *seikei bunri*, the 'separation of economic affairs from politics'. Even though the need for such a principle implied subordination to US policy in Asia, there was also a positive side in that it helped Japan to develop the confidence eventually to pursue its own policy. Japan could not afford to take any step which might prejudice its alliance with the United States. Nevertheless, this did not preclude non-political contact between the Japanese people and mainland China, and various contacts in the fields of trade and culture were promoted without any modification of the policy based on *seikei bunri*. A cabinet member of the Ikeda government declared, 'We are glad that more recently Communist China has come to show an attitude flexible enough to accept our point of view.'[9] These were encouraging signs for the ultimate *economization*, or *depoliticization*, of Japan's relations with China and other Asian countries as well.

Japan's 'economics-centred' diplomacy was extended to a wider area when Prime Minister Ikeda toured South-east Asia in November 1961. On this tour he talked to Asian leaders such as Ayub Khan of Pakistan, Jawaharlal Nehru of India, U Nu of Burma, and Sarit Thanarat of Thailand. A main theme of the talks was the problem of economic development. Ikeda pointed out that his country had recently learnt a great deal about the value of a free economy as an instrument for nation-building; in view of Japan's impressive achievement, a similar course might perhaps recommend itself to other Asian nations as an alternative to a state-controlled economy. Throughout the tour Ikeda was struck by the discrepancy between Japan's economic power and that of other Asian countries, and he became aware of the leading role that Japan must play in the regional co-ordination of trade, aid, and investment. His impulsive decision to extend a 'special yen loan' to Thailand symbolized the contribution that he felt Japan could make.

Pre-trilateralism

By the early 1960s Japan's high-growth economy was beginning to attract international attention. Thus, for example, a survey in *The Economist* – 'Consider Japan' – which appeared in September 1962 pointed to Japan's extraordinary achievement, and suggested that it held important lessons for Britain and other Western countries. Europeans were eager to know what it was that made the Japanese economy work the way it did. At the same time, the Japanese came to realize Europe's importance as an integrated economic and political power in the free world. It was against this background that Prime Minister Ikeda went on a tour of six West European countries in the autumn of 1962.

The purpose of Ikeda's tour was, in particular, to break into the Western economic club. In Europe he saw a forceful movement aiming at economic integration through the elimination of tariff barriers and other trade restrictions within the region. Japan wanted above all to avoid being left out of the economic reorganization of the free world that would result from the likely expansion of the European common market to include

Britain, and from the development of a new-style American trade and political partnership with a 'United Europe'. President Kennedy delivered an important speech in Philadelphia in July 1962, talking about the two pillars – American and European – on which the common Atlantic structure should rest in the future. Under such circumstances, Japan wished to have access to the European market. In November 1962, when Ikeda visited London, a Treaty of Commerce and Navigation was concluded between Japan and the United Kingdom which led to the removal of discrimination against Japanese imports into Britain. Other European countries followed suit. Ikeda's European visit seemed to remove doubts on both sides about Japanese membership of the Organization for Economic Co-operation and Development (OECD); Japan became its only Asian member country in April 1964.[10]

By exploring the possibility of improving relations with Europe, Japan would be able to prevent itself being left out of the free-trade movement on the one hand, and to escape from the excessively lopsided relationship with the United States on the other. That might have been a strategic motivation behind Ikeda's European tour. If so, Yoshida's 1954 tour and Ikeda's 1962 tour had the common feature of playing off the United States against Europe. Just before the tour, Ikeda said in Tokyo that Japan's policy of looking only to the United States was lopsided. In view of the uncertainty of the world economy and international political situation, Japan could not ignore Europe, for European opinion might influence the policy-making of the United States.[11] A foreign correspondent in Tokyo hinted that another object of Ikeda's tour was to seek British and other European backing for issues on which Japan did not always see eye-to-eye with the United States – for instance, relations with China.[12]

Autumn 1962 was a time of acute international tension following the Cuban missile crisis. On the brink of nuclear war, every government in the free world was taking a crucial risk in aligning itself with President Kennedy's confrontation strategy, and the Japanese government was no exception. Prime Minister Ikeda accepted the urgent American request for full support, and issued a statement on the same lines as that of the United States. But this was no easy decision, and Ikeda could relax only when he found that his view was fairly close to those of West European leaders on the subject. Nevertheless, he tasted the bitterness and powerlessness of a 'small' nation among superpowers, finding Japan in the position of having its fate determined by others. Ikeda visited Europe immediately after the Cuban crisis, although some people in Tokyo urged him to go straight to the United States for talks with Kennedy.

During talks with European leaders such as President Charles de Gaulle (France), Chancellor Konrad Adenauer (West Germany) and Prime Minister Harold Macmillan (Britain), Prime Minister Ikeda exchanged views on world politics and international tension, including the crises in Cuba and Berlin, and the Sino-Indian border conflict of October 1962. The focus was on the Far East and South-east Asia, Japan's chief concerns. In every European capital, Ikeda was asked a particular question on communist China and Sino-Japanese trade. His answer was that although it would be premature for Japan to normalize relations with China, trade could be carried on under the principle of *seikei bunri*. Moreover, Ikeda thought that the time would come when Japan and Europe would collectively influence the United States; in a way, a repetition of Yoshida's approach. The talk with General de Gaulle, as Ikeda described it later, was about Asia and Europe, no doubt touching upon trade with China and Japan's attitude towards it, a theme which inevitably transcended the interests of a 'transistor radio salesman', as he was cynically described by de Gaulle himself.

As well as economic issues, the Ikeda–Macmillan talks focused on the Asian situation in the light of the Sino-Indian dispute and Indonesia's confrontation with Malaysia. In comparison with previous discussions on the same topic between Yoshida and Eden in 1954, a significant shift could be seen in that Ikeda, instead of being the mere recipient of a briefing, made a positive response to Macmillan's overtures on the confrontation. 'You are the only person who can influence Sukarno,' Macmillan said to Ikeda. 'Please do something.'[13] This suggestion was seriously considered by Ikeda, and proved to be an important motivation behind his second visit to South-east Asia the following year.

In September 1963, when he visited Jakarta, Ikeda advised Sukarno to refrain from his coercive diplomacy towards the Asian countries of the British Commonwealth as well as from such actions as hauling down the Union Jack at the British embassy. Sukarno paid a return visit to Tokyo in January 1964. A tripartite summit meeting of South-east Asian leaders, including Sukarno, Tunku Abdul Rahman of Malaysia, and Diosdado Macapagal of the Philippines, was held in Tokyo in June. Even though the summit ended inconclusively, Japan's 'assembly room' diplomacy showed a more positive political attitude towards the regional problems of South-east Asia.

A passage from Ikeda's essay 'Awakening with diplomacy' can provide a final assessment of Japan's diplomatic perspectives as conceived in his tours of the United States, Europe, and Asia:

> During part of the post-war period, Japan was able to manage diplomatic affairs by being dependent on Japan–US relations alone. But we are now confronting a wider world. I have maintained for some time the concept of three pillars in the free world which consists of the United States, Europe and Japan. But Japan cannot stand as one of the pillars by itself. My idea implies that Japan is

one of these three pillars in agreement with the countries of Asia.[14]

The perspectives reflected herein are threefold: first, the acquisition of a non-discriminatory status for Japan in the trilateral world market; second, the development of relations between Europe and Japan similar to those between the United States and Japan; third, the securing, with the agreement of the Asian countries, of Japan's position as one of the three pillars of the free world. The Ikeda government saw Japan both as a member of the democratic bloc of free nations and as a fellow of the Asian nations. In East–West relations, Japan was aligned with the West, but it was also very much concerned with the North–South problem of helping underdeveloped countries. Already a member of the DAC, Japan believed that its aid programme entitled it to full OECD membership.

The Japanese government also regarded it as important for the West to disappoint any Soviet hopes that the free world would split into three blocs consisting of Britain and Western Europe, the United States and Canada, and Japan and the rest of Asia.[15] Under these circumstances, Japan's aim was to avoid being isolated by North America and Europe, for it saw little prospect of forming any comparable kind of economic and political bloc in the Asian Pacific region. The best hope for Japan seemed to lie in strengthening the nexus between the three pillars, one of which would be 'Japan in Asia'. In this way a kind of prototype for Japanese trilateralism was created, though Ikeda may never have thought that his broad idea would become reality in the form of the Western economic summit meetings more than a decade later.

The end of the post-war era

When Ikeda resigned through illness just after the 1964 Tokyo Olympic Games, Sato Eisaku, the younger brother of the former Prime Minister Kishi, took over the reins of government. Ikeda and Sato were at one time considered to be political rivals within the ruling party, but both of them were faithful to the political leadership of Yoshida. Sato stayed in power for nearly eight years, becoming the longest-serving Prime Minister in Japanese constitutional history. In following his predecessors' achievements in such things as equal partnership with the United States, the economization of the alliance, and the introduction of the concept of world trilateralism, the Sato government developed further the policies of alignment with the West and association with non-communist Asia.

The development of Japan's external relations during Sato's period of government coincided with several major events which can be seen as n.arking the end of the post-war period. Those events included the return of the Okinawa islands to Japan and the 'Nixon shock', and comprised harmonious as well as divisive elements, affecting especially the security and economic relationship between Japan and the United States. By the early 1970s the pattern of political and security relations between Japan and the United States in East Asia had become essentially more stable, whereas the economic relationship was increasingly one of complementary/competitive interdependence.

The first diplomatic task of the Sato government was to approach the United States for close consultation on the international situation and on matters of mutual interest. Prime Minister Sato and President Lyndon Johnson met in Washington in January 1965, and reviewed the situation in North-east and South-east Asia in particular, focusing on China, which had acquired a nuclear capability, and on the crisis in Vietnam. Recognizing that the question of China had a vital bearing on the peace and stability of Asia, Sato and Johnson exchanged frank views on the position of their respective countries and agreed to maintain close consultation on this matter. Johnson emphasized his firm support for the Republic of China and his grave concern over communist China's militant policies. Sato stated that it was the fundamental policy of the Japanese government to maintain friendly ties with the government of the Republic of China and at the same time to continue to promote private contacts with the Chinese mainland in such matters as trade, following the principle of the separation of political from economic matters.[16]

As regards the critical situation in Vietnam, Sato and Johnson agreed that perseverance would be necessary to secure freedom and independence in South Vietnam. They also recognized that improvements in living standards and social welfare were essential for the political stability of developing nations in South-east Asia and throughout the world. On the question of the reversion of the Okinawa islands, they recognized the importance of military installations on the islands for the security of the Far East. Sato then expressed the desire that administrative control over these islands should be restored to Japan as soon as feasible. Appreciating this wish, Johnson stated that he looked forward to the day when the security interests of the free world in the Far East would permit the realization of Japanese desires.[17] Clearly the future of Okinawa was inseparably linked with the strategic interests of the United States in Asia.

Soon after his return to Tokyo from Washington, Sato took the bold step of normalizing Japan's relations with South Korea. The Japan–Korea Basic Treaty was initialled in Seoul in February 1965, and officially signed in Tokyo in June. But the opening of diplomatic relations with one half of a divided Korea was strongly criticized by the communists of North Korea and China as well as by opposition parties in Japan. The *rapprochement* between Tokyo and Seoul, however, represented a historic event which ushered in a new era for two nations which had had bitter experiences before and during the war, and had overcome numerous difficulties throughout the protracted negotiations on the normalization of diplomatic relations in the following two decades.

In August 1965, Sato flew to Naha, the capital of Okinawa, becoming the first Prime Minister of Japan to visit the city since the war. He made it an opportunity to declare his conviction that, until Okinawa was returned, Japan would not have completely emerged from the post-war period. Despite growing interest in the return of Okinawa to Japan, prospects for serious negotiations on the matter were deemed to be still remote, in the context of the intervention of the United States in Vietnam (which required the use of its military bases in Okinawa), which had just begun to escalate into full-scale warfare.

The Japanese desire for the return of administrative control over the Okinawa islands had first been expressed in the Kishi–Eisenhower joint communiqué as long ago as 1957. From the outset, the United States stuck to its position that so long as threats and tensions existed in the Far East, the present status would have to be maintained. Faced with the firm attitude of the United States, the Japanese government could only rely upon a policy of trying to enhance the welfare and well-being of the inhabitants of the Okinawa islands, thereby indirectly increasing its voice in the civil administration there. As the Japanese economy grew faster in the early 1960s a widening gap appeared between living standards in Japan proper and in Okinawa. Meanwhile the US government came to appreciate Japanese co-operation in promoting Okinawa's economic and cultural advancement. In response to this, the Ikeda and Sato governments substantially increased economic assistance to Okinawa, which was channelled through the American budget. As a result, gradual economic integration paved the way for the final restoration of administrative rights to Japan in the early 1970s.

The Sato government carried out a broader policy of increasing economic assistance to South-east Asia from the mid-1960s onwards. Prime Minister Sato presided over the Ministerial Conference for the Economic Development of South-east Asia (MEDSEA) which was held in Tokyo in April 1966, the first-ever international meeting sponsored by Japan after World War II. Nine nations from South-east Asia, excluding North Vietnam, were invited; but Burma, as a neutral state, refused to come, and the non-aligned Indonesia and Cambodia (now Kampuchea) attended only as observers (Indonesia became a full participant from the next meeting). Japan pledged a substantial increase in economic aid to the countries of the region, promising to reach as soon as possible the aid target –1 per cent of GNP – recommended by the United Nations Conference on Trade and Development (UNCTAD).

The Japanese government also became very interested in the establishment of the Asian Development Bank (ADB), a central financial institution to promote trade and investment in the region. The original scheme for the bank was taken up by the Economic Commission of Asia and the Far East (ECAFE), which organized the formalities of incorporation. With headquarters in Manila, and under Japanese presidency, the bank started operations in 1966. Membership of the bank comprises recipient and donor countries. (By the late 1980s Japan had become a prime contributor of investment capital, providing, like the United States, 20 per cent of the total authorized funds.) As well as the Japanese president, there are three vice-presidents, representing the United States, West Germany, and India. This organizational structure shows a Western presence which Japan had long regarded as important, as shown in earlier proposals such as Yoshida's concept of an Asian Marshall Plan and Kishi's plan for a South-east Asian development fund. In other words, Japan realized that it could not back Asian development programmes without Western participation. As indicated by these institutional networks, Japan's Asian diplomacy was passing through the 'take-off' stage.

Prime Minister Sato then carried out a two-stage programme of foreign tours: he went first to Burma, Malaysia, Singapore, Thailand, and Laos in September 1967; then to Indonesia, Australia, New Zealand, the Philippines, and South Vietnam in October. Sato also visited Seoul in July and Taipei in September, and immediately after the visit to Saigon he went on to Washington. The 'twin-track' diplomacy of Sato's tours echoes his brother's tours exactly ten years before. In Asia and the western Pacific, Sato repeatedly expressed the view that regional security from the communist threat should rely ultimately on economic welfare. In Washington he stressed that the maintenance of peace and security rested not merely on military factors but also on political stability and economic development.

In spite of this emphasis on economic development rather than military methods to deal with the South-east Asian crisis, the Sato government gave the impression of following a hard line in backing anti-communist forces in the region. Indeed, Sato dared to call on Seoul, Taipei, and Saigon one after another, regardless of criticism from inside and outside Japan, 'My tour in South-east Asia this time,' Sato told the press in Saigon, 'should have a good effect on the November meeting in Washington.'[18] This revealed the real purpose behind the plural approach.

The positive involvement of Japan in South-east Asian economic development and Sato's politico-diplomatic tours combined to produce a successful conclusion to the negotiations for the return of Okinawa. The Okinawa question moved towards an eventual solution when a Japan–US joint communiqué, issued in November 1967, mentioned a target date for an agreement possibly 'within a few years'. Yet there were still considerable hurdles to be cleared.

The latter stages of the Okinawa negotiations overlapped with the textile dispute which generated a serious economic crisis between Japan and the United States. In the 1968 presidential election campaign Richard Nixon had promised the domestic textile industry that he would negotiate restraints on exports of Japanese wool and man-made fibre products to the United States. President Nixon moved quickly in May 1969 to fulfil his election pledge by sending an envoy to Tokyo to seek the co-operation of the Japanese government. At their meeting in November, Nixon won a secret concession from Sato which, however, proved politically impossible to implement, because of Japanese resistance to 'unreasonable' US demands. The main theme of the summit was not the textile problem but final negotiations on the reversion of Okinawa. These came to a successful conclusion, assuring Japan that residual sovereignty over the islands would be restored to it during the year 1972. The textile problem, however, continued to be a source of tension for two more years, although Nixon and his special adviser, Henry Kissinger, tried to use a linkage policy for the solution of these two issues.

By the mid-1960s Japan's trade balance had improved remarkably, to the extent of being in overall surplus of up to $1 billion, with, in 1965, the first instance on record of the balance of Japan–US post-war trade being favourable to Japan. The Japanese trade advance was a consequence of the US-led international trade liberalization initiated by the Kennedy Round, which brought about the largest tariff reduction in history, but at the same time unleashed pressures for import restrictions, especially in sensitive sectors such as the textile industry. In comparison with the Japanese performance, American exports to Japan grew so slowly that the US government became critical of the limited extent of Japan's trade liberalization.

The USA's international trade balance was worsening against the background of its substantially increasing overseas military expenditure as the Vietnam war further escalated in the late 1960s. President Johnson proclaimed the 'defence of the dollar' in his special message to Congress in May 1968, and requested co-ordinated action from Western allies, including Japan. Japan's response was not enthusiastic. This reluctance on Japan's part only resulted in a protectionist backlash in the US Congress. The Nixon administration was then unable to contain domestic pressure, especially from the textile industry, which demanded an import quota Bill. In August 1971 President Nixon delivered his strong measures: the 10 per cent import surcharge and the floating of the dollar.

In July 1971, one month before the 'new economic policy' which took Japan as its main target, President Nixon shocked Tokyo with his announcement on Sino-American *rapprochement* – the United States was to open relations with China, without having consulted Japan. This two-fold 'Nixon shock' threatened the basis of Japanese trust and confidence in the alliance with the United States. Japan no longer had any justification for taking for granted a relationship of political and economic dependence on the Americans. The Japan–US alliance was in fact entering a new era, one of more sophisticated interdependence.

Another aspect of the new era in Japan's external relations emerged from its concern to maintain peace and security in East Asia. For the first time since the war, the Japanese governement officially expressed an interest in the security of East Asia when it recognized that 'the security of Japan could not be adequately maintained without international peace and security in the Far East and, therefore, regional security was a matter of serious concern for Japan'.[19] Such recognition was apparent in the Sato–Nixon agreement, which confirmed the application of the Treaty of Mutual Security to Okinawa. It can be said that, through the negotiations for regaining possession of Okinawa, Japan became seriously concerned with regional security beyond its own territory, in wider East Asia (e.g. in the Korean peninsula). Prime Minister Sato bluntly asserted that Japan, as 'the guardian of Asia', would have to shoulder new and expanded responsibilities not only for its own defence but for the security of Asia.

Parallel with such developments as the annual meeting of MEDSEA and the establishment of the ADB, there arose another forum for the nine nations of Asia: the Asian and Pacific Council (ASPAC). South Korean President Park Chung-hee took the initiative of organizing it, and the first meeting was held in Seoul in June 1966, with delegations particularly from those countries involved in the Vietnam war. The Japanese government sponsored the fourth ASPAC conference at the resort of Kawana in June 1969. The Kawana conference gave an opportunity for Prime Minister Sato to advocate a concept of 'Pacific Asian co-operation', with the following five key points: (1) it should promote peace and progress in the region; (2) it should not aim at a military alliance; (3) it should be guided by a consensus of member states; (4) its activities should be initiated with a feasible programme; and (5) its membership should expand.[20]

Although Sato's proposal was not accepted, his attempt to tone down the anti-communist, militaristic colour of ASPAC and concentrate its activities on economic development could be regarded as typifying the Japanese approach. The concept of Pacific Asian or Asian Pacific co-operation had been envisaged in the later 1960s by Japanese political leaders such as the Foreign Minister, Miki Takeo, who foresaw an eventual shift from a politically biased Afro-Asian movement to an economically oriented Asian Pacific co-operation. In a Diet statement in March 1967, Miki first used the term 'Asian Pacific region' to describe the basic context of Japan's foreign policy. In another speech, two months later, he said that the most important question for Japan's Asian Pacific diplomacy would be how the 'have' countries in the Pacific should assist the 'have-not' countries in Asia. These perceptions influenced the Japanese government's approach to Asia on various occasions, including the MEDSEA and ASPAC conferences.

To conclude the examination of the Sato government's achievements during this precarious transitional period, it is not inappropriate to refer to the key phrases in Sato's Nobel Peace Prize lecture on 11 December 1974. First, 'Peace and stability in the East Asian region surrounding Japan have been strengthened, as a result of the political solution for the Okinawa question.' The return of Okinawa, he said, was a shining example of a peaceful transition. It helped to place Japan–US relations on an even firmer foundation, and to relax tension with China as well as in the western Pacific. Second, with the Treaty on Basic Relations between Japan and the Republic of Korea, a major issue in post-war Japanese diplomacy had been solved. Although the negotiation to normalize relations with South Korea had encountered numerous difficulties, largely owing to the historical legacy of the past domination of Korea by Japan, and to the division of the Korean peninsula into two camps, the realistic approach of seeking to establish friendship with close neighbours had proved effective. Third, looking at South-east Asia in the 1960s, economic development had occurred over the entire area at a comparatively steady pace, despite the grave problem of the Vietnam war, which fortunately had not spread beyond Indochina. Japan had been able to make some contribution to this progress. The leaders of South-east Asia appreciated the role Japan had played in the non-military area of the economy and technology. Finally, despite these achievements and contributions, the overall relationship between Japan and the outside world still suffered from some constraint, a sense of isolation. So Sato had to admit that 'Japan is basically a difficult nation to understand because the foundation of our culture differs so much from those of the West and of other Asian countries'.[21]

From isolation to involvement

With President Nixon's historic visit to China and the Shanghai communiqué of 1972, political bipolarity in East Asia gave way to triangular or quadrilateral arrangements, although the bipolar global system remained as a central component of the balance of power, as evidenced by the first SALT (Strategic Arms Limitation Treaty), which symbolized US–Soviet nuclear parity. The confrontational mood of the cold war was replaced with *détente* in East–West relations. At the same time the Sino-Soviet dispute became a major source of tension within the communist world, and China initiated an unprecedented improvement of relations with the West, notably the United States and Japan. The overall political environment in East Asia was in this way converted into a multipolarity which might give Japan more room for manoeuvre, even if the Tokyo government were to show little intention of acting independently of Washington.

Furthermore, the coming of the Sino-American *rapprochement* in 1972 – and the Sino-Soviet split in 1961 – were, as Richard Nixon described them:

> the most significant geopolitical events of the post-World War II era. [Under the circumstances,] the West has no higher priority than to pursue policies which will convince the Chinese leaders that their hopes for security and economic progress will be realized if they turn West rather than to the polar bear in the north.[22]

The US policy of separating China from the Soviet Union also gave Japan greater economic access to China.

Despite the initial shock and sense of political isolation created by Nixon's *volte-face* on China, Japan quickly seized the opportunity to negotiate diplomatic normalization with Beijing. In September 1972 the new Prime Minister, Tanaka Kakuei, moved swiftly to deal with this issue, making a parallel approach to the United States and China. In Hawaii, Tanaka confirmed with Nixon that Japan's normalization of relations with China was compatible with its adherence to the Japan–US security treaty system. The same proposition was affirmed as a fact in the Beijing meeting between Tanaka and Zhou Enlai.[23] These events meant that the United States could now enjoy good relations with both the two most important Asian countries, Japan and China. Japan was, in turn, liberated from one of the most divisive issues in post-war domestic and foreign politics once the China question ceased to be a burden on its security relationship with the United States. As a result, the Japan–US alliance survived a shaky transition, and achieved greater political stability. For perhaps the first time since the war, Japan had adopted compatible policies towards the West and Asia.

The next areas concerned in the 'multipolar diplomacy' of the Tanaka government were Western Europe and the Soviet Union, which had long been outside the Japanese foreign-policy perspective. In autumn 1973 Prime Minister Tanaka made the first official state visit to three European capitals since Ikeda's in 1962 and the first such visit to Moscow since Hatoyama's 1956.

The climax of the tour was the Soviet–Japanese summit talk in Moscow. After difficult negotiations, Tanaka signed a Japanese–Soviet communiqué which stated: 'Both sides confirm that the settlement of outstanding questions left over since World War II and the conclusion of a peace treaty would contribute to the establishment of good-neighbourly relations.' In comparison with the cordial outcome of the Sino-Japanese talks a year earlier, the Moscow meeting ended on a half-hearted note. However, Tanaka's manoeuvres demonstrated Japan's growing political involvement with the world outside and its emergence from the diplomatic shadow of the United States.[24] In connection with Japan's moves in the early 1970s to normalize relations with both China and the Soviet Union, it is interesting to note that several questions were raised in the minds of Americans about the direction of Japanese foreign policy. Was Japan moving away from the United States and towards much closer relations with its large mainland neighbours? If so, would Japan try – and succeed in – balancing its relations with Moscow and Beijing, or would geographical and historical factors lead Japan to move much closer to Beijing than to Moscow? If so, how would the latter react?[25]

There seemed to be grounds for US concern because the Japanese people and political parties, including conservatives, revealed their anxiety about the reliability of the US connections, in the wake of the 'Nixon doctrine', which heralded disengagement from Asia, the ground troops' withdrawal from Vietnam in 1973, and North Vietnam's victory in 1975; and President Jimmy Carter's proposals to remove US ground forces from South Korea in 1976–7. Yet Japan remained in the American strategic orbit. There was no alternative.

In the context of multilateral diplomacy, Tanaka's West European tour before his Moscow trip had no less significance, particularly as a means of counterbalancing Japan's relations with Europe against those with the United States. Before leaving Tokyo, Tanaka disclosed his intention of trying to develop a balanced triangle of economic and political relations between Japan, the United States, and Europe. He said, 'There has been a big pipeline between Japan and the United States and between the United States and Europe, but the pipeline between Japan and Europe remains very small.' The concept of a 'balanced triangle' can be traced back more than a decade to Ikeda's concept of the 'three pillars' of the free world, launched in 1962. The renewed suggestion would have attracted considerable attention had Japan's enhanced economic status been reflected in its relations with Europe. Tanaka's visit to Paris was certainly very different from Ikeda's trip, when he was cynically dubbed the 'transistor radio salesman'. Tanaka was not a salesman, but a potential purchaser of Concorde.[26]

In May 1973, prior to Tanaka's European tour, Ohira Masayoshi, the Foreign Minister, visited France and Belgium as well as the United States. He met French leaders in Paris and talked to leaders of the European Community in Brussels, against the background of growing tensions over the Japanese export thrust which had previously been absorbed by the US, but was now directed towards the European market. Ohira's talks with François-Xavier Ortoli, president of the EC Commission, and Sir Christopher Soames, its vice-president, resulted in an agreement on regular biannual high-level consultations on trade and economic issues. The first high-level consultation was held in Brussels in mid-June. Despite this new link, the general atmosphere in Europe remained cool and cautious towards Japan, which was trying to establish closer ties with the European Community to offset its one-sided relationship with the United States.

Europe's vigilant mood was aptly illustrated by a cartoon in the mass-circulation newspaper *France-Soir*, showing President Nixon heading for Europe in a rowing boat, pulling Japan behind him. This also seemed to be a comment on European reaction to presidential adviser Henry Kissinger's April proposal for a 'new Atlantic charter' which, among other things, defined Japan as a 'principal partner in the common Western enterprise'.[27] In the design of Nixon and Kissinger, the multipolarized world emerging from the shocks of summer 1971, especially the economic measures which led to the breakdown of the Bretton Woods system, would be based on a 'pentagonal' system, in which the Europeans and Japanese would participate in a regime dominated by the world's five greatest economic powers. Before the Paris press, Ohira expressed his support for Kissinger's proposal, referring to the Japanese government's official view, which envisaged the scheme as a global strategic plan not only for the Atlantic community but for the entire world, including Japan. But French leaders showed great reluctance to accept the Kissinger scheme, deeming it necessary to deal very cautiously with the proposal since political and military considerations were also involved.

Theoretically the Europeans agreed that Europe, the United States, Canada, and Japan had a common interest in the security of the Western world. The question was whether this interest was served by substituting a new overall relationship in the place of the existing web of defence and economic relations which had been developed separately in the Atlantic and the Pacific. For most Europeans, Japan remained a distant and still somewhat exotic country. On trade, the Europeans were beginning to regard Japan as an ever more threatening competitor. On defence, no two policies contrast more sharply than those of Japan and France, for example. Whereas the former depended almost totally on the United States for its external defence, the latter was independent of the unified NATO command system.[28] After his European tour, Ohira made the sad confession that he had somehow sensed, in the European leaders with whom he had conferred, an 'absence of trust in the Japanese pledge of commitment to international society'.[29]

A few months later, when Prime Minister Tanaka visited Paris, President Georges Pompidou did not conceal his doubts about Dr Kissinger's concept of a new Atlantic charter, and explicitly rejected the idea of Japan operating on an equal footing with the European Community and the United States within an overall Western relationship. In London the two Prime Ministers, Tanaka and Edward Heath, agreed that closer contacts should be developed between the three centres of power in the non-communist industrialized world. In Bonn, Chancellor

Willy Brandt stressed to Tanaka the necessity of strengthening ties between the European Community and Japan. Both Heath and Brandt, however, were fairly vague about the practical agenda for the solution of economic problems. The biggest disappointment for the Japanese was the lack of European interest in the co-ordination of energy resources. Among the proposals made by Tanaka were joint development of enriched uranium with France, exploitation of North Sea oil resources with Britain, and the establishment of a joint energy resources commission. In addition to these, there was the delicate problem of the development of the Tyumen oilfield in western Siberia. But on none of these issues was any conclusion reached during the Japanese–European summit talks. In the end, Tanaka found that it was possible to be given the red-carpet treatment and the cold shoulder at the same time, and he realized that Japan and Western Europe still had a long way to go to overcome their years of lack of mutual interest.[30]

Following the fourth Middle East war in October 1973, the subsequent Arab oil embargo, and the OPEC price increases in 1973–4, the oil problem became increasingly urgent for Western industrialized countries and Japan. In negotiations over a common energy policy towards the Arab states, European countries could not avoid a split with the United States; Japan also failed to follow the American initiative. The Tanaka government shifted towards a 'pro-Arab' stance in a bold action which ran counter to US policy. It can be said that a 'resources diplomacy' prevailed against the historical primacy of the Japan–US alliance.

Tanaka's resources diplomacy was not restricted to Arab oil. It ranged from aluminium refining in Indonesia, a petrochemical project in Singapore, timber planting and exploration for uranium ore in Brazil, to the exploitation of tar sand in Canada: a long shopping list for his tour of five countries of South-east Asia in January 1974, and four countries of the Western hemisphere in September. It would not be surprising if such aggressive measures incurred American displeasure.

A heavy blow against excessive concentration on resource-oriented economic diplomacy came from South-east Asia, where Japan's economic penetration had become more and more conspicuous. Tanaka was this time treated to both the red carpet and students' placards demanding, 'Jap go home.' Festering hostilities over Japanese economic domination came to the boil, and lingering wartime memories were revived. The anti-Japanese movement in South-east Asia, which stemmed from those countries' constant trade dependence on Japan, was serious enough to make the Japanese rethink their business behaviour in the region. With US disengagement from Indochina and the oil crisis, the countries of South-east Asia were finding it very difficult to manage their domestic economic and political situation. In several countries the anti-Japanese demonstrations stemmed from political frustration with the national government. Under the circumstances, Tanaka's visit was really inopportune, in spite of his willingness to remove misgivings.

In reviewing the external performance of the successive governments of post-war Japan, we can recognize a unique style; that is, 'high diplomacy' through foreign tours *(gaiyu)* conducted by Premiers, starting with Yoshida's 1954 mission. The features and motivations common to these reveal two aims: first, to build a close relationship with the Western free world, especially the United States; second, to forge closer economic links with Asia, in particular South-east Asia. These two persistent aims tended to diverge in the earlier period, and gradually to converge later, according to world circumstances. For instance, in the Asian 'cold war' period, Yoshida's approach, aiming at the opening of the China trade and an 'Asian Marshall Plan' with the consent of the West, was doomed to failure. Ikeda's idea of 'three pillars of the free world' – North America, Western Europe, and Japan with Asia – and 'assembly-room diplomacy' for the Malaysian–Indonesian confrontation were unable to produce any tangible result. But, by the time of the Sato government, the international environment was ripe for a Japanese diplomacy based on coherent policies, aiming, on the one hand, at enhanced relations with the United States (and Western Europe) and, on the other, at economic co-operation with the countries of Asia. Although American influences and inhibitions were still a decisive factor on Japan's policy, this relationship of dependence ceased to act as a constraint upon Japan's relations with Asia, as changes occurred in the Asian policies of the United States itself.

Chapter four

On the Road to the Summit

The diplomatic achievements of successive governments from Yoshida to Tanaka reflected progress up the economic ladder, enhancing Japan's political status and capability as it steered its way through various crises to a more stable relationship with both the West and Asia. Japan had recovered political independence by the early 1950s, gained solid bases for security, economic growth, and trade expansion in the first half of the 1960s, and experienced and overcome vulnerability resulting from the oil crisis in the early 1970s. It then began a vigorous pursuit of scientific and advanced technological achievement. Meanwhile, Japanese leaders' diplomacy in the form of 'twin-track' overseas visits were replaced by regular participation in Western summit meetings as well as dialogue with ASEAN from the mid-1970s onward. The previous chapters broadly sketched the personal performance of Japanese leaders abroad. In this chapter the different phases will be examined in the context of the international political and economic changes which Japan has used to further its aim of becoming a summit power.

A look at recent history, and at Japan's immediate post-war and post-occupation external relations, indicates certain distinct periods in which the Japanese government pursued different diplomatic policies. These were mainly the result of reactions to events in the outside world, although Japan did also create its own style of diplomacy, a subject to which particular attention is given in this book. Although a clear-cut demarcation between periods is not possible, and some overlap between them is unavoidable, four successive phases can be marked out in Japan's post-occupation foreign policy: (1) from the early 1950s to the mid-1960s, *alignment with the West*, and limited alternatives in Asia; (2) from the mid-1960s to the early 1970s, *take-off as a world economic power*; (3) from the early to the late 1970s, *multilateralism in Japan's diplomatic stance*; (4) from the early 1980s to the present, *political maturity at summit meetings*. (See Table 2.)

Table 2: The four phases of Japanese foreign policy

Period	Japan	The world
1 Early 1950s to mid-1960s	Alignment with the West, limited alternatives in Asia	Cold war in Europe and Asia
2 Mid-1960s to early 1970s	Take-off as a world economic power	US intervention in the Vietnam war
3 Early 1970s to late 1970s	Multilateralism in diplomatic stance	East–West *détente*, US–China *rapprochement*, oil crises
4 Early 1980s to the present	Political maturity at summit meetings	New cold war, relative decline of the superpowers, economic recession

Alignment with the West, alternatives in Asia

The first phase began with the conclusion of the San Francisco peace treaty and the Japanese–US security treaty in 1951, reached a peak with the revision of the security treaty in 1960, and tailed off in the mid-1960s. The fact that the San Francisco peace treaty, designed to reinstate Japan in the world community, was not concluded until six years after the end of the war reflected the influence of the East–West confrontation in the post-war world which came to be known as the 'cold war'.

During this period of incorporation into the US system in the Asian Pacific region, the most difficult problem facing the Japanese was how to approach the re-establishment of relations with their Chinese neighbours, now divided between two territories under different regimes. While Japan was preparing for a separate peace with the United States, the People's Republic of China repeatedly expressed severe criticism of the US occupation of Japan and of the possibility of Japanese rearmament. The leaders of the Beijing government regarded US policy as a means of preserving Japan's militarism and preventing its 'democratization'. But it is interesting to note that as soon as the San Francisco treaty was concluded, the Beijing government recognized that immediate revolution in Japan was impossible. It therefore began to take a more flexible view of the Japanese government.[1] Meanwhile the question of whether Japan would choose Taiwan or Beijing had become a matter of the gravest concern to the United States.

The Japanese government decided to choose Taiwan, mainly because if it did not re-establish normal relations with the Chinese Nationalists, ratification of the Japanese peace treaty by the US Senate might well have been delayed or rejected. Nevertheless, the Yoshida government wanted to avoid a situation in which a deeper relationship with Taiwan would mean that Japan found itself unable to acknowledge the existence of the Beijing regime.[2] The Japanese could not negate their traditional relationship with mainland China without considerable fear and hesitation. The agonizing choice over the China question was a typical case, reminding Japan how limited was the freedom of its diplomacy during the cold war period.

The problem of China continued to be a major question confronting Japanese diplomacy throughout the first phase, extending from the early 1950s to the mid-1960s, and further still into the early 1970s. Basically, the split between nationalists and communists in China complicated Sino-Japanese relations to an extreme degree. Then, in view of the East–West confrontation and political and military tensions in the Straits of Taiwan, Japan was obliged to avoid any step which might upset the precarious international balance of power in that part of the world. However, from the historical perspective, it appeared quite natural for Japanese and mainland Chinese to engage in exchanges of various sorts, in the fields of trade, culture, and art. So a practical alternative was found in a policy based on the 'principle of separation of political affairs from economic affairs'.

Parallel to this unique approach was another consideration prominent in Japanese minds at the time, that 'the best antidote to the spread of Communism in Asia was a prosperous South-east Asia'.[3] The fundamental policy of Japan and the Western countries towards that region, the Tokyo government considered, should be to make a co-ordinated effort to hasten its economic development by contributing human and material resources. If, as a result, South-east Asia could achieve prosperity, peace would come with it.[4] It was with these considerations in mind that Japan addressed itself to the problem of economic development in the region. Japan found a profitable trade in exporting manufactured goods to and importing raw materials from South-east Asia, as a valuable alternative to the China market which had predominated before the war.

Japan had become a member of the United Nations in 1956, shortly after establishing diplomatic relations with the Soviet Union. While Japan rated its UN membership highly, it had already become obvious that the real basis of its national security and economic well-being would be maintained not necessarily by the UN system but by the framework of the Japan–US alliance. A landmark on the road to a more equal and favourable status was reached when the security treaty between Japan and the US was replaced by a new mutual co-operation and security treaty in 1960. The Soviet Union showed strong opposition to this and hardened its attitude towards Japan, refusing even to acknowledge the existence of the territorial question. Moreover, it began to expand its military forces in the northern islands, apparently in order to strengthen its strategic position in the North Pacific. In this way Japan was placed in a position to justify further close security co-operation with the United States on the one hand, and to maintain minimum diplomatic relations with the Soviet Union on the other.

The cold war structure in East Asia has continued to inhibit change in the international order under which Japan has been aligned with the United States and detached from the continent of Asia. The state of 'cold war' in Asia, however, underwent a shift from total confrontation with a monolithic communist force when the Soviet Union and communist China split, as shown by the departure of Russian technical specialists from China in 1960. The prediction made by Yoshida became a reality. Unlike the Soviet Union, communist China adopted a more conciliatory policy towards Japan as soon as the Kishi government resigned after the revision of the Japan–US security treaty. Through an unofficial Sino-Japanese trade agreement, concluded in Janaury 1962, Japan became the only country in the world to trade both with Taiwan and with the Chinese mainland with substantial freedom.[5]

Again, after the revision of the security treaty, the Japanese–US relationship broadened its base into more positive economic co-operation. The United States under the Kennedy administration needed Japan's support for its initiative for low tariffs and trade liberalization in the 1962 revision of the Trade Expansion Act. Japan's relations with European countries were gradually consolidated through its membership of the OECD, and resulted in regular consultation being established with individual countries. The basis for these expanding external relations was to be found in the vigorous recovery and development of the nation's economy. The economic resurgence, which owed much to Ikeda's famous 'double-income policy' paved the way for the second phase of its post occupation diplomacy, which might be termed its 'take-off' period as a world economic power.

The risen sun as an economic power

In the second half of the 1960s Japan became the third greatest industrial power in the world, after the United States and the Soviet Union. When Japan entered the OECD in 1964, its GNP was the fifth largest in the non-communist world. It subsequently overtook the three strongest European nations, West Germany, France, and Britain. Japan's GNP rose to $133 billion in 1968, exceeding West Germany's $132 billion.[6] That was a symbolic achievement fulfilled precisely in the centenary year of the Meiji Restoration. The Japanese economy achieved a world-beating annual growth rate of 12.2 per cent in the second half of the 1960s, and continued to expand further into the early 1970s.

Corresponding to this remarkable economic growth, a significant change occurred in Japan's trade relations with the West. Until 1964 the United States had enjoyed what was essentially a favourable balance of trade with Japan. In 1965, however, Japanese exports to the United States began to exceed imports for the first time since 1932. A few years later, the same reversal was seen in Japanese–European trade. Trade relations between Japan and Europe had been unequal and unbalanced since the beginning of modern commerce. For a hundred years the balance was tipped in Europe's favour, save for the period of the two world wars. After 1968, however, for the first time in history the trade balance started to move steadily in Japan's favour.[7] All the signs indicated that the Japanese economy had reached the stage at which it could fully compete with the advanced countries of the West. As a result, Japan launched itself into a new phase with the completion of its reinstatement in the international community.

'The risen sun' drew the world's attention to its impressive economic expansion, as can be seen by prominent Western commentators' surveys or essays on Japan. Norman Macrae of *The Economist* wrote a survey, in 1967, which offered a full explanation of the Japanese forces that had thrust this prodigy of an economy head-and-shoulders above any of its competitors. Herman Kahn, the American futurologist, expanded his famous prediction, 'The twenty-first century will be Japan's', by saying that the Japanese government and people would meet the target of surpassing America in terms of GNP *per capita* by the year 2000. Furthermore, Robert Guillan, a veteran French journalist, published a book entitled *Le Japon – Troisième grand* in 1969, in which he described Japan as a nation that had finally caught up with the advanced countries of Europe in the hundred years since the times of Meiji.

Japan as one of the world's top economic powers then led Western observers to the next question: what sort of new political creature was likely to emerge from this triumphant economic chrysalis? Non-Japanese asked whether it was really conceivable that the world's third strongest international economic power could go on behaving like a rather diffident Belgium or Denmark in international politics; and above all, whether the Japanese would be in a position to use this continuing economic strength in the service of a more active foreign policy.[8] In a sense, the success of Japan's low-profile and economic-oriented policy seemed to have irritated the Western nations no less than the countries of Asia. Japan, economic giant but political dwarf, had to face these questions, in view of the policy options available in the region in which it had been most profoundly involved.

Japan's vital interest lies in East Asia and the Pacific: the north-eastern and south-eastern periphery of the continent of Asia on one side, and North America on the other, with Australia and New Zealand at the lower edge. This is where economic and military power and political influence are so unevenly distributed. Militarily weak, Japan is confronted with two active but rival military powers – the Soviet Union and communist

China – while being itself protected by an alliance with the United States. As a trading nation it was in the position of having to maintain economic and security interests particularly in the small or less developed countries on the western rim of the Pacific. Under the circumstances, the Japanese government was primarily concerned not to be dragged into a risky regional political and military situation; and at the same time it needed to prevent itself from being isolated in the region. Hence the only practical policy option for the Japanese was to be found in promoting economic associations with its neighbours.

As the Vietnam war escalated in the later 1960s, the Sato government explicitly supported the US Vietnam policy, including the bombing of Haiphong. But what Sato actually did in his 1967 summer pilgrimage to the western Pacific was to extend substantial economic assistance loans to many non-communist countries in the region. After 1967 Japan's exports to South-east Asian countries began to surpass those of the United States to that region. In the same year, Japanese exports to non-communist countries in Asia (from Korea to Pakistan) accounted for 25 per cent of its total exports. On the other hand, Japan never ceased to trade with North Vietnam throughout the war period. While the Americans were making war in South-east Asia, the Japanese were carrying on business in the region. In Japan's view, trade and business precede politics: they can contribute to the opening of local markets and can overcome ideological barriers between different social systems. Perhaps these things could not easily be appreciated from the American point of view of anti-communist campaign in Asia. But it was clear to the leaders of public opinion in Japan that the idea of containing and rolling back communism by military means would eventually be proved false. Successful containment should not rely exclusively on military methods, but rather on peaceful trade. The most effective means to be adopted was the 'rollback of poverty'.[9]

In 1968 US policy in Vietnam reached a turning-point when the Johnson administration was forced to change course from what had been all-out confrontation with Hanoi to a compromise through peace negotiations; the Tet offensive of January 1968 confirmed the new US policy. In 1967 the presidential aspirant Richard Nixon contributed an article to *Foreign Affairs* which cautiously adopted a 'long-run' policy of pulling China back into the world community. This reorientation of US Asian policy coincided with an assertiveness in Japan's economic diplomacy in Asia. The 1967 Sato missions across the whole region gave a stimulus to the beginning of operations in the various regional organizations simultaneously. In this particular year a series of important international meetings were held, such as the Manila Conference for South-east Asian Development and the Bangkok talks between the leaders of ASPAC member countries which followed the inauguration of MEDSEA, the establishment of the ADB and the introduction of the Agricultural Development Fund for South-east Asia in the previous year. Although MEDSEA and ASPAC were destined to be disbanded after the fall of Saigon in 1975, another organization founded in 1967 – ASEAN – survived a crucial transitional period and endured into the next stage of regional economic and political co-operation.

The United States lost the war in Vietnam, but its defeat did not lead to the communist take-over of the whole of South-east Asia predicted by the 'domino theory'. Of course, US intervention in Vietnam and the rest of Indochina had negative effects such as the terrible physical devastation inflicted by the war itself, but it also had a positive impact on the regional economy. The substantial war funds injected by the United States did in fact help South-east Asian countries to take off economically. Another factor which contributed to economic growth and political stability in South-east Asia was the political development of mainland China. China was in a state of total chaos with the Cultural Revolution which began in the summer of 1966 and was at its peak until the spring of 1969. During this period, and even after, China could not exert much influence over the politics of the region outside, and virtually lost its role as a model and leader for the revolutionaries of the region. Freed from their concern with domestic communist insurgencies supported by Beijing, South-east Asian leaders were now more inclined to relax their rigid controls somewhat and allow their respective economies a freer rein.[10] The leaders in the region, like Suharto (Indonesia), Ferdinand Marcos (the Philippines), Lee Kuan Yew (Singapore) and Park (South Korea), who came to power around the early and mid-1960s, responded to the situation with the practical wisdom which can be described as 'development-minded politics' in their efforts at nation-building.

The US retreat, however, meant a subsequent decline in its military spending in South-east Asia. As a result, it was thought imperative that more Japanese money should be provided – in aid or investment or credits – to sustain the sort of growth rates these countries had to have if they were to go on being good markets for Japanese exports. Early in the 1970s, two-thirds of Japan's foreign aid programme went to the Asian Pacific region, mainly to South-east Asia. Most of the outflow of private investment also went to this region. After the first step towards capital liberalization had been taken in 1969, Japanese direct foreign investment in the five ASEAN countries multiplied constantly, with the cumulative total of approved outgoings rising from $490 million in 1970 to $1,481 million in 1973, a threefold increase in four years. With such fast-growing investment not only in industrial projects but also in resource development and the consolidation of infrastructure, Japan quickly assumed a dominant position over the markets in the region. Given this rapid economic expansion and deeper involvement in the

Asian Pacific, Japan faced the crucial question whether to adhere to a diffident low-profile diplomacy or to accept a more active international role going beyond mere export policy. 'Trade and investment,' a Western editor argued, 'do not take place in a vacuum: they have effects on other people, and those people react, and their reactions require decision from Tokyo. Economics, on the Japanese scale, and politics cannot be kept in separate compartments.'[11] Response to this proposition was divided between 'immobilism', unable or unwilling to take political decisions and so continuing post-war Japan's passive stance, and a positive commitment to a policy aimed at preserving peace by economic and diplomatic means, thus preventing the local situation from moving into internal instability. In the long run, the shift was from the former to the latter, but Japan's position remained far removed from that of a fully-fledged actor on the stage of international politics; it lacked the prestige commensurate with its status as the world's third largest economy. In the meantime, abrupt changes in US policies towards Asian and international politics, as well as changes in the world economy, increased the impact of Japan's next crucial phase in the early 1970s.

The emerging context of multilateralism

A variety of major events, such as the US *rapprochement* with China and the US departure from the gold–dollar link in 1971, the oil crisis in 1973–4, and the end of the Vietnam war in 1975, combined to shake Japan's confidence in its policy on Asia and its alliance with the United States. Japan then entered the third phase of its foreign policy, one of 'multi-faceted' diplomacy both in the East Asian political arena and in world economic affairs.

While the world moved towards multipolarity and the Tokyo government intended to change its foreign policy accordingly, Japanese diplomacy was still geared to the bilateral plane, Japan having become accustomed to dealing with international problems through the United States. Even when the Japan–US relationship was shaken by Nixon's deceitful China initiative or strained by Tanaka's cunning reversal of policy towards the Arab states, for example, Japan did not find it possible to change the bilateral alliance into a multilateral arrangement with a third party. One obvious option would have been to focus on trilateral collaboration between the world's major industrialized groups, Japan, North America, and Western Europe. But, as we have seen from the visits to Europe of Premiers Ikeda and Tanaka and even as far back as Yoshida, Japan's successive overtures to the Europeans in its search for a counterbalance to the United States were given the cold shoulder. On the other hand, Japan did not have any close relations with neighbouring Asian countries to which it could appeal to develop a regional partnership:

no possible parallel to West Germany's integration into the European Community and NATO.

Japan's involvement in trilateral co-operation became inevitable, however, soon after the 1973–4 oil crisis, which caused a grave recession and dislocation in the world economy. US intellectuals such as George Ball, Edwin O. Reischauer, and Zbigniew Brzezinski inspired the early rhetoric of trilateralism, which sought a new conceptual foundation on which the 'Western' community could reconstruct the crumbling international economic system.[12] The initiators of the non-governmental Trilateral Commission came out in favour of multilateral summit meetings which should include Japan. Meanwhile, in June 1975, in an interview with James Reston, who asked why a new summit formula should be devised in addition to the various existing Atlantic forums, the French President, Giscard d'Estaing, replied that the novelty was the inclusion of Japan.[13]

When the Prime Minister, Miki Takeo, was invited to the summit conference of Western industrialized nations at Rambouillet in November 1975, Japan had the opportunity, for the first time in the post-war period, to take part in multilateral discussions on the management of the world economy. That the Japanese were from the outset included in the trilateral process of economic policy adjustment concerning the energy problem, the massive upheaval in the balance of payments system, and international monetary matters, was attributed to the fact that none of these problems could be properly solved without the participation of the second biggest economic power in the non-communist world. It was a boost for Japanese dignity to be recognized by the West as a leading nation, and the only industrialized country in Asia.

At the summit meeting, Prime Minister Miki introduced the question of trade into the discussions: Japan was expected to make a contribution to rectifying payments imbalances by reinforcing economic growth. But Miki attached the utmost importance to the North–South problem. He urged participants to make a positive effort to extend economic assistance to the poor nations of the South, using money saved through disarmament. This 'idealistic' proposal met with a cool reaction from the other participants, who preferred to consolidate a united Western position towards the developing countries. Nevertheless, the Japanese delegation succeeded in incorporating its general ideas on the North–South problem into the Rambouillet declaration. So Japan's first campaign at a summit proved to be satisfactory, but resulted in some discord between it and its 'Western' partners.[14]

The economic summit at Rambouillet provided for the establishment of a multilateral management system for the advanced economies of the world. It has persisted to this day. From the Japanese perspective, the purpose of participation in this capitalist apparatus has been twofold:

first, to ensure participation in the mainstream of economic interdependence centred on the Western community; second, to ensure participation in the economic development of the Third World, especially the Asian region.

After the precedent set by Prime Minister Miki at the annual summits of Rambouillet and San Juan (Puerto Rico), successive Premiers followed the same two policies almost throughout the history of the Western summits. At the 1977 London summit, Prime Minister Fukuda Takeo accepted the role of 'locomotive' country for Japan, which would lead a recovery in world business. He also supported the idea of a fund for commodity price stabilization for the developing countries. At the 1978 Bonn summit, Fukuda repeated his commitment to high economic growth, and announced a plan for doubling Japan's development assistance within the next three years. He mentioned the development fund which in the previous year, 1977, he had offered to the ASEAN countries, with extra finance to be allocated for joint regional projects. Fukuda thus considered he should be able to avoid criticism over Japan's trade surplus accumulation.[15]

Parallel to its multilateral diplomacy towards the West, Japan's Asian policy was soon also to diversify in response to new circumstances. With the Vietnam war ending in communist victory in 1975, the most immediate concern in East Asia focused on the so-called 'domino theory'. The countries of South-east Asia were terrified of being forced to assume an adversarial stance towards the United States after the withdrawal of US ground troops from Indochina. Despite the Sino-American *rapprochement* and the Sino-Vietnamese dispute, Chinese intentions in South-east Asia continued to be a source of anxiety, as it was feared that they might support communist insurgencies in Malaysia and Indonesia. The Soviet alliance with Vietnam and the Vietnamese domination of Laos and Kampuchea increased anxiety throughout the region, especially in Thailand. These threats, however, contributed more than any other factor to stimulating the ASEAN nations into joint action as a collective group for the first time since the organization was founded in 1967.

The leaders of the ASEAN nations carried out an active programme of exchange visits, and ASEAN's first summit was convened in Bali, Indonesia, in February 1976. During this crucial period the ASEAN leaders united together under the concept of 'resilience', aiming at socio-economic development and political stability through regional co-operation. In this context, the Bali summit adopted two documents, the Declaration of Concord and the Treaty of Amity and Co-operation. In a quick response from Tokyo, Prime Minister Miki sent a special message conveying Japan's support for the effort to consolidate the political, economic, and social foundation of the five ASEAN countries. The Foreign Minister, Miyazawa Kiichi, issued a statement expressing Japan's positive assessment of the meeting, and its hopes of economic and technological co-operation with the ASEAN countries and stable relations of mutual trust and confidence through a broad range of dialogue and exchanges.

In August 1977 ASEAN observed the tenth anniversary of its formation by holding its second summit meeting and its first summit talks with Japan, Australia, and New Zealand. Prime Minister Fukuda first attended the Kuala Lumpur summit, and then visited each of the five member states and Burma. In the course of this tour he promised development funds totalling US$1 billion for five major ASEAN industrial projects. Winding up his tour with an important speech in Manila, he proclaimed a four-point policy guideline: Japan would not become a military power; it would promote 'heart-to-heart' contacts with ASEAN; it would co-operate with ASEAN on the basis of equality; and it would help to bring about stable and peaceful relations between the countries of ASEAN and Indochina. The 'Fukuda doctrine', as it came to be known, ushered in a special relationship between Japan and South-east Asia.

To further its close partnership with the ASEAN countries, the Tokyo government invited the members' heads of state to visit Japan. Between April and September 1977 President Marcos of the Philippines, Singapore's Prime Minister Lee, Thai Prime Minister Thanin, and Malaysian Prime Minister Hussein Onn all visited Japan. From the next year, 1978, Japan became a regular participant in annual dialogue with the ASEAN Foreign Ministers.

Viewed in the light of the peace and stability of East Asia as a whole, the conclusion of the Japan–China Treaty of Peace and Friendship in August 1978 was very significant. After the normalization of relations with China in 1972, the two governments had concluded a number of agreements on trade, air transport, shipping, fishery, and trade marks, thereby increasing the volume of trade and visitors. At the final stage of the negotiations on the Treaty of Peace and Friendship, the Fukuda government capitulated to China's insistence that an 'anti-hegemony' clause be included. The Soviet Union expressed deep concern over this, declaring that the clause was directed against Moscow and that Japan might fall into the Chinese orbit. But the Japanese government tried to placate Moscow by asserting that the treaty did not affect either contracting party's relations with third parties. In this way, Prime Minister Fukuda claimed that Japan was able to maintain its stance of 'equidistant' or 'omnidirectional' diplomacy.

To summarize, the third phase of Japanese foreign policy in the 1970s began with fears of political isolation and economic alienation from Asia and the Western world; it ended with deeper involvement in the management of world affairs. Japan's ability to adjust to the changing world environment enabled it to expand its international role. Despite and because of the Nixon shocks, Japan entered into close relations with the countries of East and South-east Asia, and assumed its rightful position among the Western industrial democracies.

These relations, however, did not mean that Japan was treated as a full member of the Western alliance, or that it had achieved a close *entente* with the countries of Asia, implying a joint position on political and security matters. For instance, Miki, who represented Japan at the San Juan summit, was not invited to the Western four-power talks at which US President Gerald Ford, West German Chancellor Helmut Schmidt, French President Valéry Giscard d'Estaing, and British Prime Minister James Callaghan discussed political and security matters, since they dealt with European affairs. On the Asian scene, the ASEAN nations were indifferent to Japan's political initiative for the solution of the Indochina conflict. Integration into the trilateral Western summit meetings and the ASEAN dialogue had given Japan greater opportunity to take on economic responsibilities, but friction still continued over trade questions. The expansion of Japan's economic influence had not been matched by its assumption of a responsible role in international politics.

Towards political maturity

At the turn of the decade Japanese diplomacy entered the fourth phase, distinctive for its more politically oriented involvement in international affairs. As interdependence among nations has grown, political, economic, and other activities have become closely intertwined. As Japan's economic strength increases, the international community expects it to play an active role in achieving world peace and prosperity. But there is not much evidence that it has abandoned its pragmatic post-war approach of being reactive and defensive to external events. Japan's path towards political maturity and positive participation in the decision-making processes of international society is therefore a long one, being trodden by the governments of the 1980s.

The new phase will be reviewed at length in Part II. It is first necessary to discuss the internal dynamics of Japanese foreign policy-making, identifying the factors in domestic politics which impose strong constraints on foreign policy.

> In the traditional conception, . . . foreign policy begins where domestic policy ends. . . . If the domestic structures are based on a commensurable notion of what is just, a consensus about permissible aims and methods of foreign policy develops. . . . But, when the domestic structures are based on a fundamentally different conception of what is just, the conduct of international affairs grows complex.[16]

A crucial factor in Japan's internal dynamics, which complicates its conduct of external affairs and militates against major departures in foreign policy, is the memory still haunting Japanese consciousness of their bitter experiences during World War II.

> Most countries shape their foreign policy according to the lessons they learned the generation before. . . . Japan had an active foreign policy from 1931 onwards, and the lesson we Japanese learned was the danger of thinking we were strong, and could use our strength in adventures abroad.[17]

This precept contributed to forging the post-war national consensus embodied in the 'peace' Constitution with its celebrated renunciation of war in Article IX.

But a widening divergence between world realities and Japan's post-war consensus has led to a crucial conflict between the different political parties' foreign policy: conservative opinion adheres to a policy firmly based upon the Japan–US alliance, and the opposition insists on a position of unarmed neutrality or anti-Americanism. This division has created periodic crises in the conduct of major international affairs.

The first such clash occurred in the debate over the 'partial' peace treaty which was negotiated by the Yoshida government. National opinion was split between those in favour and those against the alignment with the West. The second clash came in the battle inside and outside the Diet when the Kishi government tackled the important issue of renewing the Japan–US security treaty in 1960. Kishi's daring policy, which put his own political future at stake, was assessed as a sign of growing maturity as well as a recognition of the harsh realities of world politics.[18] The third example was Japan's response to the abrupt shift in America's China policy in 1971. The Sato government, which continued to be loyal to Washington's previous policy, lost its *raison d'être*. But with the normalization of relations with Beijing in 1972, the China problem ceased to be a source of major domestic controversy. Furthermore, the subsequent improvement of relations, the conclusion of the peace and friendship treaty in 1978, and Deng Xiaoping's Tokyo statements on the importance of maintaining the Japan–US security treaty and on Japan's need to strengthen its defence capabilities combined to emphasize the outmoded and irrelevant nature of the foreign policy of the Japanese left, particularly the Socialists, whose opposition to the security treaty and support for unarmed neutrality had been linked to a pro-Beijing position.[19]

In retrospect, what happened in Japanese domestic politics during these three decades showed that ideological confrontation between right and left was being replaced by a more mature political pluralism, in which the opposition was compelled to give implicit approval to the policies of the ruling party and government, although the Socialists still insisted on the position to which they were formally committed. One significant departure was that political controversy over security and defence policy shifted from the issue of the legitimacy of the Japan–US security treaty and the Self-defence Forces to the issue of how the treaty system should be organized so as to ensure broad public support and constitutional legality. As a result, conflict over Japan's post-war foreign policy gave way to tacit consensus on major external issues.

Towards the beginning of the 1980s, great changes in the world's political, strategic, and economic fields posed a serious threat to the basic international order and Japan's regional environment. Faced with growing political and military tensions in East–West relations and economic difficulties in the Western industrialized countries as well as in the developing nations, Japanese policy-makers attempted to re-examine the basic objectives of their foreign policy, and find a new role in the international community. In the first place, they realized that because of increasing interdependence among the nations of the world and the increasing complexity of their interests, countries are more frequently influenced by incidents in which they are not directly concerned. They also recognized that developments in Japan can have a substantial influence on the world outside; consequently it can no longer consider international relations as a given but, rather, as something which it should help to form, as a responsible member of the international community.[20]

With this new understanding of its own position, how has Japan steered its course through recent crucial international development? What are the themes and issues that Japan faced, and indeed still faces, in its political and economic interactions with Western powers, and in East–West and North–South relations? How has Japan responded to its position as a summit power in the West? These issues are examined in Part II.

Part II

Japan as a Member of the West

Chapter five

A Stage for the Western Alliance

Japan acquired the status of a summit power in the West in the mid-1970s, and has consolidated its position in not only the economic but also the political and security dimension of the Western partnership since the early 1980s. The 1980s have witnessed great shifts in the world power structure in three major areas: first, East–West relations, especially over arms competition and control between the two superpowers, the United States and the Soviet Union; second, the grave dislocation of the global economic and financial system; and, third, conflicts and instabilities in certain parts of the Third World. Looking at these developments from a deeper and much longer perspective, the profound transformation in world power now taking place is the relative decline of the two super-powers, and the corresponding rise of Western Europe's and Japan's power, which helps to cushion and prevent traumatic upheavals in this interregnum in the world order.

Accordingly, Japan's involvement in Western summitry entails innovative efforts to pursue a coherent foreign policy towards the above-mentioned three arenas, in order for Japan to assume a role as a responsible member of the Western industrial democracies. Chapters 5 and 6 detail chronologically Japan's performance in the Western summit meetings. Chapter 7 presents an overview of how Japan's policy has adapted to the main themes of the summit discussions.

The chronology of Japan's participation in the seven-power summit meetings parallels its quest for a proper role in managing the crucial affairs of the Western alliance, and in speaking for its Asian neighbours. Japan started out as a summit power with considerable hesitancy, especially in talks on political affairs and security. But eventually it gained greater confidence which enabled it to play an indispensable part in crisis management and policy co-ordination not only in economic but also in political and security relations among the Western industrial democracies. The annual meetings, rotating between the participating countries, have given Japan a platform to express its opinions about world problems as seen from a corner of Asia.

In accordance with the original idea of dealing mainly with economic problems, the early summits covered a range of subjects from macro-economic policies, trade, and monetary policies to the North–South problem. The first four summits (Rambouillet, Puerto Rico, London, Bonn) concentrated on multilateral management of the world economy by jointly undertaking anti-inflationary/recession policy measures. As for political subjects, there was a reluctance, or even a resistance, to take them up as part of the summits' formal agenda: it was resisted particularly by one of the initiators of the summits, namely France, on the ground that it would detract from the summits' main purpose. Moreover the French position tended to limit international summit politics to the 'Big Four' Atlantic powers, as shown at the Guadeloupe summit in 1979. The Japanese also had different reasons for being uncertain whether to become involved in political discussion. Japan's hesitation could be attributed to its not feeling committed to political and security relations with West European countries. However, much as the French and the Japanese might desire it, a complete separation of economics and politics would not have been possible in any case, since the summits came to deal with the extremely intricate pattern of international relations from the Tokyo and Venice meetings onwards.

Through participation in the summits, Japanese consciousness of being a member of the West has certainly been enhanced. But for the Japanese to regard themselves as belonging to the Western club is one thing; for the Americans and Europeans fully to accept their membership is quite another. Indeed, the allies might part ways and embark on a collision course if economic relations were to move much beyond a tolerable degree of friction. Given the troubled nature of economic interdependence with the West and the difficulties of policy adjustment, how could Japan ensure an intimate partnership acceptable to Western countries? Besides continued efforts to overcome economic and trade tensions, an attempt had to be made to reinforce political ties with the Western nations, thereby permitting greater confidence when dealing with economic problems. This is one important perspective from which this chapter approaches the subject.

It is not intended, in the present study, to examine the whole process of the Western summits. There are already many books and articles which have dealt comprehensively or theoretically with this topic.[1] The present study is confined to a review of Japan's involvement in Western summitry, focusing on the shifting balance between its economic, political and security interests. The period to be reviewed for this particular purpose has the 1979 summit – the first to be organized by Japan – as its starting-point. Before analysing developments from the Tokyo summit onwards, we should look briefly at a summit without Japan – Guadeloupe – a paradoxical event which acted on Japan both as an inducement towards isolation from, and as an incentive to join in, world politics.

A summit without Japan

In January 1979 four Western leaders met in an informal conference – the so-called 'sunshine summit' – on the French Caribbean island of Guadeloupe. It was planned as the first politico-security summit involving the United States, Britain, France, and West Germany since World War II. The leaders of the Big Four, US President Jimmy Carter, French President Valéry Giscard d'Estaing, British Prime Minister James Callaghan, and West German Chancellor Helmut Schmidt, met to discuss the full range of world political issues and monetary issues as well. The Guadeloupe summit had no fixed agenda, no public appearances, and no official joint communiqué, merely individual statements made by the four respective leaders.

The four men had, however, much to discuss, particularly the precarious situation in Iran, where political strife threatened to cut off a major oil source for all four nations. Other main issues included the threat to European security from Soviet military expansion; the prospect of a US–Soviet strategic arms limitation treaty; and the new era in US–Chinese relations. Warfare in Kampuchea was another relevant topic. Special emphasis was placed on the more urgent economic and monetary problems. Focusing on the stabilization of the international currency system, the participants at Guadeloupe needed an agreement in principle to move from the system of floating rates under self-regarding national control to a system of joint management. Hampered by the technical complexity of the new scheme, however, the monetary discussion proved inconclusive.

In the two days of discussions, although everyone was frank and friendly, some very definite differences were aired. West Germany and France were clearly worried about Carter's continued public support of the Shah of Iran, regardless of that country's internal situation. Schmidt was reported to have felt for some time, correctly as it turned out, that the Americans were taking enormous and unwarranted risks in selling sophisticated weapons to the Shah and ignoring the possibility of economic dislocation inside Iran leading to discontent and violence. Giscard d'Estaing, too, argued that it would be unwise for the West to deny itself the option of one day doing business with the Ayatollah. He also wanted to co-ordinate Western policies on Vietnam and Kampuchea. Callaghan wanted European opinion to be given greater weight by Washington policy-makers not just on Iran but on other problems such as the threat of another oil crisis, arms limitation, the Middle East, and Soviet expansion in Africa. Carter's main objective at Guadeloupe, however, was to secure NATO support for a new strategic arms treaty before signing it at a meeting with the Soviet leader, Leonid Brezhnev. On the question of European missiles to counter the Soviet Union's SS-20 medium-range missiles, the four leaders agreed to develop a new approach, coupling the stationing of US Cruise and Pershing II missiles in Europe with progress in arms control negotiations between the superpowers.[2]

The final result of the Guadeloupe summit, as described for example by British Prime Minister Callaghan, was that, having discussed a wide range of political, security, and economic issues, the four leaders understood why and where differences of emphasis existed: they had even been able to resolve these differences in some cases. The Americans were particularly relieved at the strength of support given by the three European leaders to the conclusion and early ratification of the SALT treaty. The Europeans stressed that the relationship between the West and the Soviet Union remained central to the security of Western Europe. As a specific measure, it was decided that it was essential to pump financial aid rapidly into Turkey to support the crumbling economy of a country on NATO's vital eastern flank. The four leaders agreed that developing economic and political contacts with China should not affect the crucial relationship between the West and the Soviet Union. They finally succeeded in overcoming various difficulties in order to co-ordinate policies, make deals, and demonstrate the fundamental common interests that bound them together, even if some of them were reticent on particular issues.[3]

'The Guadeloupe summit is over, Japan was excluded from it. Why?'[4] This was the editorial comment of a leading Japanese newspaper on the exclusively Western summit. Another Japanese editorial writer commented: 'The so-called Sunshine summit at the Caribbean resort was, after all, a family affair among the four major Western allies, and Japan, therefore, had no reason to attend.'[5] Japan's feelings towards the Guadeloupe summit were ambivalent – a mixed reaction of taking exclusion for granted on the one hand, and a sense of humiliation on the other. The tone of immediate Japanese press reaction was divided between cynical detachment and cheerless disappointment. To some, it was almost a relief that the Japanese Prime Minister was not invited, for Japan did not have a leader of sufficient calibre to join in informal talks with these veteran politicians of the Western world.[6] To others, it was a blow to their pride that Japan was not invited although both the China question and the Iranian situation were closely connected with its national interests. Some Liberal Democratic Party (LDP) politicians and government officials, reportedly, expressed feelings of this kind.

Perhaps, in the eyes of the leaders at Guadeloupe, Japan, although an economic power, might not have appeared qualified to discuss world strategy. One important factor was that Japan's diplomatic stance was not as clear-cut as that of the United States and its European allies. While their foreign policies constituted a coherent whole of political, economic, and security interests, Japan's was centred on economic interests alone. There was something opaque about its diplomacy that made it taboo even to discuss defence and security matters.[7] The ambivalence in these arguments is deep-rooted.

However ambivalent it may have been, Japanese reaction to Guadeloupe did appear to be unusually heartfelt, in the sense that it provoked a reappraisal of Japan's own status and role in the world. In this respect, the cheerless disappointment was to become even deeper when the Japanese meditated at length on the reasons why their nation was excluded from the Guadeloupe summit while West Germany, which is also committed not to possess nuclear weapons or despatch troops abroad, was invited.[8] One of the reasons for this was the contrast between the two countries' diplomatic stance *vis-à-vis* the United States. Whereas West Germany could take its own view of international crises, as exemplified by Schmidt's warning to Carter on the Iranian situation during the Guadeloupe discussions, Japan had almost no individual perspective on Iran and the Middle East in general. Although Japan had differed from the United States in protecting its oil sources in the 1973 Arab–Israeli conflict, in the main Japan relied upon and followed the US position. After the Guadeloupe conference, and in the midst of the Iran crisis, West Germany played an active role, for instance, in manoeuvring backstage to try to have the US hostages in Teheran freed. Japan could not take a role anything like equivalent to Germany's in Iranian affairs.

Lacking their own particular world perspective, and handicapped by the language factor, Japanese leaders have found active involvement in international affairs to be no easy exercise. Prime Minister Fukuda himself admitted that attending the Bonn summit in 1975 was a 'trying experience', for he felt an underlying psychological ambivalence – a feeling of 'belonging' (to the Western world) mingled with a sense of alienation.[9]

Not only was Japan excluded from the Guadeloupe meeting, but so also were NATO's smaller and medium-sized members such as Belgium, the Netherlands, Italy, Denmark, and Canada. In contrast to Japan's rather inconclusive reaction, in public at least, Italy, Belgium, and the Netherlands clearly resented being excluded from the discussion on European security, which was no less crucial for them than for the 'Big Four'. They feared that vital strategic decisions would be taken over their heads. The hostile and apprehensive reactions from this minor group implied a profound criticism of the original aspirations of the summit, which was intended to represent a very limited number of countries with major responsibilities.

Participants at Guadeloupe – especially President Giscard d'Estaing – seemed to favour holding highly restricted meetings whether politics or security were being discussed, but the critical reaction from those not invited made this 'directorate' format impossible and outdated. Thus the consequence of the Guadeloupe meeting, paradoxically, was to give the excluded members of the seven-nation summits – Japan, Italy, and Canada – a strong incentive to develop the economic summit into a more formal and visible vehicle of political discussion.[10]

Tokyo: at the eleventh hour

Just six months after Guadaloupe, the Tokyo summit – the first one to take place in Asia – was held in June 1979. Japan's first experience as host to a major international meeting was a hard lesson in how to preserve national interests within multilateral arrangements for crisis management in an economically interdependent world. However premature it may have been in handling discussions on the world's economic crisis and political issues, the Tokyo summit at least took positive steps towards formulating joint approaches to international action. The Tokyo summit also gave Japan an opportunity to draw world attention to problems in Asia. The Prime Minister, Ohira Masayoshi, who was to host the summit, staked his personal prestige on the success of the meeting which was to mark Japan's achievement of an enhanced international role. He expressed in advance his hope that the leaders of the major Western countries would deepen their understanding of the problems of the Asian Pacific region when they gathered in Tokyo. Other Japanese political leaders, such as ex-Premiers Miki and Fukuda, who had attended previous summits, counselled Ohira to take up the North–South problem from the perspective of a newly emerged industrialized country which could represent the aspirations of the developing nations.[11]

A month before the Tokyo summit, Ohira visited Washington for talks with President Carter. Obviously, this was a sort of pre-consultation aimed at co-ordinating the actions to be taken by the two countries at the Tokyo summit. A joint communiqué between Ohira and Carter confirmed that the two countries would work with others at the summit to ensure that it made a substantial contribution to a healthier world economy, particularly through bilateral and multilateral co-ordination among the industrial nations to improve the world energy outlook. The two leaders stressed the need for a 'productive partnership' on issues that went beyond purely bilateral considerations. For example, the communiqué also referred to the flow of refugees from Indochina, which was a cause of instability and a matter of great humanitarian concern in the countries in South-east Asia where they arrived. At a parallel meeting, Japanese Foreign Minister Sonoda Sunao managed to persuade

Secretary of State Vance to accompany him to the ASEAN dialogue meeting scheduled for immediately after the Tokyo summit, so setting a precedent for joint Japan–US action in support of ASEAN and thereby linking the Western summits and the ASEAN dialogue.[12]

Immediately after the Washington visit, the Prime Minister flew to Manila, where UNCTAD V was being held, in order to demonstrate his intention that the Tokyo summit should be part of a Japanese effort to reflect the interests of the developing countries, especially those in South-east Asia. In a keynote speech at the Manila conference, Ohira put forward a new scheme, *hitozukuri* (development of human resources), the area which would be singled out for Asian Pacific co-operation during the 1980s. As a parallel diplomatic gesture, the Ohira government sent a special prime ministerial envoy to the member countries of ASEAN in early June. He met the leaders of ASEAN and heard their expectations of what Japan could do for the region at the Tokyo summit. From the outset of Western summits in 1975, such missions from Tokyo to the ASEAN capitals have been a routine part of Japan's diplomatic efforts, whether or not ASEAN's desires were eventually conveyed accurately or satisfactorily to each summit.

The Tokyo summit was dominated by a single major issue – the energy problem. It was the first summit to attempt to solve a crisis by co-ordinated responses within the industrial world. The second oil crisis in 1979, which was triggered by the Iranian revolution, had a tremendous political and economic impact on the rest of the world. The acute oil shortage and massive price hike by OPEC on the very eve of the Tokyo gathering had a direct effect on the proceedings. The participants opened their discussions in a very tense atmosphere: how to deal with the differing interests of the individual countries in response to the crisis? The opening formal session, under the chairmanship of Ohira, plunged into disorder; he found himself taken by surprise by Giscard d'Estaing's unexpected plan to restrict the seven nations' oil imports at the 1978 level for the next few years. Giscard d'Estaing's proposal for the adoption of specific country-by-country oil import quotas quickly gained the agreement of President Carter, Mrs Margaret Thatcher (Britain), and Chancellor Schmidt.

There were signs that the French scheme derived from an informal night meeting of the Atlantic 'Big Four', later dubbed 'Tokyo Guadeloupe'.[13] Appalled at the stringent limits to be imposed upon Japan's oil consumption, Ohira cracked a joke at a luncheon party, 'Anxiety has made me lose my appetite.'[14] To accept the French proposal would be a fatal blow to the future growth of the Japanese economy, and to refuse it might lead to the failure of the Tokyo summit through Japan's fault. Both possibilities were avoided at the eleventh hour. A helping hand came from the US delegation, which offered a compromise, allowing Japan to keep its oil imports within tolerable limits, at a level not to exceed between 6.3 and 6.9 million barrels a day as a 1985 target. After intense bargaining, which continued right to the end, the Tokyo summit actually turned out to offer the best example of crisis management in that it reached a fairly concrete agreement.[15]

With two-thirds of the economic sessions occupied by the energy problem, the Tokyo summit could hardly propose policy measures in other areas. A macro-economic policy to give priority to the fight against inflation, a trade policy to defeat protectionism, and a monetary policy to ensure stability in international exchange markets: all these were a mere formality in the final communiqué. The North–South problem, to which Japan attached such special importance, was neglected apart from a few empty phrases to the effect that the North had consistently worked to bring developing countries more fully into the world trading system.

It was in fact an Asian political issue – the question of refugees from Indochina – which attracted a great deal of attention in the first Asian-based summit meeting. In line with the previous US–Japanese agreement, President Carter took the initiative of announcing in Tokyo that the United States would double the number of refugees from Indochina it would accept, as part of a seven-nation commitment to increase significantly aid to the homeless 'boat people' of South-east Asia. The other leaders all pledged themselves to do more to help the refugees. There was a criticism of Japan's passive attitude to the intake of refugees, but the government decided, by way of compensation, to contribute up to half the financial aid needed for their settlement overseas. The results of the Tokyo summit were reported by US Secretary of State Vance and Japanese Foreign Minister Sonoda to the five nation ASEAN Foreign Ministers' meeting in Bali, Indonesia, in July.

The refugee question was the only non-economic subject discussed at the summit. It was an international political issue, but it should be regarded more as a humanitarian matter. Although the special statement on refugees helped to establish the precedent that summits would react to international crises or political events, there was no sign of any willingness to discuss global political and security issues to the same extent and degree as the Guadeloupe meeting. The North American and European participants had not expected to devote much of their time in Tokyo to discussing international politics or even security matters regarding NATO. The Japanese hosts, for their part, had little to say on this score, and apparently did not wish to project a misleading image to the sceptical Soviet leaders who might then incorrectly identify Japan as 'a sixteenth member of NATO'.[16] Nevertheless, the limits to Japan's 'non-aligned' stance on NATO had already been revealed when the government decided in May 1979 to extend yen credits to Turkey. Although heralded as an example of Japan's 'independent assistance policy', it was in fact assumed to be part of a commitment made by Japan as a result of West German and US persuasion just before the Tokyo summit. The geopolitical distance which separated Japan from the West was still great, but it would not be long before Japan was involved in security discussions with its Western partners.

Venice: all in the same gondola

The experience and the fate of Venice in the fifteenth century – how the powerful merchant city, with its traditional trade and political relations with the East, was disrupted by the fall of Constantinople, and how it declined as a political and commercial power in Europe owing to its failure to make fundamental adjustments in policy and approach – should be a reminder to the democracies of Europe, North America, and Japan of the costs of an inadequate response to current problems.[17] One key question emerged before the twentieth-century Venice summit: could democratic political systems – traditionally focused on demands emerging from within national borders – address pressing problems and new opportunities from a global perspective?[18]

Despite the intensive preparations made by President Carter and other leaders, the June 1980 Venice summit's response to the urgent political and economic issues proved to be inadequate and ineffective. The reason was not lack of enthusiasm for tackling international crises, but constraints imposed by domestic factors such as the impending elections in several countries (the United States, France, and West Germany), and the sudden death of the Japanese Prime Minister, Ohira, just before the summit. All these kept the leaders from clear commitments to adjustments in policy.

However inconclusive it may have been, the Venice meeting marked an epochal departure from the 'economic' summit practice in that, against a background of acutely deteriorating East–West relations owing to the problems of Afghanistan and Iran, political and security questions were formally inscribed on the agenda for discussion together with economic questions. It was also a new opportunity for Japan to participate in high-level discussions on affairs of strategic importance – a privilege limited in the past to key members of the Atlantic alliance.

The Japanese government was now fully prepared to join in discussions on political issues. Foreign Minister Okita Saburo, who attended the Venice summit in the place of Ohira, showed his understanding of the political nature of the meeting by saying in advance that the manner in which Western countries foresaw and coped with future moves by the Soviet Union would be a major topic for discussion in Venice.[19] When the Afghanistan crisis broke out in December 1979, Ohira, the then Prime Minister, well understood the profound strategic implications of the

Soviet threat to the entire Western world, Japan included. Faced with this grave situation affecting the vital interests of the industrial democracies, the Japanese, government and public alike, no longer showed ambivalence over aligning their policy with the West on the Afghanistan and Iran crises.

The political discussion in Venice focused mainly on the Soviet invasion of Afghanistan and the Iranian seizure of American hostages. The joint communiqué issued after the summit called for joint action against the Soviet threat towards central Asia and on the political instability in the Middle East. The summit meeting, however, failed to work out specific measures which might effectively check the Soviet Union, apparently because the United States and its European allies did not see eye-to-eye on how they should approach the Afghan problem, the Middle East situation, and East–West relations in general. The US-proposed economic sanctions against the Soviets and boycott of the Moscow Olympics met with a cool reaction from West European leaders, who were reluctant to make any commitment to such concrete measures.

The leaders adopted broadly different interpretations of the Soviet gesture, made just before the summit, of partially withdrawing troops from Afghanistan. According to Okita, Giscard d'Estaing, who received a message from Brezhnev, at first appraised the Soviet move positively, whereas Carter and Mrs Thatcher took a rather cautious view.[20] On policy towards the Middle East, the United States and Western Europe were in disagreement – for instance, over the hostage problem. The Europeans had been very critical of Carter's attempt to carry out a military rescue of the American hostages in Teheran.

Japan did not side explicitly with either party. It merely joined in the statement calling for the complete withdrawal of Soviet troops and condemning the Iranian taking of hostages. But, in the last analysis, Japan's position on the Afghan issue was close to that of the United States, while on the Middle East problem it was rather similar to that of the European countries. Okita tried to draw attention to the Kampuchean conflict, which he thought just as important as the West thought the Soviet invasion of Afghanistan, but virtually no one showed any concern. Nevertheless, it was at the Venice summit that Japan first took part in the formal process of Western political co-ordination, despite the limitation inherent in its absence from NATO and from European political co-operation.[21]

In the economic discussions, the Venice summit gave top priority to the reduction of inflation, but, as at the Tokyo summit, much time was devoted to energy. The energy problem was approached with a view to breaking the link between economic growth and oil consumption. This strategy implied conserving oil and substantially increasing the production and use of alternative energy resources. The final communiqué called for a large increase in the use of coal and nuclear power in the medium term, and a significant increase in production of synthetic fuels, solar energy, and other renewable energy sources over the longer term.

Coupled with the energy problem, economic difficulties in developing countries were discussed, especially from the point of view of helping non-oil-producing countries liable to suffer both a sharp increase in oil prices and debt. The discussions were influenced by the Brandt Report, which urged a massive attempt to offset the impact of oil prices on the developing countries. West German Chancellor Schmidt was sufficiently impressed with the urgency of the North–South problem to push the Brandt Report on to the summit agenda. The Germans were pressing for OPEC to give more in the way of grants to help the Third World. An imaginative initiative on recycling oil money was desperately necessary,[22] but the immediate practical problem was how agreement on effective measures could be reached between the summit countries. Although Japan had a strong desire to assist the Third World, it could not make any specific commitments of economic aid to developing countries during the Venice summit, partly because of the death of Ohira, who had been thinking of pledging to double Japanese assistance to the Third World in the next five years. In the end, the North–South problem was left to be discussed as a major issue at the next summit; in the meantime participants would review aid policy and procedures and other contributions to developing countries, and report back their conclusions to the Ottawa summit.

After the conclave in a former monastery on the Isola San Giorgio, Okita used a single phrase to sum up the situation: they were all, he said, in 'the same gondola', and had to find a common policy to meet a common danger.[23] Chancellor Schmidt was more sober-minded and unusually frank when he said that it was not good enough for the leaders to agree on common principles only once a year at the summit conference. The difficulties arose, he insisted, when they parted; then, under political pressures at home, they seemed to forget the promises and principles they had agreed upon at the summit.[24]

Ottawa: patching up the alliance

The July 1981 Ottawa summit saw a radical change in the line-up and consequent divergence of political and economic philosophies. The elections in France and the United States as well as the changes of government in Japan and Italy altered the personal representation at the summit more than at any previous meeting. The European Commission also sent its new president to Ottawa. This reshuffle meant less concerted action among the leaders on virtually every issue: foreign-policy issues like Poland, the Middle East, and Africa, and economic issues such as macroeconomics, trade, the North–South problem, and East–West economic relations.

A clear difference could be observed in the macro-economic policy adopted by the individual summit countries. Whereas the new Socialist government in France introduced Keynesian, expansionary economic measures, the British, Germans, and Japanese pursued monetary orthodoxy, and the newly elected US President, Ronald Reagan, shifted policy abruptly from control of demand to a mixture of monetarism and expansion of supply. Controversy focused on high US interest rates and the volatility of the dollar. The Europeans were much concerned with the dampening effect that US interest rates were having on investment at home and with the fact that increases in the value of the dollar had raised their energy import costs. Furthermore, they feared that President Reagan might have got his fiscal policy wrong and that a failure to reduce the budget deficit far enough left monetary policy as the only weapon in the fight against inflation. The Japanese shared European views.

In spite of the underlying divergence of policy between the United States and other industrial democracies, the economic discussions at the Ottawa summit finally ended in agreement that efforts should be made to defeat inflation and unemployment, to avoid trade protectionism, and to assist the developing countries. They avoided short-range policy co-ordination, and preferred a longer-term compromise without a precise agreement on how to accomplish their objectives in the immediate future. Making no concession on macro-economic policy, the United States provided some compensation on the North–South problem, which the host government had intended to put forward as a centrepiece of the summit.

The North–South problem had been the 'homework' the participants were to study after the previous Venice summit. The Canadian host, Prime Minister Pierre Trudeau, made an extensive trip to sound out opinion and to seek support for a North–South dialogue among his European partners as well as leaders in the Third World, prior to the Ottawa summit and as a part of the preparations for the North–South summit meeting scheduled to be held in Cancun, Mexico, at the end of October.[25] When the Japanese Prime Minister, Suzuki Zenko, was on his way home from Washington, he met Trudeau in Ottawa in early May, before Trudeau's foreign tour. They agreed that the North–South problem should be given the 'highest priority' at the Ottawa summit. But when President Reagan visited Ottawa, Trudeau realized that the new US leader had little enthusiasm for the issue in general or for the Cancun meeting in particular. In Europe, Trudeau found strong supporters in the new French President, Franc·ois Mitterrand, German Chancellor Schmidt, and the European Commission, but the response in Britain was lukewarm. In the developing countries Trudeau sensed a great suspicion of the West's sincerity in global trade negotiations.

President Reagan and Mrs Thatcher were very sceptical of the proposal from the 'Group of 77' for global negotiations on North–South economic co-operation to be sponsored by the United Nations. Reagan was reluctant to expand the industrial nations' assistance to developing countries and tended to view foreign aid from the strategic standpoint of East–West relations. With high unemployment in Britain, Mrs Thatcher could not afford to increase foreign aid. But at the summit Reagan agreed on a language of compromise, expressing his willingness to participate in preparations for a mutually acceptable process of global negotiations. With this major change in attitude on the part of Reagan, and also Thatcher, the summit marked a personal triumph for Trudeau.[26]

Suzuki also felt satisfied because he had been able to play a 'leading role' in the field. This seemed to him important because Japan saw itself as the sole representative of Asian countries, particularly the ASEAN nations which he had visited in January of that year. To prove its sincerity, the Japanese government had decide to double Japan's official development assistance (ODA) in five years; this was the second such decision, Fukuda having made a commitment to double ODA at the 1979 Bonn summit. In line with Japan's position at the Venice summit, where it had appealed for a peaceful solution to the Kampuchean conflict but had been virtually ignored, Suzuki took the matter up again in Ottawa, asking that the importance of finding a solution to the problem of Kampuchea be included in the summit's closing report. This was achieved, through a brief reference in Trudeau's political report.

The greater political orientation of the Ottawa summit compared to previous summits was evident in the 'Trudeau Report' issued at the end of the meeting. In it Trudeau called for a two-pronged strategy comprising dialogue and military build-up to confront the Soviet Union. The report acknowledged the need for a large defence build-up by Western nations, an apparent concession by other Western nations to President Reagan's tough anti-Soviet strategy, but it also stated that the Western nations were ready to resume dialogue and co-operation on disarmament with the Soviet Union. Moreover, Trudeau identified the Arab–Israeli conflict as the major international concern, not the Soviet military threat as had been strongly advocated by Reagan. Trudeau thus skilfully patched up differences between the Western nations.

For both political and commercial reasons, of course, differences still existed inside the Western alliance over East–West economic relations. The United States wanted to maintain its technological advantage over the Soviet Union, with mainly strategic considerations in mind. The Europeans, for their part, tended to look to trade with the East not only to fill their order books, but also to build bridges between the political blocs.[27] The leaders agreed to co-ordinate action to ensure that 'our economic policies continue to be compatible with our political and

71

strategic objectives'. But there was no evidence that either side had shifted where matters of substance were concerned, even though the communiqué implied that both President Reagan and the Europeans were willing to consider each other's viewpoint.

The Japanese position on East–West political relations was explained by Suzuki: 'The West must restore the military balance with the East in order to ensure a fruitful dialogue between the two sides for disarmament in the future.' This was precisely in keeping with the line articulated in Trudeau's political statement. But Suzuki rejected pressure from the United States and the West European allies for commitment to a greater defence build-up. In this respect, he clearly maintained a position compatible with Japan's own defence policy and constitution renouncing war. In Japan there was a mixed reaction to the prominent place given to political issues at the Ottawa summit and President Reagan's obvious success in bringing the Soviet threat to the fore. Some people feared that the summit had intensified East–West confrontation by stressing its military preparations rather than opening a dialogue on disarmament with the Soviet Union.[28] Japan's position on the issue seemed clearly closer to the European countries, which emphasized dialogue with the Soviet Union. This had already been indicated by press comments expressing the hope that Prime Minister Suzuki would work with his West European colleagues to modify Reagan's hard-line policy towards Moscow.

On the highly politicized question of foreign aid, Suzuki promised the other participants that Japan would step up its economic assistance to regions of East–West conflict, such as Thailand, Pakistan, and Turkey. This move seemed to be influenced somewhat by the US strategic view which regards foreign aid as an instrument for containing communism in the Third World. On international trade issues, Tanaka Rokusuke, the Minister of International Trade and Industry, tried to forestall the EC's criticism of Japan's soaring trade surplus with Western Europe by revealing a new programme to encourage imports. He said the government was willing to facilitate the entry of a wider range of foreign goods into Japan. At the same time, 'Japan would suggest to the Western countries that the solution lies in making structural adjustments,' said a Japanese diplomat, meaning that Japan's competitors should improve their own systems of production.[29] The EC failed in its attempt to insert a reference into the communiqué about restraint by exporting nations. Criticism of the large Japanese trade imbalances was rather muted, and Foreign Minister Sonoda emphasized that Japan had not been required to make any new undertakings.[30]

Outside the seven-nation summit proper, Suzuki and Reagan met separately, in an attempt to patch up a row over the joint communiqué issued after their May meeting in Washington. Controversy had arisen over a reference, for the first time ever in a Japan–US communiqué, to the bilateral relationship as an 'alliance', and also to Suzuki's remarks about defending sea lanes up to 1,000 nautical miles from Japan. This new definition and new commitment had been taken to imply an expanded military role for Japan. On his return to Tokyo Suzuki lamely denied this. US–Japan relations consequently soured because of the apparent contradiction between Suzuki's utterances in Wahington and his defensive explanations at home. The differences over defence and the management of the bilateral relationship seemed in fact to stem from Suzuki's preference for a 'comprehensive security' concept in which economic and diplomatic means weighed heavier than military ones as against Reagan's belief in a strategic military build-up. Suzuki's reaffirmation of his commitment to the May communiqué appeared to serve the immediate purpose of rectifying relations with Reagan. However, the roots of the differences had still not been aired and Japan had still not been absolved from the need to improve its defence capability.[31]

Versailles: transatlantic strife

The Western summit conference was held in each of the seven member states in turn, and in 1982 returned to its first location, France. From Rambouillet in 1975 to Versailles in 1982, crisis management of the world economy continued to be the dominant theme of the summits, without any significant improvement being achieved. A solution could emerge, President Mitterrand argued, if leaders reached what he termed 'a minimum of consensus' in the formulation of strategies aimed at promoting world-wide economic growth. 'Rarely have the allies,' Mitterrand dared to say during a pre-summit interview with American journalists at the Elysée Palace, 'been so indifferent to one another's fate.'[32]

The overall outlook for the world economy had been becoming more and more unfavourable since recession had started to spread round the world several years before. By 1982 unemployment in the industrialized nations had risen to nearly 30 million, almost twice as many as in 1975, when the first economic summit was held. Industrial production in the seven summit countries had decreased by an average of 2.8 per cent in the previous year, though the rate of inflation was being steadily reduced. The burden of debt in the developing countries had reached an alarming level. The interest rates recorded in many countries were higher than they had been since the 1930s. All the signs pointed to the danger of a breakdown in the world economic system.

Faced by growing strains in the free-trade system, the June 1982 Versailles summit gave top priority to international monetary policy. An ideological clash occurred between the French and the Americans: the former advocated a reform of the world monetary system by means of direct intervention to stabilize exchange rates, the latter insisted on floating rates to avoid artificial support in the market. In the background was the Europeans' continued criticism of high US interest rates, large deficits, and, above all, the stubborn policy of the Reagan administration. Schmidt was resentful at the Americans for keeping interest rates up and so robbing the rest of the world of some of the benefits of this painful medicine. The European assault on high US interest rates was countered by US objections to the planned natural gas pipeline from Siberia and the terms of credit proposed for the Soviets, which might make Western Europe too dependent on East–West trade.

Transatlantic strife of such magnitude could hardly be reconciled in a few days' meeting. In their final communiqué the leaders of the seven nations pledged themselves to pursue 'prudent' monetary policies and a 'prudent and diversified' economic approach to the Eastern bloc. What 'prudence and diversification' actually meant was that participants had been unable to adopt any real joint measures because they had been unable to resolve their basic differences.[33]

To achieve multilateral control of the world economy, the Europeans had hoped, but failed, to get President Reagan to promise a change in his monetary policy. Donald Regan, the US Treasury Secretary, said unequivocally, 'All the intervention in the world will not bring interest rates down in the United States.' In addition to this rebuff, the Americans had pressed the West Europeans and Japan to limit trade credits to the Soviets, in the interests of East–West strategy. Suzuki, however, insisted to President Reagan that Japan's Sakhalin oil development project, agreed even before the US-led economic sanctions were imposed, should be exempt from the proposed credit restriction.[34] For the European side, the French led resistance to US moves.

Political discussions at the Versailles summit focused on two urgent issues: the British–Argentine 'war' in the Falklands and the Israeli attack on Lebanon. Afghanistan, Poland, and disarmament were also examined. However, all these discussions took place outside the main meeting. The fact that the political and security issues were set apart from the formal conference and confined to individual sessions or private talks seemed due to the host country France's preference that summit meetings should limit themselves to the 'economic' sphere. As a result, the trend towards more extensive and formal discussion of political and security matters was interrupted at Versailles.[35]

The Falklands crisis cast a long shadow over the Versailles summit. It could not be the subject of any formal statement, but Western solidarity with Britain on this matter was confirmed. The UN resolution calling for an immediate cease-fire and withdrawal of troops had been vetoed by Britain and the United States. However, the United States had originally wanted to abstain, rather than veto, which suggested some degree of rift. Japan voted for the resolution, in line with its consistent view that the issue should be settled through the United Nations. Mrs Thatcher complained to Suzuki at Versailles, saying she had hoped Japan would abstain. Despite these embarrassments, all the seven leaders gave full support for the British cause, and Mrs Thatcher declared her satisfaction. The Lebanon crisis erupted during the summit meeting; President Reagan sent messages to all interested parties in the region calling on them to refrain from any intervention, and to Menachem Begin, Israel's Prime Minister, he sent a personal message appealing for an end to hostilities. However, the only response he received from Begin was a statement that Israel had advanced into Lebanon to put its settlements out of reach of attack. The European countries and Japan could do nothing. As these episodes make clear, purely political questions played a smaller part at the Versailles summit than at previous summits, due partly to insufficient co-ordination among participants.

A positive theme at the Versailles summit, however, was the French strategy for promoting higher levels of international economic growth through collaboration in technology. In spelling out this strategy, President Mitterrand urged the other leaders to agree to give priority to co-operative efforts between governments and public and private companies in high investment areas such as energy, telecommunications, robotics, electronics, space, and other new technologies. The Japanese government positively supported the French initiative, and Suzuki emphasized the need to facilitate such international co-operation not only among developed nations but also between developed and developing countries. Suzuki also stressed that the proposal should be advanced as part of the international effort to revitalize the stagnant world economy.

The United States and Britain, by contrast, were more concerned to focus on the unfair disadvantages to private companies resulting from increasing government intervention – notably by France and Japan – in the high-technology sectors. Both President Reagan and Mrs Thatcher emphasized the importance of the private sector in the development and application of research. The summit's declaration on technology reconciled the two different approaches, emphasizing the need to remove barriers both to the development of new technologies and to technology transfer. After the summit a working party was formed to follow up President Mitterrand's proposals, but in the event the French initiative came to nothing.

A degree of subtle agreement was reached on the North–South issue, when the Reagan administration came a step closer to its allies by accepting the UN-sponsored 'global negotiations', on condition that the influence of authoritative agencies such as the International Monetary Fund (IMF) should not be diluted in favour of the General Assembly. The issue of global negotiation on the problems of trade, finance, agriculture, and poverty in the Third World had remained stalled since the Cancun meeting in October 1981, and it was hoped that the new agreement at Versailles might mean a breakthrough for North–South dialogue. Still, there was no clear indication that the stalemate could be broken, given the obstructiveness of the hard-liners in the 'Group of 77'.

Preoccupied with monetary policy and East–West economic relations, the economic discussions at the summit left little space for international trade issues. Yet the Western industrial nations were becoming seriously worried about the prospect of a slide into protectionism. Here again the 'Japanese problem' was evoked by the Americans and Europeans, who wanted the Versailles summit to focus on Japan's disproportionately large trade surplus. In the United States, Congressional demands mounted for what was called 'reciprocity', meaning that restrictions would be imposed on Japan's or other countries' imports if they did not derestrict their markets to levels equal to the US levels.[36] The US government hoped and expected the EEC to side with it in bullying Japan into opening its markets. Japan narrowly escaped being singled out as the target of criticism at the summit, however, by announcing, in advance, a new package of measures to reduce import tariffs on over 200 items. This move was carefully timed for maximum publicity before and after the summit. Yet it did little to ease the underlying frustrations of the rest of the world.

Chapter six

Forging the Political Partnership

Although Japan's participation in the annual Western summits has been part of a gradual and continuous process of transformation in its foreign policy, a new head of government may bring a sort of mutation in policy on basic issues. This was particularly true of Prime Minister Nakasone Yasuhiro, who attended his first summit at Williamsburg in 1983. This chapter examines the five consecutive summits attended by Nakasone and the first attended by his successor, Takeshita.

Williamsburg: security on a global basis

Political and security issues again came to the fore at the 1983 Williamsburg summit. After nearly a decade of Western summits, none of the original initiators of the meetings was still participating, for the last founding member, Helmut Schmidt, had given up his seat to Helmut Kohl, the new Chancellor of West Germany. Other newcomers were the Japanese Prime Minister, Nakasone, and the Italian Prime Minister, Amintore Fanfani. The host, President Reagan, insisted that the participants be free to discuss whatever they wanted without being committed to a prearranged agenda. So Williamsburg became the first summit where Western defence and East–West arms control were taken up *ad hoc* as issues for a joint statement.[1]

Nevertheless, macro-economic policy, East–West trade, and Third World debt and development, issues which were carried over from the previous summits, could not be treated lightly, especially after the failure of previous attempts to co-ordinate policy had cast serious doubt on the validity of the summit meetings. By the time of the Williamsburg meeting, the world economy was over the worst, and was heading towards recovery from stagflation and the pressures of high oil prices. Estimates of economic growth in most of the leading industrial countries had been revised upwards; a useful stimulus to growth was provided by the fall in the price of oil; and the rate of inflation had been brought down. However, structural obstacles to sustained, non-inflationary economic growth remained, including the US budget deficit, exchange-rate instability and the international debt problem.

The Reagan adminstration's determination not to let summit politics interfere with domestic measures proved a major stumbling-block to the attempt to co-ordinate macro-economic policies among the industrial democracies. The policy of refusing to give way adopted not only by the United States but also by other countries had dashed hopes of harmonization even at the stage of drafting the summit agenda. Barely touching on the crucial divergence between monetary and exchange-rate policy, and overlooking chances for essential agreement on macro-economic strategy, the final communiqué repeated platitudes on the need for a better co-ordination of Western efforts to promote world economic recovery by pursuing 'a balanced set of policies' designed to obtain inflation-free growth, low interest rates, reduced budget deficits, higher productive investment, and greater employment opportunities.

At a meeting of OECD Foreign Ministers in Paris in early May 1983, President Mitterrand of France had proposed that a new Bretton Woods-style monetary conference be convened to study different methods of stabilizing exchange rates. But the American response was cool, and apart from West Germany, other countries were only lukewarm. The Japanese government did not consider it realistic to talk about a return to the fixed-rate system which had broken down a decade before.

On trade issues there was an expectation that the summit would call for a new round of GATT ministerial meetings to negotiate broader liberalization of trade. The Americans had also been pressing for more specific institutional links between trade and financial issues, but the French attitude to such an initiative was negative. Thus the whole area of trade was littered with banana skins.[2] Disagreement over East–West trade and relations with developing countries was, once again, unresolved.

In contrast with the sterile argument on economic issues, the Williamsburg summit produced a fruitful political statement on security. Western defence and arms control policies provided the centre-piece of the summit's political debate. It was a personal success for President Reagan, who obtained agreement on a statement by reconciling marked differences between the Western nations, including France and Japan – both non-members of NATO.

To begin with, in his capacity as chairman, President Reagan judged that the summit should respond firmly to the Soviet Union, which had issued a 'pre-summit' challenge in the form of a threatening statement made in late May. The statement said that Soviet missiles might be deployed closer to Western Europe if the deployment of new US Cruise and Pershing II missiles there went ahead. Reagan suggested that the Foreign Ministers prepare a strong statement on the issue, to be adopted at the summit. Mrs Thatcher supported this idea, as she considered that it could be useful for her election campaign, stressing as it did the West's commitment to arms reductions alongside its strong determination to defend peace and freedom.

However, the French protested against the US proposed statement, in line with their belief that the summit should not try to issue policy guidance, especially on political and security questions. More important, they felt that Reagan was confirming their worst fears, attempting to turn the Western summit into a US-dominated 'super-NATO' – a permanent forum for discussion of East–West and security issues.[3] Finally, after they had obtained considerable modifications, which placed more emphasis on arms control and less on the deployment of the new US weapons, the French reckoned that they had made their point and went along with the final statement.

In agreeing to the Williamsburg statement on security Japan took a bold and significant step towards reassessing its role as a member of the Western alliance. Prime Minister Nakasone came to the summit determined to represent a Japan which, in his words, was not 'just an economic animal', but was ready to speak out, take stands, and shoulder responsibilities on matters important to the survival and prosperity of the global community. Of course, Nakasone's actions in Williamsburg inevitably attracted stern criticism and controversy, not least in Tokyo. For example, the leader of the Japan Socialist party, Asukada Ichiro, commented that the summit statement confirmed the link between the Japan–US security treaty and NATO.[4]

A crucial phrase in the joint statement was the one proclaiming: 'The security of our countries is indivisible and must be approached on a global basis.' It was placed in the statement at Japan's request. A Japanese declaration of close adherence to the NATO military alliance was a symbolic step linking the US–Japanese security arrangement in the Pacific and the US–European security system in the Atlantic. This link caused serious anxiety to those who opposed a larger Japanese military role in the world. Nakasone and Foreign Minister Abe Shintaro ruled out any drastic change in their defence policy. Nevertheless, the new definition of Japan's role as 'indivisible' from Western security *vis-à-vis* the Soviet Union represented a major departure from its previous position, in which security concerns had been confined to defence of the homeland.

The immediate impetus of Japan's shift of policy came from Soviet statements made in January 1983, suggesting that SS-20 nuclear missiles removed from Europe as a result of the Geneva arms control negotiations might be moved to Asia. Tokyo's fear of this eventuality led to its insistence that no arms control deal should permit the Soviet Union to reduce its military power in Europe while increasing it in Asia. In that context, the US attempt to bring the Japanese and Europeans together met with success in the form of an unprecedented assumption of joint responsibility.[5] Some of the Western press commented on the 'surprising' efforts of Mitterrand and Nakasone to make a success of the summit, but it was not known at the time that Nakasone's shrewd diplomatic sense had played such a crucial part.[6] During the summit, prior to the formal session on East–West relations, Nakasone had made overtures to both Mitterrand and Fanfani. Aware that France had often objected to Japanese involvement in Western security discussions, Nakasone first spoke to Mitterrand in broken French. Unnoticed by the 'Anglo-Saxons', Nakasone won over the two 'Latin' leaders with his un-Japanese personality.[7] In a historical perspective the Williamsburg political statement may seem even more important than it did at the time, as a landmark in Japan's involvement in Western security discussions.[8] 'Western unity can have a political result – bringing the Soviet Union to the negotiating table,' Nakasone said. 'If we are not united, the Soviet Union may just laugh at us and never sit down to negotiate. As a realistic statement, that is how I think.' No Japanese leader had spoken out as resolutely and explicitly at a summit meeting before.[9]

London II: resisting protectionism

The London summit in June 1984 was the tenth annual Western summit meeting, and coincided with the fortieth anniversary of D-Day. The seven heads of government took the occasion to issue a 'London Charter' on democratic values. This was seen as an affirmation of commitment to the summit meetings over the last ten years and to shared traditional values by the Western industrial democracies. For the former, it was a time of stocktaking; for the latter, a time for reappraisal of unity.

Prior to the tenth summit, the Trilateral Commission (a private group of US, Japanese, and European leaders) published the report *Democracy must Work*, which argued that no single summit meeting would be able to solve all problems: each summit would need to monitor developments and decide on fresh action in the light of experience. The summit discussions, it continued, would need to extend beyond economic matters to other issues relating to the effective working of democracy, political stability, and military security.[10] Reflecting these expectations, the London Charter declared that in the political and economic system of the democracies, governments should create conditions for the greatest possible range and freedom of choice and personal initiative. Like the ten previous meetings, the London summit did not produce a programme of action. But, on balance, it stiffened resistance to protectionism and gave some impetus to the liberalization of trade.

At Williamsburg in 1983 the seven summit nations were able to detect clear signs of economic recovery from world recession. Now, in

London, it could be seen that the recovery was established on the sound basis provided by determined efforts in the summit countries and elsewhere to reduce inflation. The economic declaration then emphasized that unremitting efforts should continue to reinforce the basis for enduring growth and for the creation of new jobs. For a number of reasons, no participant dared to wage an open dispute over policy options. Mrs Thatcher, as hostess for the first time, wanted to preside over an uncontentious summit. President Reagan hoped the meeting would be a smooth and harmonious conclusion to successful trips to Ireland and the Normandy beaches. Other participants had no desire to 'embarrass' Reagan, who was facing a presidential election in November.[11]

Despite, or perhaps because of, the wish not to embarrass Reagan, the summit again failed to check high US interest rates and budget deficits. The final communiqué said that high interest rates and failure to reduce inflation further could put recovery at risk, but the United States was not singled out for any public criticism at the summit itself. The communiqué merely repeated a hackneyed message: prudent monetary and budgetary policies of the kind that have brought us this far will have to be sustained and, where necessary, strengthened. Not surprisingly, the outcome of the discussion on macro-economic policy was strongly criticized by leaders of the British opposition parties for its failure to find any positive formula to promote further international recovery: in particular the lack of measures to reduce unemployment was questioned severely. Mrs Thatcher, in a BBC interview, referred to Japan and the United States as examples which other countries, including Britain, would do well to imitate in terms of their business recovery under fine entrepreneurship.

The issue of international trade liberalization versus protectionism had been a source of continuous conflict from the beginning of the Western summits in 1975. The London summit urged all trading countries, industrialized and developing alike, to resist continuing protectionist pressures, and to make renewed efforts to liberalize and expand international trade. However, these fine words did little to produce a breakthrough in trade negotiations. The Japanese delegation, with the support of the United States, had come to London in a positive frame of mind to place one specific initiative on the conference table: a new multilateral GATT trade round. Takeshita Noboru, Minister of Finance, put this proposal in the context of wider economic recovery: 'A strong trading system can revitalize the world economy.' Japan regarded free trade as a *cause célèbre*, and hoped it would emerge as one of the central points of agreement at the London summit.[12] Yet Japan's enthusiasm was to be soon dashed, as the West European countries, especially France, were not to be persuaded. Japan also would have liked to take a new initiative, this time together with the European countries and

Canada, for a more specific commitment on debt and development aid to the Third World, but in this case it was the United States which was simply not prepared to agree.

As far as economic discussions are concerned, all indications point to the conclusion that the summits of the seven industrial countries have not yet succeeded in co-ordinating the action necessary for revitalization. The participants should understand that, as US President Calvin Coolidge once said, the job of governments is not to do good things but, rather, to prevent bad things from happening. As an American summit veteran has commented, the summits were most successful when they made it politically easier for governments to remove or reduce obstacles to sound growth (e.g. oil price controls) rather than when they proposed goals (e.g. specific national rates of growth) which their members lacked the means to achieve.[13]

On the political and security fronts, three statements emerged from discussions on such crucial topics as international terrorism, the Iraq–Iran conflict, East–West relations, and arms control. The most notable of these was the statement condemning the growth of so-called state-sponsored terrorism, as exemplified by the shooting at the Libyan embassy in St James's Square, London, in April. The statement expressed the leading Western nations' determination to stamp out further abuses, but did not go beyond general proposals which included co-ordinated action through competent international organizations and in the international community as a whole to prevent and punish terrorist acts. The second statement was a short expression of concern over the continuing Iraq–Iran war and attacks by both sides on neutral shipping.

The third statement, on East–West relations and arms control, stressed the primary need for solidarity and resolve among the Western allies. At the same time, it expressed a determination to pursue the search for extended political dialogue and long-term co-operation with the Soviet Union and its allies. There was a clash between President Reagan and Prime Minister Trudeau, the former showing his anger at the latter's personal '*détente* crusade', which blamed the United States for the impasse in East–West relations.[14] Nevertheless, substantial agreement was reached on the need to explore all suitable opportunities for East–West dialogue.

Following up its acceptance of the Williamsburg statement on defence and security on a global basis, Japan supported the London statement calling on the Soviet Union to accept the Reagan administration's offer to restart nuclear arms control talks anywhere, at any time, without preconditions. It is not surprising, given that the London statement did not imply a commitment to any specific defence effort, that Japan's endorsement of it provoked much less criticism at home than had the statement at Williamsburg.

The London summit scored a fair point in the reappraisal of unity among the seven nations through the 'declaration on democratic values'. Though full of clichés and banalities, it is still valuable. 'Just the day before,' a veteran participant said, 'we had a long celebration of D-Day.' He continued: 'The Germans and the Japanese were our enemies then, and we wanted to say that 40 years have passed. Maybe the people in Japan and Germany will read the declaration and think that, well, we did mourn D-Day but now we're working together.'[15]

Bonn II: an equal sacrifice by three parties

The 1978 Bonn summit had claimed 'far-reaching economic measures of agreement'. The Bonn summit of May 1985 might similarly have seen the macro-economic debate between the United States and other parties as evidence of a turning-point. In the expectation that the American budget deficit was about to be brought under control, the participants wanted to discuss how a rectification of the US fiscal imbalance would benefit the economies of Western Europe (and Japan).[16] But what actually happened in Bonn was far from satisfactory. No concrete agreements resulted from the political debates, either, which were overshadowed by legacies from the past and vague proposals on the future.

The host country, West Germany, through Chancellor Kohl, seemed to have deliberately timed the summit to coincide with the fortieth anniversary of VE-Day in order to usher in a period of reconciliation. The 'historic' reunion in Bonn was, however, marred before it even started by a tremendous row stirred up by Reagan's visit to the war cemetery at Bitburg with Chancellor Kohl. This was so mishandled that Allied–German reconciliation seemed still to be required to overcome the bitterness which had lingered on for forty years. There was another opportunity, not in Bonn but in Strasbourg, for the visiting US President to make an emotional appeal to Europeans to unite, but the speech was heckled by left-wingers in the European Parliament.

The economic context underlying the Bonn summit appeared to be a promising one, given the prospects for US-led recovery. A 'positive and encouraging message' of sustained growth and higher employment came from the declaration. It contained three conditions for a common economic strategy: (1) the reduction of the USA's budget deficit by limiting public spending; (2) increased Japanese imports and a greater international role for the yen; (3) in Europe, the creation of a genuine internal market without barriers. Thus the three parties could compromise by making 'equal' sacrifices on their most difficult problems. The concept was said to have been proposed in the preparatory meetings by the Japanese.[17] The collective approach, however, did not mean a mutual commitment, because of the hard negotiations which had to be held on specific policy measures.

The talks on international trade again ended in open failure, with no specific date being set for a new round of GATT negotiations. The French obstructed the resolution on trade for a number of reasons. President Mitterrand had some valid points in relation to the fact that the trade issue could not be settled among the developed countries alone; some of the most difficult questions concerned access to Western markets for the products of the Third World. His main point was that no liberal trading system could long survive persistent, unpredictable, and unrealistic exchange rates. All this was more or less openly aimed at the French electorate, principally the farmers.[18] A White House spokesman harshly criticized France for its stubbornness, saying, 'we just don't think it's a good thing for one nation to be able to hold us up. France is the odd man out.'

Thanks to France's 'non', Japan's huge trade surplus with the United States and European countries was not the centre of the summit discussion. In this respect, Prime Minister Nakasone felt he had achieved the most difficult objective of avoiding open criticism on the 'Japanese problem'. Yet immediately after the main summit conference, the British Prime Minister, Mrs Thatcher, voiced her exasperation with Japan's failure to improve the trade imbalance. In doing so, she pointed out a number of Japanese practices which Britain considered unfair, in particular the case of the Bosphorus bridge project, which had been secured by a Japanese-led consortium against stiff British competition. For the sake of the overall Japanese and British trade relationship, the Bosphorus case was regarded as an 'isolated issue'. However, the unveiled trade warning to Japan had to be taken seriously, for it contained profound implications, including, in Mrs Thatcher's words, 'a hint that a very real trade war, with its attendant political and diplomatic consequences, could break out between East and West' (East meaning Japan here).[19]

The political tension surrounding the Bonn summit was heightened in debates on President Reagan's 'Star Wars' plan. Reagan's initiative gave rise to heated controversy on East–West strategic relations and the arms control questions which had been the focus of the political agenda at the Williamsburg and London summits. Almost all the European governments, whether summit or NATO members, had been sceptical about the merits of the Strategic Defence Initiative (SDI), so the West European countries were confronted with a serious dilemma about whether to take part in the US-led research programme. Japan also faced a crucial choice between its own reservations about joining in any kind of strategic defence system and its desire to participate in advanced technological research.

Not in the main conference, but in their respective bilateral summit talks with President Reagan, the leaders of Britain, West Germany, Japan, and others expressed their 'understanding' for the US-proposed SDI research programme, and gave their qualified agreement to participation in the programme. Although they were on record as regarding the US plan as 'justifiable', they maintained that this did not necessarily mean endorsement of its eventual deployment. In sum their position remained tacitly 'yes' for research, but 'no' for strategic deployment. Conversely, the French maintained 'non' for the former, but 'oui' for the latter, putting forward a rival plan – Eureka – in place of the American SDI. President Mitterrand bluntly refused Reagan's invitation to take part in the SDI programme. In a superbly Gallic press conference of which General de Gaulle would have been proud, Mitterrand presented himself as the defender not just of French interests but of those of the European Community as well.[20]

The following explanation was given in Paris for France's double 'non' to both the US security initiative and the push for a new round of trade talks:

> In spite of differences at the Bonn summit, Europeans will recognize that they need to be strong, united and co-ordinated in the face of the United States and Japan. . . . In the face of this enormous industrial and economic power represented by the United States and, at the other end, Japan, Europe must exist.[21]

These words imply fear concerning Europe's ability to survive a challenge by the US–Japan 'joint front' in both trade and security. President Reagan's request to Japan to join in SDI and Prime Minister Nakasone's positive, non-sceptical response during the Japan–US bilateral talks might be taken by the Europeans to mean that the US and Japan intended to collaborate in an integrated space development scheme.

Because of these conflicting factors, the summit could not make much of a start on a joint study at the outlines of the US level, but it was primarily intended as an exchange of information rather than a debate. Thus the final political declaration did not mention a word about SDI, though the summit leaders supported the US position in arms talks with the Soviet Union.

The political declaration of the Bonn summit made reference to the fortieth anniversary of the end of World War II in Europe. Like the London Charter, it was a fairly general text. However, a note of novelty emerged in the Bonn declaration in the allusion to the reunification of Germany and of Korea in the same paragraph. As for the former, the summit leaders looked forward to a state of peace in Europe in which the German people would regain their unity through free self-determination. As to the latter, they hoped that in Asia a political environment would be created which would permit the parties to overcome, in freedom, the division of the Korean peninsula. A parallel between European and Asian politics appeared for the first time in the history of the Western summits.

Tokyo II: in the shadow of the soaring yen

The Tokyo summit of 1986, like that of 1979, was preceded by a number of serious developments which acted as a backdrop to it. In place of the steep rise of spot oil prices in 1979 came the soaring yen, which reached a record post-war high in 1986. In place of the Soviet military build-up in East Asia came the Chernobyl nuclear power disaster. In place of Ayatollah Khomeini's rise to power in Iran came Colonel Qaddafi's terrorism and the US bombing of Libya; and finally, in place of the massive outflow of Indochinese refugees came the fall of President Marcos in the Philippines. These events stimulated much discussion at the first summit in Asia for seven years. From Ohira to Nakasone, the contrast between a 'stumbling' summit and the 'best ever' plainly indicated Japan's maturity on the level of both personal leadership and the deeper national involvement in the world economy and politics.

In parallel with the pre-summit meeting between Ohira and Carter in 1979, Nakasone visited President Reagan in mid-April 1986. He committed himself to a 'historic change' in the management of the Japanese economy by endorsing the main theme of the report of a high-level advisory group headed by the former governor of the Bank of Japan, Maekawa Haruo. The report recommended that Japan switch from an export-or-die economy to one dependent on domestic demand. Having pointed out Japan's unprecedentedly large trade surplus in 1985, equivalent to 3.6 per cent of GNP, the Maekawa Report stated that the time had come for the country to make a historic transformation in its traditional policies on economic management and the nation's way of life. Nakasone affirmed this new policy orientation.

Implementing the recommendations of the Maekawa Report, however, meant facing considerable hostility from the political opposition. An economic transformation of the scale envisaged by the report would be a long-term process, taking a minimum of five to seven years; sections of the ruling LDP as well as the opposition parties were unhappy with the report's sweeping recommendations, for example for major structural improvements to Japanese agriculture in an 'age of internationalization'. Reducing protection of domestic agriculture and allowing increased farm imports would be ruled out immediately by the conservatives, who still needed the farmers' vote. These obvious difficulties engendered a cynical view of the recommendations at home and abroad. Just before the publication of the Maekawa Report, Peter F. Drucker wrote, 'The Japanese only sell, they do not buy. They practice adversarial trade.'[22]

Before the Maekawa Report's offer of a reorientation of Japan's policy, the United States made its own reversal of policy when the G-5

(Group of Five) masterminded the Plaza agreement in New York in September 1985. This move to bring down the value of the dollar, in order to reduce the huge trade deficit of the United States, meant that the Reagan administration was abandoning its long-standing opposition to intervention in the currency market. As we have seen in the discussions of the Bonn summit, the Reagan administration was determined to bring the budget deficit under control. The US Treasury Secretary, James Baker, used the G-5 Plaza agreement to reverse American fiscal and monetary policies to a more flexible line pointing towards possible joint intervention in the international currency market.[23] Baker emerged from the May 1986 Tokyo summit with an impressive success of his own in macro-economic policy co-ordination.[24]

Secretary Baker's persuasiveness led to broad agreement on a complex surveillance scheme to bring about closer co-ordination of international economic policy among the summit nations. The economic declaration also confirmed the usefulness of concerted market intervention to achieve exchange-rate stability. Having expressed their appreciation of the improved co-ordination under the Plaza agreement, the Tokyo participants agreed to form a new G-7, including Italy and Canada. There had been reluctance over this, but the Italian Prime Minister, Bettino Craxi, threatened to walk out of the summit if the G-5 was not expanded to include his country and Canada.[25] Other European summit nations still had doubts. A compromise was reached at Baker's suggestion, to forge an accord creating a new G-7 but retaining a role for the existing G-5.

The summit commitment that the G-7 governments and central banks would intervene in currency exchange markets has not always led to concerted action, particularly in the case of the Japanese yen. But the summit agreement to strengthen multilateral surveillance of economic policies did not contain a requirement that the yen be kept at a stable rate. On the contrary, Prime Minister Nakasone's plea for concerted intervention by the summit nations to stabilize the currency markets at their present level, the yen having appreciated by 40 per cent against the US dollar over the previous six months, was rejected by President Reagan and other leaders.[26] In the meeting with Nakasone, Reagan said that the yen's appreciation would help rectify Japan's trade imbalance. The British Chancellor of the Exchequer, Nigel Lawson, also said that European countries wanted a further strengthening of the yen. These remarks fuelled a bullish sentiment for the yen on the international exchange markets.

As a result, massive speculative moves gave the yen a hoist to a record high rate of ¥165.20 against the US dollar on the Tokyo foreign exchange market, on the final day of the summit. The Tokyo summit did not only leave serious burdens for Japan to shoulder in its bid to resolve remaining problems such as trade and current account imbalances;[27] it also left uncertainty over the future of international exchange rates. Japan's current account surplus had reached as much as $50 billion for 1985, exceeding Saudi Arabia's peak of $41.4 billion in the aftermath of the 1979 second oil crisis. A tough warning had already been levelled at Japan by a senior US official who said: 'Japan is playing a very dangerous game in the conduct of international trade. A nation cannot be all exports and no imports'.[28]

Compared with the previous summit in Bonn, the Tokyo summit was relatively trouble-free, in both economic and political discussions. The host country had only one minor embarrassment, when Japanese radicals fired five hand-made rockets in the direction of the guest house where the summit meetings were taking place. But they fell far from the building and caused no injuries of significant damage. The rocket attack came on the same day that mildly radioactive rain fell in some areas of Japan as a result of the Chernobyl accident in late April. These events provided an ironic backdrop to the political discussions.

In the heated discussions on international terrorism, President Reagan and Mrs Thatcher were most adamant in their insistence on singling out Libya by name, and they succeeded in persuading their reluctant allies into accepting a tougher statement than was issued after the 1984 London summit, not only condemning terrorism but also promising more forceful action against it. The French delegation announced that its government did not consider that the sanctions being called for against Libya were strictly obligatory. However, President Mitterrand's position was not so secure this time, partly because the leader of France's conservative Gaullists, Prime Minister Jacques Chirac, had also come to Tokyo and there was a tacit agreement between the two leaders to stick to a policy of 'one voice, two mouths'. To avoid any political differences with Chirac, Mitterrand backed down on the issue of naming Libya and agreed that the statement should include a list of concrete measures against terrorism. Even so, his aides immediately made it clear that France still considered the list to be merely a series of non-binding recommendations.

This statement was the first time Japan had publicly agreed to identify Libya as a source of state-sponsored terrorism. Though Nakasone stressed that it was not directed against the Arab world as a whole, the decision to approve a statement jointly with countries such as the United States and Britain was enough to give the impression that Japan had abandoned its neutral policy on the Middle East for a pro-Western position. However, as host country Japan was obliged to seek consensus.

The statement on Chernobyl, by contrast, was not provocative but predominantly sympathetic to those affected by the accident. It offered assistance, in particular medical and technical aid, to be made available as and when requested. It expressed the view that every country engaged in nuclear power production bore full responsibility for the safety of the design, manufacture, operation, and maintenance of its installations.

It anticipated Soviet participation in post-accident analysis through the International Atomic Energy Agency (IAEA). Initially the Soviet government reacted with displeasure to the summit statement's reference to the Chernobyl disaster, but the Tass news agency soon issued an official statement thanking those nations which had offered condolences and assistance after the accident.

In the Tokyo declaration, as well as these two statements, the leaders of the seven nations recalled the agreement between the United States and the Soviet Union to accelerate work at the Geneva arms control negotiations. They called for a positive attitude on the part of the Soviet Union towards a high-level dialogue addressing East–West differences. In summing up the three-day Tokyo summit, Nakasone said that as well as calling for dialogue between the superpowers, it had called for all Soviet forces to be withdrawn from Afghanistan and for North and South Korea to be admitted to the United Nations. He also said the leaders had expressed their support for peace initiatives by ASEAN to solve the Kampuchean conflict and for the efforts made by President Corazon Aquino to overcome the economic problems of the Philippines. Nakasone had also insisted that the importance of the Asian Pacific region should be noted in the Tokyo declaration.

'Nations surrounding the Pacific,' the Tokyo declaration reads, 'are striving dynamically through free exchanges, building on their rich and varied heritages.' It also mentioned the countries of Western Europe and North America, which 'are firm in their commitment to the realization in freedom of human potential'. Nakasone thus realized his ambition to make co-operation overarching the Atlantic and Pacific a major theme of the Tokyo summit. He described the meeting as a 'superb' success in his own speeches, and American and European leaders praised the Tokyo summit as the best ever.[29]

Venice II: a seasoned partnership

The June 1987 Venice summit was dubbed the 'bland canal' conference, as the mood was one of avoiding obvious risks. Indeed, participants appeared more afraid of dissent than of vacuity.[30] There was a great deal of verbiage, but neither the economic nor the political declaration offered an effective strategy for tackling vital questions. Given the 'lame duck' status, politically, of many of those present, including the host, Prime Minister Fanfani, the summit leaders were in no position to take any initiative on such critical issues as budgetary policy, trade and monetary measures, the lowering of agricultural subsidies, Third World debt, the protection of shipping in the Persian Gulf, or the elimination of intermediate-range missiles from Europe.

Nakasone, who feared he might be the main target of criticism, was determined to forestall US and European accusations over Japan's trade practices and surpluses. So the Japanese government had orchestrated, in advance, an impressive catalogue of programmes designed to placate Japan's major trading partners. After arranging a ¥6 trillion ($43 billion) emergency economic package to raise domestic demand through tax cuts, increasing public spending, and drafting a $30 billion programme to channel some of the trade surplus to poorer Third World nations, government officials under Nakasone's leadership embarked on a diplomatic offensive to stifle criticism abroad. The Prime Minister himself visited Washington in early May, and gave a cool performance in the aftermath of Reagan's sanctions over Japanese semiconductors and in the face of Congress approval of a controversial protectionist trade Bill.[31] Then, in Venice, he felt able to speak more assertively, not only defending his position but even criticizing US policy.

Immediately before the opening of the plenary session, Reagan informed Nakasone of his decision to bring a partial end to the US sanctions on Japanese electronic goods, by removing 17 per cent, or $51 million, of the $300 million in penalty tariffs imposed in April. Reagan's goodwill gesture was welcomed, but fell far short of Japanese expectations that sanctions be lifted entirely at the earliest possible date. The punitive tariffs imposed on Japanese goods in retaliation for alleged violation of a 1986 semiconductor trade agreement had already aroused fears in Japan that the matter had become excessively politicized. Reagan's action was aimed at appeasing Japan's opposition and the critics in the US Congress as well as in the European countries. However, this political motivation would not bring a long-lasting and fundamental solution to an economic issue.

The economic discussions at the Venice summit focused on the international co-ordination of fiscal and monetary policies, notably by the United States, Japan, and West Germany, the three biggest industrial countries. The crucial problem was how to achieve a 'fiscal rebalancing' in which the Big Three would agree to measures to reduce the US budget deficit and stimulate each other's growth. In contrast with Japan's reiterated and robust promises, the German government refused to take any action to stimulate growth beyond a DM14 billion ($7.8 billion) tax cut. Washington, which pledged to bring its fiscal deficit down to 2.3 per cent of GNP in the fiscal year 1988, did not agree on how to bring this about. Japan's promises received a warm welcome matched by a degree of scepticism, as illustrated by Mrs Thatcher's words: 'We will believe it when we see it.'

Argument centred on the question of curbing the US budget deficit, which, in Chancellor Kohl's words, had become the 'central problem' of the global economy.[32] West Germany and the other European countries demanded that the United States take significant measures to cut its budget deficit, rejecting US demands for more stimulus from Europe. Britain and Japan joined in each other's criticisms of US fiscal policy. Despite such discord between President Reagan and his partners, the participants endorsed a plan for establishing medium-term goals for their economies through a multilateral surveillance system, using economic performance indicators, including growth rates, inflation, trade surplus, government deficit, and monetary exchange rates. To follow the plan through, the Finance Ministers of the seven nations agreed to meet at least three times a year to co-ordinate their economic policies. This was a small but substantial step towards multilateral management of the world economy.

In addition to co-ordination of macro-economic policy the summit leaders agreed, in the economic declaration, on a six-point plan for effective structural policies, including a commitment to job creation in member countries, the reduction of agricultural surpluses and the lifting of national barriers to trade. Much of the economic discussion focused on the world debt crisis. The leaders adopted the UN target of giving 0.7 per cent of their GNP as aid to developing nations. The debt problems of the poorest nations – mostly those in sub-Saharan Africa – were particularly acute, and required 'special treatment'; the leaders mentioned the possibility of cutting interest rates on loans to those countries. However, none of the agreed measures was in fact new, and none amounted to more than the endorsement of negotiations agreed upon at a meeting of the OECD in May. In this respect, the Western summits have not shown the same capacity for policy initiative and decision-making in the economic field as the OECD and the G-5 and G-7 meetings.

By contrast with the less intense economic discussions, the political agenda, such as East–West relations and the increased tensions in the Persian Gulf, attracted relatively greater attention at the Venice summit. In a set of three statements, the Western leaders urged the Soviet Union to negotiate on arms reductions in a positive and constructive manner; they demanded freedom of navigation in the troubled Persian Gulf; and they condemned all forms of international terrorism. One significant phenomenon was the more subdued role of the United States in the political discussions, and the correspondingly more assertive stance taken by Western Europe and Japan.[33]

The declaration on East–West relations called on the two superpowers to achieve verifiable arms reductions, but made no reference to the negotiations for eliminating intermediate nuclear forces (INF). The reasons for the omission were both technical and substantive. The summit leaders decided to address this question in general terms because NATO Foreign Ministers were soon to meet to hammer out a Western approach to the issue of medium and short-range missiles. But, more fundamentally, the European leaders, particularly President Mitterrand,

did not want the summit to become a forum for specific policy decisions; consequently the declaration was limited to mere moral support
for the US negotiating position. It was made clear, however, that the
Soviet Union should not have a free hand to intervene in regional conflicts
while talking about arms reduction. Japan, as a non-member of NATO,
could not become directly involved in arms reduction talks, but Nakasone
tried to moderate the conflicting interests of the Europeans and Americans
at the final stage of discussions. The text of the declaration on East–
West relations was based on a Japanese draft and Nakasone's role
deserves recognition.[34] An aide said that Nakasone was 'very satisfied'
with Japan's contribution.

A declaration called for an immediate end to the Iraq–Iran war and
for freedom of navigation in the Persian Gulf. Yet here again participants
made no specific political commitment, leaving the declaration to be
issued only as the 'personal contribution' of the representatives. As a
result, President Reagan had to be satisfied with this limited statement
of his allies' support. He did not receive the increased material help which
the US expected of its allies for its arms reinforcement policy after Iraq's
attack on a US Navy frigate in May.

Constitutionally, Japan cannot deploy military forces abroad. During
the bilateral meeting with President Reagan, Nakasone said that Japan
was not in a position to give military support, but would study forms
of non-military co-operation, such as economic and diplomatic initiatives
towards the Arab countries. He announced that he would send his Foreign
Minister to Iran and possibly to Iraq, Japan having maintained diplomatic
relations with both countries. Foreign Minister Kuranari Tadashi visited
Teheran on his way home from the Venice summit, in what officials
described as part of an unceasing search for a diplomatic solution to the
seven-year-old Gulf war. Japan was satisfied that, without being
associated in a stand against Iran, it could maintain a kind of intermediate
position on Middle East problems, even if it did not play a leading role
in the solution of conflicts.

With this relative success in Venice, where he asserted Japan's
interests and responsibilities, Nakasone scored some political victories
and secured goodwill for the remaining tenure of his premiership. Indeed,
an American newspaper commented that he could be the first Japanese
Premier to return to office for a second time.[35] Whether a good
domestic reception and a good international one are the same thing is,
of course, another question.

After completing a five-year period in office – the third longest served
by a Japanese Prime Minister since the war – Nakasone stepped down
in early November 1987. With much of his political strength intact, he
was able to choose Takeshita as his successor. During the contest for
the premiership, all the contenders, Takeshita, Abe, and Miyazawa,

committed themselves to continuing Nakasone's tradition, which was outstanding in his more self-assertive and flamboyant diplomatic style, as illustrated by the 'Ron–Yasu' relationship and record *gaiyu* (foreign travel; see Table 3), his challenges to various taboos in Japanese society (such as making an official visit to Yasukuni Shrine, where war dead are enshrined), and his attempts at administrative reform through successful privatization of the nation's public corporations and amendments to the tax and education systems.

Table 3: Japanese Prime Ministers' foreign missions, 1951–87

Name	Term in office	No. of foreign visits
Yoshida, S.	7 years, 2 months	2 (7)
Hatoyama, I.	2 years	1 (1)
Kishi, N.	3 years, 5 months	5 (28)
Ikeda, H.	4 years, 4 months	5 (17)
Sato, E.	7 years, 8 months	10 (14)
Tanaka, K.	2 years, 5 months	9 (18)
Miki, T.	2 years	3 (2)
Fukuda, T.	2 years	6 (14)
Ohira, M.	1 year, 7 months	6 (10)
Suzuki, Z.	2 years, 4 months	8 (20)
Nakasone, Y.	5 years	23 (29)

Note: Figures in brackets refer to number of countries visited.
Source: *Nihon Keizai Shimbun*.

Takeshita, the new Prime Minister, made his international debut at the Manila summit conference of the six-member ASEAN in December 1987. He then visited Washington to see President Reagan in January 1988. So, at the outset of his tenure, Takeshita could be seen to be following his immediate predecessors' diplomatic technique of giving priority to Japan–US relations, reinforced by Japan–Asia ties. Substantial aid and loans to Japan's Asian neighbours, especially the Philippines, were intended to prop up Japan–US co-operation in the Western Pacific region. The future of economic security in the Asian Pacific will depend to a large extent on the maintenance of good Japanese–US relations. In Washington, Prime Minister Takeshita and President Reagan reaffirmed their support for the economic policy co-ordination process adopted at the Tokyo and Venice summits; Takeshita renewed his commitment to continuing the structural reform of the Japanese economy and to increasing its foreign assistance budget, and Reagan promised to reduce the US budget deficit and to veto protectionist trade legislation. They looked forward to their next meeting in Toronto in June 1988.

Another traditional technique which Takeshita borrowed from his predecessors was to seek closer ties with Europe, reinforcing the weak link of the trilateral Western partnership; otherwise Japan would lose to the Europeans in the battle for US friendship. In a two-round tour of Europe in April–May and June 1988, Takeshita met all the leaders who were to attend the Toronto summit, so as not only to introduce himself but also to take a preliminary sounding of European views on points on the summit agenda which seemed to be different from those of the US. These points included East–West relations, how to respond to changes in the Soviet Union, and also macro-economic adjustment and agriculture. The tour also provided an occasion to highlight Japan's new role in global issues.

During his visit to Britain in May 1988, Takeshita announced a new 'International Co-operation Initiative', which articulated his basic policy for the construction of a Japan with a contribution to make to the world. The initiative comprised three pillars, namely the strengthening of co-operation to achieve peace, the promotion of international cultural exchanges, and the expansion of Japan's ODA. His London speech dwelt primarily on the second of these. In the middle of the two-round European tour, he visited New York to attend the Third Special Session of the UN General Assembly on Disarmament, and delivered a major policy statement dealing mainly with the first of these initiatives – co-operation for peace. He outlined the practical diplomatic measures that Japan would implement to facilitate the peaceful settlement of regional conflicts.[36] During Takeshita's second trip to Europe he also had an informal meeting with Reagan, who was on his way back from the Moscow summit. Their meeting in London was the occasion for both a briefing on the US–Soviet summit and a final effort to solve the bilateral dispute over beef and orange imports. It was thus not a meeting primarily designed to enhance the Japanese Prime Minister's image. Takeshita was then ready for his maiden battle in Toronto.

Toronto: a shift of leadership structure

With the 1988 Toronto meeting the Western economic summits concluded their first two cycles, having been held twice in each of the seven member countries. A glance back over the fourteen years in which the forum had developed from an informal conclave limited to economics into a platform for views on every world issue can provide a clear perspective on the profound changes which have taken place in the industrial world and its power structure.

In the first place, as the Toronto economic declaration stated, a sharp contrast was apparent between the 1970s, a decade of high inflation and declining growth, and the 1980s, the longest period of economic growth in post-war history. Yet this sustained growth coincided with the emergence of a large external imbalance in the major industrial economies. Bitter disputes over trade and difficult macro-economic adjustment have resulted in the emergence of regional blocs, as evidenced by the Free Trade Agreement between Canada and the United States, and the European Community's internal market, which is due for completion in 1992. Despite the summits' affirmative statements on these developments, and other moves towards regional co-operation (perhaps Asian Pacific co-operation), it cannot be denied that 'Toronto confirmed the emergence of a new "multipolar" form of decision-making, in which power will increasingly be shared between three major regional blocs, in North America, Western Europe and Asia.'[37] Whether this multipolarization will support an open and free international trading system remains to be seen.

The second change, as Mrs Thatcher has said, has been the transformation of crisis control from a short-term to a long-term perspective.[38] It was, in fact, at the 1981 Ottawa summit that the participants first tried to replace short-range policy co-ordination by a longer-term agreement. At the time all they were really trying to do was find an excuse for their failure to reach agreement on policy for the immediate future.

The third notable change, affecting the Japanese in particular, is that they are now hardly criticized for their trade surplus, in consequence of their having accommodated their critics on larger issues. It may be recalled that the EC delegation tried to target Japan obliquely by a coded reference to orderly selling practice, when they raised the question of the mounting Japanese trade surplus at the Ottawa summit in 1981. Seven years later, in Toronto, Willy de Clercq, EC Commissioner for External Relations, said, 'They [the Japanese] feel that they have done quite a lot to help. Something has changed with them. They feel comfortable and strong. That's the new Japanese look.'[39] At the Toronto summit, which was relatively free of major differences, Japan could play a key role in the debates on development aid and the debt problem as well as on macro-economic adjustment. Although Prime Minister Takeshita was not as flamboyant as his predecessor Nakasone, being more restrained in the Suzuki style, he was able to command even higher respect from the other participants.

Japan, which has spent most summits being attacked by its allies, was able to claim in Toronto in 1988 that it had done more than most other participants to honour its international obligations.[40] With a flourishing growth rate (an annualized 11 per cent in the first quarter of 1988), substantial imports, and a dwindling trade surplus, Japan could set an example to others of successful macro-economic management. Takeshita made an impressive statement on economic co-operation with the developing countries of the Third World. In his third initiative on the subject, he proclaimed Japan's intention to increase its ODA to more than $50

95

billion for the next five years, remodelling and increasing his predecessors' aid pledges. In addition, Japan made public a $5.5 billion debt-waiver plan, taking the lead from France, West Germany, and Canada, which had also proposed similar debt-relief plans for the poorest nations. For middle-income debtor nations, mainly in Latin America, Finance Minister Miyazawa unveiled a Japanese scheme for defusing the debt crisis. Although it was turned down by US Treasury Secretary Baker, Japanese government officials predicted that the plan would have a great influence on future debates on the issue among industrial nations. If all these Japanese initiatives gained acceptance, they would pave the way towards the solution of North–South problems.

During the main sessions in Toronto, especially the economic discussions, the prime actors were US President Reagan and British Prime Minister Margaret Thatcher; both attributed the sustained economic growth of the 1980s to the free-market policies that had been the hallmark of their tenures. When Reagan first presented his ideas for reinvigorating the US and Western economies through market forces at the Ottawa summit in 1981, he was mocked by some of his colleagues. But when he was about to leave the world stage, he showed awareness of his achievements, for example in his remark that 'we are on the right track and we have to stay on it'.[41] Mrs Thatcher also stressed that further economic growth depended on a commitment to continuing the market-oriented economic policies that set the industrial democracies on a new wave of expansion after the recession of the early 1980s.

The political discussions largely concentrated on assessing the evolution of East–West relations following the Reagan–Gorbachev summits of December 1987 and May–June 1988. The final communiqué welcomed the beginning of the Soviet withdrawal from Afghanistan, and endorsed the INF treaty, which had been signed in Washington. Western leaders expressed the hope of deep cuts in US and Soviet strategic arms. None the less, they expressed their reservations about the massive Soviet conventional forces in Eastern Europe and the military build-up in the Far East. Having urged that security and stability could be enhanced by a lower level of forces, the communiqué stressed that genuine peace could not be established solely by arms control, but must be based on firm respect for fundamental human rights. In the communiqué the participants hardened their stance on drugs and terrorism, calling notably on the US to set up a ministerial–level special task force on the international narcotics trade.

Although the seven leaders repeated the goals and values to be preserved while seeking an improvement in East–West relations, a divergence appeared, notably between Presidents Reagan and Mitterrand, on strategic views of East–West *détente*. Despite his major achievement on nuclear disarmament by the superpowers, Reagan was taking a wait-and-see attitude towards further progress in the negotiations on strategic missile reductions and also towards the prospect of a new East–West relationship following the Gorbachev reforms. Mainly because of strong pressure from Congress, the Reagan administration was forced to take a tough stance on the possible impact on Western security of loans, trade credits, and direct investment to the Soviet Union. By contrast, Mitterrand represented a view emerging among the West European leaders that Gorbachev's efforts at reform should be encouraged by the West offering new economic prospects. This viewpoint made the European leaders increasingly reluctant to follow the US lead.[42]

The European Community now emerged from the obscurity in which it had been shrouded during its ten years of attendance at the summit meetings. Against the background of the single European market, due in the early 1990s, the EC Commission began finally to make an impact, adopting a higher profile on issues such as trade and agriculture. In an angry exchange with President Reagan, the Commission's president, Jacques Delors, summarily dismissed the US demand for more substantive commitments on agricultural subsidies.[43] A vague compromise was reached, but the United States was forced to drop its proposal to eliminate subsidies by the year 2000 in the face of European and Japanese resistance.

Japan also tried to adopt a higher profile, but of a different kind. Just prior to the summit, Japan and the US had managed to resolve their protracted dispute over beef and orange imports. This gave Takeshita a freer hand at the summit. As noted earlier, other participants were favourably impressed by the Japanese line on macro-economic adjustment, ODA, and the debt problem. Japan had played the key role expected by the host Prime Minister, Brian Mulroney, after his meeting with Takeshita in Ottawa in January. Moreover, Japan was representing Asia's interests, including those of the newly industrializing economies (NIEs, the term used instead of NICs), demanding international aid to the Philippines and support for the Seoul Olympic Games, and recalling the need for a peace settlement in Kampuchea.

Thus the Toronto summit provided Japan with an occasion to demonstrate the scope of its 'twin-track' approach towards the West and Asia. Japan has now assumed an anchor role in sustaining the Western economies, and at the same time an ambassadorial role on behalf of Southeast Asia and the Pacific. Japan's greater clout means, however, that its economy, including its agriculture, must suffer further restructuring to adjust to multilateral policy.[44]

Chapter seven

Agenda for the Summit Powers

Japan's active involvement in the Western summits, particularly since the 1979 Tokyo and 1980 Venice summits, has had repercussions on its foreign policy, changing its somewhat insular position to a global perspective. Given the very intricate international environment, in which events in one region may immediately affect the entire world, Japan could not remain aloof even from those events in which it was not itself a principal actor. The era of so-called passive foreign policy was at an end, and Japan now had to embark upon an active foreign policy, taking a global perspective.[1]

More significantly, the new era in foreign policy implied a departure from the old system in which Japan's security and prosperity were essentially guaranteed by the United States. Although there was no basic change in Japan's ultimate dependence on the United States for its security, the relationship between the two countries could no longer be taken for granted in the drastically altered environment. Events at the turn of 1979–80 – such as the Iranian crisis and the Soviet invasion of Afghanistan – posed an acute test for the Japan–US alliance, the Americans becoming more adamant in demands for their allies' loyalty to their global strategy, and Japan becoming more uncertain about its future economic security. For Japan, supporting the United States was no longer merely a matter of speeches and votes in the United Nations; it now demanded the sacrifice of material interests, such as oil from Iran and economic relations with the Soviet Union. The old order, which rested on the limited obligations incurred under the Mutual Security Treaty and allowed the pursuit of global economic interests unfettered by political considerations, had come to an end.[2]

In December 1979, when US Secretary of State Vance met Japanese Foreign Minister Okita at an International Energy Agency meeting in Paris, the US government complained of the 'insensitivity' of the Japanese in buying large amounts of Iranian oil on the spot market even after the Americans had imposed an embargo. In April 1980 the US government asked Japan to follow the American example of economic sanctions against Iran. The Japanese government then sent Okita to Luxembourg for private discussions with the Foreign Ministers of the European Community to plan a united European–Japanese policy. 'At that time Japanese diplomacy was distressingly sandwiched between Iranian oil and United States friendship!'[3] Significantly, this was the first time that the Japanese government had approached the EC for consultation on a joint reaction to unreasonable American pressures.

The Soviet military invasion of Afghanistan and the US reaction to it placed East–West relations under serious strain. Participation in the 1980 Moscow Olympics and economic sanctions against the Soviets raised difficult problems for Japan as well as for the West European countries. The Japanese followed the Americans loyally, if reluctantly, while the Europeans contented themselves with speeches. The Afghan crisis and the subsequent increase in East–West tension also posed difficult questions regarding Japan's defence policy. In March 1980, when Okita visited Washington, Secretary of State Vance and Defence Secretary Brown asked the Japanese government to make a sustained, significant effort in the manner of defence. But the Ohira government took a cautious attitude towards arguments for a substantial build-up of Japanese defence forces, believing that only under extreme circumstances should any change in Japan's post-war policy of keeping a minimal self-defence force be contemplated.[4]

These experiences brought Japanese policy-makers to this conclusion: 'That Japan should have a common basic perception and strategy with the advanced democracies, including the United States, does not necessarily mean that this country's specific policies should be the same as those of other countries.'[5] Such a position suggests that, where vital economic interests or security questions are at stake, Japan should keep an appropriate distance from the United States and take into consideration European attitudes to US policies. This also implies transcendence of the bilateral alliance with the United States that has been such a feature of Japanese post-war foreign policy.

The security treaties and relationships of the Western alliance were originally separated into two different axes, the US–European and US–Japanese, resting on the fulcrum of US leadership and command. There has been no direct security relationship in the third link between Europe and Japan. However, the changing international environment promoted a shared perception of security interests between these two parties, despite differences in their regional backgrounds and difficulties in co-ordinating policies.[6]

Political consultation on East–West relations

New developments in international politics and in the central strategic relationship between the superpowers have combined to make European and Japanese perceptions of global security questions converge in recent years. First, in the face of steadily expanding Soviet military capabilities, it has become impossible to consider the security of the Euro-Atlantic area and the Asian Pacific region in isolation from each other. Some attempts to examine common security problems have already been made in specialist Euro-Japanese meetings as well as in bilateral consultations by government officials on specific issues such as the Soviet invasion of Afghanistan, the Polish question, and the Soviet deployment of SS-20 missiles.

Second, since the beginning of the 1980s the United States has ceased to be able or willing to meet the Soviet military challenge alone, but has had to work in closer association with Europe and Japan. Moreover, Americans want Europeans and Japanese to participate in a global security system, in the conviction that Western security is indivisible. In this context, European countries and Japan are expected to shoulder the main burden of their own defence, and at the same time to provide more positive diplomatic and economic support to the United States in certain areas vital to Western interests around the world. The US has thus helped to push Europe and Japan towards a joint policy on East–West strategic issues.

Third, US expectations have not always received a positive response from Europe and Japan, because of their different perceptions on security. The United States tends to insist that Western countries co-ordinate their policies on diplomatic, economic, and ideological matters according to the viewpoint of its global strategy against the Soviet military threat. But Europe and Japan do not see security from the Soviet threat in global terms, only in purely military terms and in a regional or local context. Moreover, both Europeans and Japanese are perhaps more conscious than Americans of the need to learn to live with the Russians. Therefore they do not want the United States to dictate the conduct of their relations with the Soviet Union.[7]

These three closely linked aspects have influenced the framework of trilateral interactions, creating a Euro-Japanese nexus *vis-à-vis* the United States. Of course, the United States remains the fulcrum of the trilateral relationship, because, for the survival of Japan, economic and security relations with the United States are of much greater importance than those with Europe; and the same logic can be applied to US–European relations. However, it is also a fact that Western Europe and Japan have collaborated most successfully in their relations with the United States when discussing East–West and related questions. The absence of a relevant treaty between Western Europe and Japan has not severely affected the pace and degree of their consultations on security.[8]

The record of Japanese participation in talks on East–West relations shows that it was from the 1980 Venice summit onward that Japan joined in the official resolutions on global political and security issues, as at least an 'honorary member' of the Western alliance. The Europeans had initially seen Japan's participation in discussions on East–West affairs only as a matter of form, in so far as its position was regarded as identical to that of the US. But gradually, on certain issues, Japanese and European policy began to converge, the two sides moving closer to each other than to the United States. For example, the Japanese shared the Europeans' opposition to the strict US embargo on the supply of strategic materials to the Soviet Union during a heated Euro-American dispute on the subject at the Ottawa and Versailles summits.

As for the issues of global security and the importance of political consultations, the congruence of Japanese–European concerns were affirmed during discussions between Foreign Minister Abe and West European leaders in January 1983. Then, in the statement at the Williamsburg summit in June that year, Prime Minister Nakasone Yasuhiro agreed with the other participants that Western security was indivisible and must be approached on a global basis. This statement was regarded by the West European countries as an important demonstration of Japan's sympathetic stance on Western security as a whole, and it became a significant factor behind subsequent co-operative relations between Japan and Western Europe.[9] Europe and Japan also appeared to collaborate successfully in persuading the United States to adopt a more open policy on political dialogue and negotiations with Moscow, although it is difficult to illustrate a clear-cut contrast between the American, and European and Japanese positions. The Williamsburg summit thus laid the political foundations of the INF treaty negotiations.

Nakasone's bold moves to join in the discussions on global strategy removed the taboos Japan had felt in the post-war security debate. His January 1983 remarks in Washington, about Japan being an 'unsinkable aircraft carrier' and providing a blockade of the three most strategic straits through the Japanese islands, as well as his support for NATO's policy on INF at the 1983 Williamsburg summit, were a far cry from 1977, when Ohira was reported to have asked one of his aides, 'What is the SS-20, anyway?' after a meeting with West German Chancellor Schmidt, who had voiced concern over the Soviet missiles to his obviously uncomprehending Japanese counterpart.[10] Another marked difference was between Suzuki's and Nakasone's lectures delivered in London in 1981 and 1984 respectively. In clear contrast to Suzuki's lecture, which dealt mainly with economic matters between Japan and Western Europe, Nakasone's lecture took the grandiose theme of a strategy for world peace, with particular reference to the free world's shared views on East–West relations.[11] Equipped with a definite strategic view, Nakasone was considered to be the first post-war Japanese Prime Minister who had a sense not only of his country's international economic role but also of its geopolitical responsibility. Under the Nakasone government Japan enhanced the quality of its participation in world politics.[12]

The relative decline of the superpowers

In the long-term perspective of a shifting world power system, it is the relative decline of the superpowers, especially the United States, which has led to the emergence of a triadic Western alliance with a new link between Western Europe and Japan. The reasons are twofold: first, as noted earlier, the United States can no longer meet the Soviet military challenge without Europe and Japan to share the defence burden; and, second, the relative decline of US power has meant the relative rise of other Western powers, namely the European Community and Japan. In consequence, many Japanese came to feel that the Europeans could exert considerable political influence in Washington.[13]

US power had begun to wane as early as the 1968 Tet offensive in the Vietnam war. Nixon and Kissinger attempted to stave off the effects of this relative decline by relying more on a skilful diplomacy which advocated a multipolar world with five clusters of power: the United States, the Soviet Union, Japan, China, and the European Community. Carter attempted to sidestep containment of the Soviet Union by demoting the superpower relationship from its central position in US foreign policy. The Carter administration put more emphasis on North–South issues and human rights in its attempt to maintain a leadership role. But the fundamental difficulty common to both Nixon and Carter was that they had accepted the limits of American power. Reagan, in contrast, rejected the idea of such limits. He attempted to revert to tradition by restoring US military power, adopting interventionist policies in the Third World, and launching the Strategic Defence Initiative to establish US superiority. All these were combined in the effort to restore US leadership of the alliance, especially in NATO. All the attempts, however, have turned out to be counterproductive and have simply intensified anxieties in Europe about the nature of that leadership.[14]

US leadership of the Western world was further shaken when Wall Street and international stock markets plunged in the great crash of 'Black Monday' in October 1987, the same day, coincidentally, as Takeshita became Prime Minister – an indication of the magnitude of the problems facing a relative novice in international affairs. 'Black Monday' can be said to have symbolized the decline of US dominance of the world economy; but other countries were as yet unwilling or unable to take over the US role.[15] As Helmut Schmidt often remarked, the West was suffering from a 'leadership vacuum'.

Despite their loss or decline of economic and military hegemony, the

United States – and the Soviet Union – are not ready to withdraw from their global commitments and political leadership. The Americans hoped to shed some of their military burdens without losing their political hegemony. On the other hand, the Europeans have expected the US protectorate to continue, but with no consequences for their increasingly independent diplomacy. 'Hegemony on the cheap' has been matched by 'independence on the cheap'.[16] As to the Japanese position, perhaps 'peace constitution on the cheap' has been justified by the principle of abiding by non-military means despite US pressure to assume some responsibility for the security burden overseas.

However, the long-term indicators suggest that the world is shifting from a hegemonic structure in which military strength and economic and financial control are concentrated in one country, to a new order – a new international distribution of responsibility essentially among the summit powers in the West. As far as economic power is concerned, such an order already exists, Japan's GNP now having overtaken the Soviet Union's, and the European Community's having overtaken America's. In the future, this is likely to be translated into a multipolar system at the military level as well.[17] These economic and military transitions have already led to a redistribution of certain defence burdens within the Western alliance. Political leadership is less easily redistributed.

In this interdependent world the West European countries and Japan are key players, carrying great responsibility, for they can act as partners, sensitive to their respective interests and problems. In other words, the world has moved from leadership to partnership. The security of the Western democracies depends on the United States, but the United States needs active support, and sometimes constructive criticism, from its allies and friends.[18] Yet how can economic interdependence and 'asymmetrical' dependence in security matters combine with a harmonious and viable political partnership? When the US administration attempts to use the political influence provided by European and Japanese military dependence to extract concessions on financial and commercial issues, considerable strains are created within the alliance. When the US administration attempts to impose its view of global security and East–West relations, it does not always seek its allies' support and co-operation in advance. In the final analysis, dependence on the United States for security can be justified only when America's allies are able to influence the formulation of policy in Washington, and consequently reassert their position as the privileged partners of the dominant power in the international political system.[19]

The geopolitical circumstances, the historical experience, and the domestic political, economic, and social conditions of each country will ultimately affect and determine its security perceptions. Given the interconnection of these factors, concerted efforts for trilateral Western security can take place only through extensive consultations in which the allies' different perceptions and preoccupations are aired. The United States must not impose its perceptions on its allies, and must accept their independent initiatives in order to encourage them to play an active role in efforts to preserve Western security. The Americans and the Europeans need to show sensitivity to Japanese perceptions and domestic constraints regarding security. Otherwise Japan will not be able to make a constructive contribution to tripartite Western security endeavours.[20] The Europeans in particular should broaden their outlook from the narrow interests of the Atlantic alliance to a truly global perspective. While Europeans are bound to look on security issues in East Asia as being of secondary importance, the dynamics of the region affect the interests of all the trilateral partners.[21] Moreover, it is in the West European interest to involve Japan in political consultations and thereby increase the weight of allied influence on the United States.[22] The two partners have no 'natural reflex of consultation'[23] but the Europeans need the Japanese and vice versa. Finally, the Japanese must be prepared to share responsibility for Western security, not by military means but in a manner commensurate with their economic strength, by communicating their understanding of security to those key areas of the Asian Pacific region and the Third World where their interests are linked not only with those of the United States but also with those of Western Europe.

Economic friction: an image gap

To turn now to the troubled economic relations of the Western industrial world, what are the factors underlying the widely observed problem of friction over economic and trade issues in which Japan finds itself? How has Japan responded to this question, which has to a large extent resulted from its rapidly increased trade surplus in recent years? How can Japan contribute to solving the problem and restoring global economic equilibrium? The co-ordination of international policy, particularly through summit meetings called to solve trade disputes, is of central importance, especially for Japan, the target of universal criticism for the so-called 'Japan problem'.

The major arguments over external economic issues and trade liberalization in Japan fall into three broad areas. The first is related to the nation's cultural tradition, social value system, and historical experience, which do much to explain the closed nature of its domestic market and the aggressiveness of its export drive. The second concerns the nature of external pressures or threats, as other countries demand greater access to the Japanese market and call for protectionist measures against Japanese exports. Finally, domestic political leadership can play a central role in the opening of the Japanese market, and in the recycling of some of the trade surplus through foreign investment and economic assistance. By examining these three closely interwoven factors, the perceptions, motivations, and actions regarding the disputes over trade can be explored.

A stereotyped image of the 'Japan problem' that is rooted in the Western perception is that modern Japan's statecraft is determined by its historical experience as a 'latecomer' striving to catch up with the West, and by the government's neo-mercantilistic policies, which helped to promote unlimited industrial and export expansion while impeding the development of an economy open towards the outside world.[24] Japan's cultural tradition has also produced a commercial practice and industrial system which tend to exclude foreigners; for example, distribution networks and hierarchical patterns of the industrial structure constitute barriers to foreign penetration. These cultural and historical developments, which are quite different from those of the West and even from those of the rest of Asia, compound the economic disputes. These ultimately concern not only the very structure of the Japanese economy, but also characteristic aspects of Japanese society and the Japanese way of life.[25] It has been no easy task for Japan to reconcile the mental and psychological make-up of its people, the result of thousands of years of history and tradition, with the norms and values of the Western world.[26]

The Japanese have reacted to the Western criticism with a mixture of reluctant compliance and outright refusal. The word *Kokusaika* (internationalization), which is now popular in Japan, implies two things at once: opening up the nation while guarding its culture, and altering another country's relative wealth more than one's own through the expansion of trade. Western commentators have also differed in their interpretations of the Japanese industrial complex. A 'modern-equals-Western' school (including such observers such as Karel van Wolferen) tends to single out Japan as a developmental exception, while others, such as Ezra Vogel, favour the 'Pax Americana-Nipponica' concept of interdependence. Thus the image gaps amplify the economic discord.[27]

Japan's statecraft favours bureaucratic decision-making processes which hamper autonomous trade liberalization and the opening of the market. It is widely known that the Japanese are reluctant to change the existing system, because of the pressure of interest groups and bureaucratic rivalries. Moreover the absence of a single leadership in the bureaucracy often contributes to immobilism. These inhibitions and inaction provoked the West to put pressure on Japan. Ironically, this has enabled the Japanese government to overcome domestic resistance to change. Ever since the 'black ship' incident, when Commodore Matthew Perry of the US Navy sailed his ships into Japanese waters and

105

forced a reluctant Tokugawa government to open Japan to the West in the 1860s, Western public opinion has generally believed, 'Tell the Japanese what to do, and they do it.'[28]

'Black ship'-style coercion has been repeatedly adopted by the Americans during major crises in their post-war trading relationship with Japan. Since the early 1970s these crises have gone through roughly three phases. The first reached its climax in the 'Nixon shock' in 1971, when, against a background of the textile disputes, a 10 per cent surcharge was imposed on all US imports and the dollar was allowed to float. US pressure forced Japan to revalue the yen. The Japanese responded with measures such as 20 per cent tariff cuts on manufactured goods and processed agricultural products, as well as an emergency import plan totalling $1.1 billion.

The second phase of tension was marked by the US trade diplomacy of the period 1977–8, through 'Carter's trip', which put cautious and calculated pressure on Japanese exports of steel products and colour television sets. The United States also called for the liberalization of Japan's remaining agricultural import quotas (i.e. on beef and oranges) and government procurement contracts. The Carter administration, worried about the trade imbalance, advocated that the three strongest 'locomotive' economies – the United States, Japan, and West Germany – should stimulate domestic demand in order to draw in imports from other, weaker economies. The Fukuda government responded with a high-level growth target backed by the rapid expansion of fiscal expenditure.

In comparison with the previous two phases of crisis, which were relatively short-lived, the third, which began in 1981–2, continues to the present day. At the outset, tension focused on agricultural problems and non-tariff barriers, but then spread to items such as automobiles, semiconductors, and video tape recorders (VTRs). Discord also resulted from a sharp increase in Japanese exports of small cars following the 1979 second oil crisis. In 1981, however, Japanese car manufacturers and exporters started a policy of voluntary self-restraint in order to ease the situation. Not only Americans but also Europeans became involved in serious competition with Japan in VTR exports. In 1982 the European Community adopted a concerted approach after the French government's decision to regulate all VTR imports through the small port of Poitiers. The 'Poitiers shock' opened the way, in 1983, for a Japan–EC voluntary self-restraint agreement on VTRs, light trucks, and motor cycles. Growing US resentment over Japan's overwhelming share of the US semiconductor chip market and alleged dumping in third-country markets led eventually to 'Reagan's sanction' – the $300 million retaliatory tariffs – in April 1987. One month later, revelations of Toshiba Machine Corporation's illegal sale of sophisticated propeller-milling equipment to the Soviet Union – in breach of COCOM regulations – brought 'Japan-bashing' to a head.

Needless to say, the worsening trade imbalance for the United States was at the heart of the dispute. Throughout the 1980s Japan has been running a huge current-account surplus, whereas the United States and the main West European countries, except West Germany, show a substantial trade deficit. Japan's surplus with the United States skyrocketed from $7 billion in 1980 to $51.4 billion in 1986 and $52.1 billion in 1987, and that with the EC countries from $8.8 billion in 1980 to $16.7 billion in 1986 and $20 billion in 1987. Naturally, US and European frustrations at the Japanese surplus and 'unfair' trading practices have mounted year by year.

It was against such a background that the 'Japan problem' became a 'hidden' item on the agenda of the annual Western economic summits. At the 1981 Ottawa summit, for example, the European Community sought to include a phrase critical of Japan in the communiqué, but failed to win support from the Americans, who had already negotiated a voluntary import ceiling on Japanese automobiles. An obvious difference of approach thus became apparent: the Americans preferred to deal with the Japanese bilaterally, whereas the Europeans intended to use the summit to put Japan on the spot. Caught between these different pressures, the Japanese method of defusing the conflict was to offer a package of liberalization measures in advance of the summit. For the Japanese government and people alike, it would be intolerable for the Prime Minister to lose face in the eyes of the world. At the same time, for the more internationalist forces inside Japan, the annual summit seemed a propitious moment to try to overcome domestic resistance to trade liberalization.[29] But the United States has often taken affairs into its own hands; then the EC countries have joined in the US-led campaign of 'Japan-bashing' or 'telling the Japanese what to do'.

Market opening and structural reform

In the five years from 1981 to 1985 the Japanese government came up with a series of seven packages of measures to make its markets more open to foreign products. These far-reaching measures ranged from tariff reductions and the elimination or relaxation of import restrictions to the simplification of import procedures. The liberalization of financial markets was also an important area. As a result, the ratio of tariff revenue to total imports, the yardstick of market openness, fell lower than that of other industrial countries. The rates over the three years ending in 1984 dropped to 2.5 per cent in Japan, compared with 3.2 per cent and 2.6 per cent respectively in the United States and the European Community. With further cuts later, Japan became the most open market as far as tariff levels were concerned. However, these 'makeshift' measures were not sufficient to reduce Japan's structural trade surplus. Ironically, the trade surplus showed a further increase each time new measures were introduced.

When the Japanese government committed itself to a three-year 'action programme' in summer 1985, its motivation appeared to be the positive wish to increase domestic sales of foreign manufactured goods. Nakasone gave a clear indication of this shift in a television campaign in which he urged his countrymen to be open-minded towards foreign products and so enrich their lives. The action programme was thus to be based on the general principle of minimizing government regulations and maximizing consumer choice in domestic markets. In other words, the government, which Nakasone described as naturally more protective of its citizens than its European and American counterparts, might have to play a lesser role. Coinciding with Japan's new approach, the US government put forward a Market Oriented Sector Selective (MOSS) negotiation proposal, covering four major areas: telecommunications, electronics, pharmaceuticals, and forest products. It was stressed that US trade officials would now have to sit down with their Japanese counterparts to go through the specific proposals word by word.

Despite the innovations in trade liberalization, Japan's current account surplus hit an unprecedented high of $49.17 billion, or 3.6 per cent of GNP, in 1985. Threatened by an uncontrollable trade imbalance as well as a growing tide of protectionism in the United States, Nakasone organized an Advisory Group on Economic Structural Adjustment for International Harmony, to explore means of reorienting Japan's economic structure in order to reduce its surplus. In the so-called Maekawa Report, submitted to the Prime Minister a month before the 1986 Tokyo summit, the group recognized that the continued large current account surplus had created a critical situation, and declared that the time had come for Japan to make a historic transformation in its policies.[30] But the report lacked concrete proposals and specific goals. It merely made general recommendations, in keeping with the tradition of consensus, avoiding clashes of opinion and interest. A solution seemed impossible, and the nominal surplus soared further as a result of the dramatic revaluation of the yen and the 'J curve' effect.

Over the period of the 1985 and 1986 Bonn and Tokyo summits the large US 'twin deficit' (trade and budget) generated uncertainty about the strength of the dollar and the stability of the international monetary system. Currency adjustment and macro-economic policy co-ordination became crucial. Turbulence in foreign exchange markets began with a sudden brief drop in the value of the dollar in early April 1985. In the next three years, with abrupt and intermittent fluctuations, the dollar fell, and the yen and the European currencies rose. Between the G-5 Plaza agreement in September 1985 and the G-7 Louvre agreement in February 1987, the value of the Japanese currency more than doubled, from ¥260 to ¥120 to the dollar. The yen's rapid appreciation had an enormous impact on the Japanese economy from 1986 onward.

Not only the business climate but the economic structure itself was affected.[31] The yen's steep upward valuation intensified the recession, particularly in the export-led manufacturing sector, but it stabilized domestic commodity prices and increased income in real terms. Decline in external demand contrasted with expansion in domestic demand. Such a change in the demand structure had a dramatic effect on industry, benefiting the non-manufacturing sector and dealing a serious blow to the export-led industries. Thus the Japanese economy has undergone a profound structural reversal.

One expected consequence of the structural reform was the transition from an external demand-led economy to a domestic demand-led one. As predicted, in 1986 external demand made a negative contribution to economic growth for the first time in eight years. At the same time, steady progress in the domestic demand-related sector made it possible to adjust to the structural changes imposed by the yen's appreciation.

Undergoing this dynamic structural turnabout, Japan has become the world's highest – or second highest – income nation, the world's largest creditor, and largest single aid donor. Japan's GNP in 1986 was close to $2 trillion, less than half the US level, but more than double that of West Germany for that year. After another upward valuation of the yen, GNP in 1987 reached an estimated $3 trillion. In reality, however, exchange rates are greatly affected by trade figures and may not accurately represent the purchasing power parity. (According to OECD calculations, the yen–dollar purchasing power parity in 1986 should have stood at around ¥223 to the dollar.) In the spring of 1987 a second Maekawa Report cited Japan's poor housing situation, long working hours, and high cost of living as prime indicators of the nation's living conditions. Therefore, alongside economic restructuring, comprehensive administrative, fiscal, and financial reform is needed, liberalizing trade practices, lifting restrictions, especially on farm imports, revising the tax system, and above all completing the social infrastructure so as to give the people a better standard of living.[32]

But Japan is still striving to achieve a pre-eminent position in the world economy. During the yen's rapid upward valuation, Japanese industry and business went offshore, investing directly in local production of manufactured goods, establishing overseas financial subsidiaries, and investing in insurance and real estate. Direct overseas investment in the year to March 1987 increased by 83 per cent to $22.3 billion, and in the year to March 1988 it increased again dramatically to reach $33.4 billion (see Table 4).

Table 4: Japan's direct foreign investment, by region

Region	1985 (US$ m)	1987 (US$ m)	1951–87 (cumulative total) (US$ m)	(%)
North America	10,441	15,357	52,783	37.8
Latin America	4.737	4,816	25,189	17.9
Asia	2,327	4,868	26,658	19.1
Middle East	44	61	3,079	2.1
Europe	3,469	6,576	21,047	15.1
Africa	309	273	3,951	2.8
Oceania	992	1,413	6,647	4.7
World total	22,319	33,364	139,354	100.0

Note: Column 5 total has been rounded up.
Source: Japanese Ministry of Finance; on fiscal year basis.

Japan's move into capital markets and its unprecedented increase in overseas investment will set it on the course followed by the Americans and West Europeans earlier this century, and will bring it to a level comparable with the peak economic periods of Britain and the United States. US leadership will be challenged by relentless Japanese advances in international service industries and developments in science and technology. The Japanese competitive edge will fuel further increases in national wealth, with returns flowing from investment and assets abroad.[33]

The Japan Economic Research Centre issued, in February 1988, a long-term forecast of 'the world economy in the year 2000', in which Japan's position was described as follows: the annual growth rate of its GNP should be 3 per cent by the early 1990s (sustained by domestic-led demand) and 3.5 per cent by the year 2000 (sustained by balanced external and domestic demand); its share of world imports was 6 per cent in 1986, and should be 7 per cent by the early 1990s and 9 per cent by the year 2000; and the yen's share of international currency reserves, which was 7 per cent in 1986, should be 30 per cent by the year 2000, whereas the dollar's share will be reduced from 66 per cent to 40 per cent in the same period. Thus the Japanese yen will become a dominant currency in the Asian Pacific region, replacing the US dollar.

The agenda for Japan as a summit power is how to use its national wealth and economic leverage in line with its new global responsibility 'Japan as a major economic power must demonstrate leadership that is familiar to and respected by advanced, newly industrializing, and developing nations, through effective use of its accumulated monetary assets.'[34] More specifically, Japan can contribute a great deal to the further development of the world economy and the open international trading system; like other developed countries, it is successfully shifting resources to accommodate demand in new industries without allowing economic and social rigidity to set in by protecting and preserving declining industries; at the same time, it is providing opportunities for developing countries to expand their manufactured exports, if necessary helping with economic assistance and technology transfer. In this broad context, developed and developing countries need to work towards agreement on a comprehensive package by which North and South alike can prosper within the market-oriented economic system.[35]

In other words, the future of the international trade regime depends on reaching agreements flexible enough to allow newly emerging countries to increase their share of the market while benefiting from the pressures of competition. In view of its competitiveness, of business and labour, the United States may have no choice but to work towards such a system. Japanese competitiveness may find itself able to dictate a 'pax Nipponica' within the Japan–US–EC trilateral presence in the Pacific Basin and elsewhere.[36]

The economic disputes already described constituted the outstanding political challenge to effective leadership not only in Japan but in all the other countries involved. The only effective solution was to call on political wisdom to devise a more stable order. A psychological reorientation was required: for the Japanese, to recognize that they had a part to play in finding a solution; for the Europeans, to recognize value systems other than their own;[37] and, for the Americans, to accept European and Japanese help.[38] In the Western summits, ganging up on Japan or any other country has never worked.

Third World strategy: burden-sharing

Just as the different perceptions among the Western allies have been reflected in the agenda for East–West relations and economic relations, so the Western strategy on the Third World cannot be dissociated from the various perceptions and priorities of the various allied nations. The United States regards Third World conflicts as a manifestation of the East–West confrontation, and emphasizes politico-military responses in line with its global strategy to contain or roll back communism in the Third World. On the other hand, for Europe and Japan, relations with the Third World are not dictated primarily by the political orientation of any particular country but by the complementarity of its and Japan's economic interests.[39] These differences of policy between the United States and its allies have complicated discussions on Third World problems.

The Third World has figured on the Western summit agenda under three main headings: first, the political crises of global and regional strategic importance; second, the economic and financial dislocation between the North and the South (and sometimes within the South), a problem closely connected with the oil crises; third, debt problems in the Third World in general. Examples under the first heading are Afghanistan, Iran, and Indochina; such cases have been on the agenda since the Tokyo and Venice summits (1979 and 1980). The second issue has been under focus since Venice, Ottawa, and Versailles in the early 1980s; the third has received serious consideration since Williamsburg and the second London summit.

Regional conflicts present a double challenge to the Western nations, the imperialistic opportunism of the Soviet Union being matched by the confused reactions of the Third World, which rejects both the remnants of Western imperialism and the Soviet imperialism once it has been recognized as such.[40]

The Afghan crisis, which was largely due to the Soviet military invasion, required a firm response from the West to convince the Soviets of its determination to resist any further expansionism. On the other hand, the Iranian crisis and then the prolonged Iran–Iraq war do not fall precisely within the terms of East–West confrontation. The situation in Indochina, and Kampuchea in particular, is essentially different from the other examples, owing to its involvement in Sino-Soviet rivalry. Given the complicated nature of such regional conflicts, the major Western nations need a strategy to respond to each threat and protect their own interests. In the case of the Afghan crisis, the US determination to contain Soviet expansionism received firm support from its allies. But its allies do not always fully endorse the US approach, which tends to see all major regional disputes (including those in Central America and Africa) in terms of global competition with the Soviet Union.

Furthermore, the allies of the United States are not always convinced of the wisdom of depending solely upon military means to ensure regional security in the Third World. They consider that a combination of efforts, political, economic, and diplomatic, may be necessary. Accordingly, the West European countries and Japan emphasize non-military resources and expertise as their contribution to political stability, but receive less appreciation from the Americans than they might expect. Given these different priorities, the key question is how to organize a division of labour or complementarity between the United States and its allies in order to safeguard Western interests by combining both military and non-military elements.[41]

Japan has identified its role within the concept of 'comprehensive security': this means providing economic assistance to shore up political and social stability in strategically important countries. Since 1979 the Japanese government has been giving financial assistance to Turkey, a neighbour of both Iran and the Soviet Union, and has gradually increased its annual contributions to $100 million (equivalent to that of France).

Japan also increased its economic aid to Pakistan soon after the Soviet invasion of Afghanistan; and in East and South-east Asia it has extended economic assistance to such countries as South Korea, Thailand, and the Phillippines, which all face communist threats of differing kinds. Japan has also borne 70 per cent of the cost of deepening and widening the Suez Canal (thus enabling US aircraft carriers to pass through).[42] All this can be regarded as 'strategic aid', though it has mainly facilitated the development of social infrastructures and various economic and commercial activities.

The North–South problem (i.e. relations between developed and developing countries) has been approached in different ways at the various Western summits and other international forums. In the early years of the summits, relations with developing countries were discussed in the context of confrontation between a solid Third World front demanding a New International Economic Order (NIEO) and a united Western stand against this challenge. Commodity prices and the transfer of resources from rich to poor countries in economic assistance, technology, and foreign investment are among the issues involved.

The Western summits, however, did not co-ordinate the major industrial countries' responses into a coherent strategy, failing notably to devise a scheme to stabilize the export earnings of the developing countries. But the Third World also failed to establish a common bargaining position towards the North, mainly because of the conflict of interests between the oil-producing and non-oil-producing countries, as demonstrated at UNCTAD V in 1979.

A distinct contrast between the Americans and the Europeans in their approach to the North–South problem became increasingly noticeable after the 1981 Ottawa summit. Under the Reagan administration the United States did not hide its strong scepticism about the South-led global negotiations, showing a conservative attitude to development aid in general. (Mrs Thatcher's United Kingdom took a similar position.) In President Reagan's view, North–South relations could not be divorced from the Western global strategy for containing communism in the Third World.

Among the Europeans, the Germans and the French have shown enthusiasm for North–South dialogue as important in its own right. Chancellor Schmidt tried to launch positive action at the Venice and Ottawa summits after the Brandt Report proposals, and at the 1984 London summit President Mitterrand declared the need for more official aid and a boost to world liquidity to help developing countries. At the 1983 Williamsburg summit Nakasone emphasized the importance of addressing the North–South problem, pointing out that there can be no prosperity for the North without prosperity for the South. Japan played a positive

113

role as an intermediary between the North and South at UNCTAD VI (Belgrade) in June 1983.

ODA as an instrument of policy

The establishment of means of mobilizing financial resources and expertise to help the developing countries are the official Development Assistance (ODA) programme and foreign investment; these reflect the economic and political-strategic interests of the Western industrial nations. Japanese ODA has shown a remarkable quantitative expansion since the late 1970s. At the 1978 Bonn summit the Fukuda government announced a doubling of ODA in three years; the volume in fact grew from $1.42 billion in 1978 to $3.30 billion in 1981, well over the target. In 1981 the Suzuki government announced another doubling of ODA, setting the new medium-term target for 1981–5 higher than the disbursed volume of $10.68 billion for the years 1976–80. Although the weak yen and delays in negotiations over multilateral aid disbursements held the annual rises below target, annual disbursed ODA did reach $3.74 billion in 1985. In 1986 the Nakasone government set a new medium-term target, doubling the volume of aid during the seven years ending 1992. With the sharp revaluation of the yen, disbursed ODA jumped to $5.6 billion in 1986 and $6.2 billion in 1987, putting Japan second only to the United States and overtaking France. Compared with Japan's ODA programme of only $100 million in the early 1960s, the increase is spectacular.

Nevertheless, Japan's performance has often been criticized as relatively poor in terms of quality, which is commonly measured by the proportion of grants in total ODA and the conditions of the grant element (i.e. a concessional interest rate and a long repayment period). Compared with the Development Assistance Committee (DAC) average of 90 per cent for the grant element, the Japanese figure stands at around 70 per cent. More seriously, the ODA/GNP ratio of Japan and the other major industrial states falls well below the target of 1 per cent set by the OECD. In the 1987 international ranking, Norway headed the league table with 1.1 per cent, followed by, for example, France with 0.75 per cent, West Germany with 0.39 per cent and then Japan with 0.31 per cent, Britain with 0.28 per cent and, finally, the United States with 0.2 per cent. Having accumulated a huge trade surplus in recent years, Japan will have to increase its ODA/GNP ratio as well as achieve a qualitative improvement in its foreign aid.

The geographical distribution of Japan's ODA follows the priorities of its foreign policy. Up to the early 1970s, Asia received between 90 and nearly 100 per cent of Japanese ODA. This was a reflection of Japan's own position as an Asian country and the historical background of its post-war economic co-operation, which began with reparations to the

Asian countries. However, as Japan has developed closer relations with countries in other regions like the Middle East, they have come to account for an increasingly important share of its bilateral ODA. Since the early 1980s the Asian share has been reduced to approximately 70 per cent of Japan's total ODA (the ASEAN countries alone accounting for one-third), with the remainder distributed almost equally between the Middle East, Africa, and Latin America.

This change can be attributed to a new guideline introduced after the May 1981 joint US–Japanese communiqué, in which the Suzuki government announced its intention to step up economic assistance under the new medium-term target, and to increase its aid to those areas which were important for the maintenance of world peace and stability. This might give the impression that Japan's aid policy has been much influenced by the American global strategy for containing communism in the Third World. It is, however, based upon the consideration that economic disorder in the developing countries breeds political and social unrest and that this may lead on to international tension or conflict. Thus supporting the developing countries through economic co-operation is conducive not only to political stability in the recipient country but also to the easing of tensions in the broader international community. But which specific countries fall into this category is a decision made independently by Japan.[43]

The focus of Third World issues, however, has shifted from simple economic assistance to developing countries to the relief of the debt crisis which erupted in the summer of 1982. Fears of a massive default by Mexico and other major Third World debtors posed a serious threat to the world financial system. The Third World debt doubled, during the first half of the 1980s, from a level of $650 billion in 1980 to $1,035 billion in 1986, and it is continuing to grow. As a result of the prolonged debt crisis, and a corresponding compression of imports, the standard of living and levels of income and investment in the developing countries have fallen catastrophically. Not surprisingly, political instability may result.

In order to avert a catastrophe in the world financial and banking system, pre-emptive and far-reaching strategies were required for active and long-term multilateral co-operation between the major Western industrial nations and the Third World debtors. The 'Baker plan' launched by the United States government at the Seoul annual conference of the World Bank and IMF in October 1985 was an initial step in that direction, but proved to be inadequate and ineffective. This joint approach towards the problem requires each debtor country to adopt economically effective and politically realistic measures to foster a renewal of self-sustaining growth. The Western industrial countries are then requested to take measures on a case-by-case basis in the following main areas:

115

further opening of their markets to ensure that developing countries can expand their exports and so earn the foreign exchange they need to service their external debt; a liberalized lending policy by official institutions, notably export credit agencies and the multilateral development banks; the provision of new credit at an adequate level by commercial banks; and further institutional innovations to add to the financial package and prevent renewed financial disruption.[44]

A positive Japanese contribution was imperative, as Japan's huge trade surplus had to be recycled as aid to the developing countries. In April 1986 a study group of the World Institute for Development Economics Research (WIDER) proposed a Japanese initiative aimed at 'Mobilizing the International Surplus for World Development'. Dr Okita, the former Foreign Minister and chairman of the group, is a strong advocate of this scheme for a Japanese 'Marshall Plan'. In its second report, in May 1987, the 'WIDER Plan' group recommended an annual programme costing $125 billion over five years, with mechanisms for promoting Japanese investment in the developing countries and increased lending by the Japanese international banks.[45] On 1 June 1987, at a White House ceremony to commemorate the fortieth anniversary of the original US Marshall Plan, President Reagan expressed the hope that other countries would follow the Japanese example. But overseas opinion saw Japanese ideas as a mixed blessing.[46]

In response, the Japanese government decided to budget for a three-year programme to funnel $30 billion of trade surplus into non-tied 'soft' loans to the Third World. Nakasone referred to these plans at the Japan–US summit in May 1987 and the Venice summit in June, when he advocated increased flows of Japanese resources to developing countries. At the Toronto summit Takeshita further elaborated Japanese commitments, explaining that the aid would go not only to Asian but also to Latin American and African countries, areas traditionally considered to be in the US and European spheres of influence.

Thus Japan has redefined its role as a capital-exporting or creditor nation in accordance with changes in global conditions and its enhanced status within the international community. Further details of Japan's role in channelling resources to the developing countries in the Third World, especially in the Asian Pacific region, will be discussed in Part III.

Part III
Japan and the West in Asian Pacific Affairs

Chapter eight

The Rise of a New Power Centre

Historically, the earliest encounters between Westerners and Japanese were not on Japanese soil but far to the south in the Straits of Malacca. More than thirty years before the first Western (Portuguese) contact with a Japanese island (Tanegashima) in 1542, junks from Okinawa with Japanese aboard met Portuguese traders at Malacca in 1511. Moreover, from 1513 onward the Portuguese intermittently frequented the China coast between the Yangtze estuary and the Pearl river, and throughout those years the Wako (Japanese pirates) were plundering and trading in this same area.[1] Four and a half centuries later, it is relevant to examine the context of Japanese–Western interactions in the Asian Pacific region, an area of enduring contact and mutual interest. Economically, over the centuries Japan's merchant trade towards the Asian rim of the Pacific has developed through coastal entrepôt networks inseparably linked with the Euro-Atlantic trading system. Politically, particularly since the inter-war period, the Pacific has become 'the centre of international affairs in several important respects'.[2]

A Pacific triangle – old and new

From a study of the Western maritime merchant expansion towards East Asia since the early sixteenth century, when Portuguese adventurers, Japanese corsairs, and Fukienese smugglers all combined to trade in the South Seas (a Chinese geographical term), different international trading patterns can be distinguished according to which mercantile power was dominant. In the early sixteenth century, when European imperial powers penetrated into Asia, they merely took over part of the existing trading networks from the unchallenged influence of the Chinese dynasties. Both larger companies and individual traders came into competition with the existing Chinese and indigenous merchants, and their trading outposts existed merely by permission of local rulers.[3]

A drastic change in the trading pattern came in the latter part of the eighteenth and, especially, in the nineteenth centuries, when the imperial

119

powers contemplated not only taking control of the existing system but also introducing a new system of trade based on large-scale production of various industrial crops. With the establishment of political control by the imperial powers, the structural pattern of trade was transformed from mercantile (commercial) business in the earlier days to manufacturing (industrial) enterprise in the later period. It is important to distinguish between the European impact before and after the second half of the eighteenth century.[4] In time the Portuguese and Spanish role as leading nations was taken over by the Dutch, British, Germans, and French as well as, eventually, the Americans.

At the beginning of the twentieth century the United States began to expand its territorial commitments into the western Pacific, by the acquisition of the Spanish Philippine islands and Guam. On the other hand, imperial Japan emerged as a strong new power in East Asia, symbolized in the Anglo-Japanese alliance. Then, while the European powers were preoccupied with World War I, Japan and the United States consolidated their interests and expanded their trade towards South-east Asia. It was after World War I that a triangular trading pattern in the Asian Pacific region began to take shape, with South-east Asia connected with the United Kingdom and other European countries on the one hand, and the United States and Japan on the other. British India and China were also involved in this trade. In the triangular trading pattern, the countries of South-east Asia earned foreign currency by selling their products to the United States (and to Europe and Japan as well), thereby enabling them to buy manufactured goods from the United Kingdom.[5] Some statistics show that, between the years 1913 and 1928, the major industrial centres' share of imports from South-east Asia changed as follows: Japan's share rose from 2.9 per cent to 5.5 per cent; the USA's from 6.9 per cent to 12.0 per cent; and the UK's (and Europe's) fell from 14.3 per cent (20.7 per cent) to 12.6 per cent (20.4 per cent).[6] These figures bear witness to the emergence of a more balanced triangle.

The great depression and, later, World War II paralysed the triangular trade. Western colonial rule, which had integrated Asian countries into the Atlantic power system, was interrupted abruptly in 1942 when, after a series of military victories, imperial Japan occupied the vast southern regions. During the great depression of the early 1930s the Japanese made headway in penetrating and invading the colonial markets of the Dutch East Indies (later Indonesia) and elsewhere. European and US traders could not compete with the Japanese in terms of commodity price, quality, or distribution of goods. The Japanese opened shops everywhere and employed native salesmen instead of leaving retail distribution to the Chinese. These shops dealt with a wide range of Japanese products, from cotton goods and electric light bulbs to bicycles. The Japanese also invaded the sea fisheries, took over the sugar factories, established silk factories, and undermined the colonial powers' monopoly of various enterprises by buying up native produce.[7]

Then, over the three and a half years from 1942, Japanese military rule replaced the Western colonial system with another colonialist system bent on forging an Asian commonwealth – the Greater East Asia Co-prosperity Sphere. The name Co-prosperity Sphere was partly a response to current world events and partly a reaction to the Anglo-Saxon policy of holding Japan back. Japan joined with Germany and Italy in the Tripartite Pact in September 1940. Germany wanted Japan to advance southward, and when the United States, followed by Britain and the exiled Dutch government, clamped restrictions on the export of their goods and vital raw materials to Japan the Japanese were forced to think of achieving self-sufficiency, even if it meant waging war. The Japan–Manchukuo–China bloc could neither supply sufficient raw materials nor absorb Japan's large industrial output. So it was only possible to establish autarky by including the resource-rich colonies of South-east Asia.[8]

The Japanese interregnum was short-lived, however, and failed to build a 'New Order' based on an interplay with the indigenous political and social forces of other Asian nations. Japan's innovative and radical but short-sighted reforms eventually proved self-destructive, for the mobilization of the local peoples away from Western rule brought nothing but untold economic hardship. None the less, it cannot be denied that Japan's invasion, and even its failures, gave great impetus to the rise of Asian nationalism, and led to decolonization in this part of the world after the war.[9]

Japan's revival in Asia after the Pacific war was achieved without any regional political or security dispute. Furthermore, with US protection and determination that it should actively participate in the economic development of 'Free Asia', Japan furthered its economic presence in every country of the western Pacific, with the exception of mainland China. As shown in Chapter 2, Japan's post-war economic growth was tied to US economic and military programmes, and its external economic expansion was diverted away from the continent of Asia – i.e. away from China – and towards a triangular integration with the United States and South-east Asia. Another historical analogy can thus be recognized in the trading patterns on the western rim of the Pacific. Corresponding to, and modelled on, a former triangular relationship which existed for some time after World War I, a new triangular arrangement was created with the United States as pivot, leaving Europe outside. The Japanese rise complemented the European decline in the Asian Pacific.[10]

The concept of triangular integration between the United States, Japan, and South-east Asia was on the cards before the Korean war, which then ensured and hastened its implementation. In cold war terminology, this was described as Japan's alignment with the 'free world', its commitment to the 'containment' of communism. In this way Japan again came to be described as a 'stabilizing power' in Asia, and its projected economic expansion and integration into the southern regions was again accorded the label of a 'Co-prosperity' sphere.[11] Japan's 'southward advance' was accelerated despite, and indeed partly by, the prolonged crises in Korea and Vietnam. It has succeeded in exploiting commercial and investment interests through accessible waterways, under the protection of the US Seventh Fleet. Thus Japan has caught up the United States as a major trader and investor in the Asian Pacific region.

The rapid economic advance of Japan, however, could not fail to rekindle memories of the Greater East Asia Co-prosperity Sphere. In contrast to the lack of any anxiety about a recrudescence of European dominance in the region, the fear of a resurrection of Japanese colonialism lingered on in South-east Asia. These countries were suspicious of Japan and did not want to tie themselves down to a 'special relationship' with the new economic superpower of Asia. Instead, they preferred the United States and European countries to increase their influence in the region as a counterbalance to Japan's weight. In spite of their weaker position in terms of economic influence, the Europeans have retained an enduring historical connection with South-east Asia in cultural and linguistic terms. This almost invisible heritage of the European states continues to influence the attitudes and behaviour of the local elites and peoples as a whole. It would be surprising if the national leaders' Western-oriented perspective did not have an effect on their domestic and international policy-making. Moreover, in the last two decades, these leaders have no doubt looked to the European experience in regional co-operation and integration when facing problems within ASEAN.[12]

In line with historical precedents, no initiative on regional affairs can really be effective unless the triadic relationship between Japan and the West in the Asian Pacific region is taken into consideration. In other words, Japan's overall Asian policy should not, and cannot, be divorced from its position as one of the Western nations. Hence the so-called 'twin-track' diplomacy which successive Japanese governments have pursued over the past three decades (see Chapter 3).

Open regionalism

Looking at broader inter-regional economic co-operation from the Japanese standpoint, the old Pacific triangle of the pre-war period differed from the new one of the post-war period in that Japan changed its trade partners from the Euro-Atlantic powers to the US-led Pacific powers. Yet it was the European concept of regionalism that provided Japan with a model for Pacific economic co-operation in a new stage of the post-war world economy.[13] In this respect, the Euro-Japanese nexus still survives, not in the same physical form but in a more sophisticated interaction.

Japan's initial views on Pacific economic co-operation in the later 1960s were stimulated by the establishment of the EEC and its significant impact on international trade and investment. For example, the earliest proposal for Pacific economic co-operation, which was envisaged as a Pacific Free Trade Area (PAFTA) at an international conference in Tokyo in 1965 by Professor Kojima Kiyoshi of Hitotsubashi University, was inspired by the EEC, as he himself recalled later. His inspiration was double-faceted, coming from a sense of isolation at Japan's being left outside the Euro-bloc on the one hand, and, on the other, an awareness of the economic growth which would be achieved if the Euro-bloc and PAFTA led the way to global free trade.[14]

According to this proposal, the five advanced Pacific countries – the United States, Canada, Australia, New Zealand, and Japan – would establish PAFTA, and then welcome the developing countries in Asia as associate members. Envisaging a 'tripolar world economic order' created by North America, Western Europe, and Japan, the Japanese would have the additional role of providing a strong basis of interdependence with neighbouring countries in the Asian Pacific region. Only then could it rank alongside major Western capitalist powers as an equal partner.[15] This ideal recalls Ikeda Hayato's 'Together with Asia, Japan could be one of the three pillars of the free world.'

Professor Kojima's concept, far-sighted for its time, was taken up by the then Foreign Minister, Miki Takeo. Keenly interested in promoting economic co-operation in the Pacific and Asian region, he presented a proposal based on it to the United Nations in 1967. Business circles were also interested in ideas for Pacific trade expansion, and the Pacific Basin Economic Council (PBEC) was established by the five Pacific countries in 1967. The following year a Pacific Trade and Development Conference (PAFTAD) was held in Tokyo and attended by prominent scholars from Japan, the United States, Australia, and elsewhere, with the aim of giving a theoretical basis to the 'Miki Plan' for Pacific co-operation.

At that stage, however, it became clear that EEC-type economic integration was premature for the Pacific Basin, for a number of reasons, including the fact that regional trade liberalization was still held back by measures to protect the main sectors of national economies, and by the disparity in levels of industrialization within the region. Moreover, the PAFTA proposal seemed inconsistent with the US commitment to a global non-discriminatory approach to free trade, a position which did not tie it to either a Pacific or a European regional grouping. As a result, the concept of an economic community modelled on the EEC had to be toned down to that of a consultative body for economic 'co-operation' on the pattern of the OECD.

A new stage in Pacific economic co-operation began in the late 1970s with a series of major advances such as the creation of the Pacific Basin Co-operation Study Group under the aegis of Japanese Prime Minister Ohira in March 1979, a US Congressional report on the establishment of an Organization for Pacific Trade and Development (OPTAD) in July 1979, and Ohira's visit to Australia and New Zealand in January 1980, followed by the Canberra Seminar on a Pacific Community in September. The Canberra seminar, which represented a shift away from institutional concerns and debates towards a functional approach, created a forum for the Pacific Economic Co-operation Conference (PECC). The PECC provided continuing machinery for consultation in a meeting held every 12 to 18 months, attended by tripartite business, academic, and *unofficial* government delegations.

Ohira's study group (headed by Dr Okita) proposed a Pacific Basin co-operation concept on the following lines: first, it should by no means be exclusive or closed *vis-à-vis* those outside the region; second, it should aspire to free and open interdependence in which the utmost respect would be paid to the developing countries' interests, while the industrialized countries should take the initiative in opening their markets; and, finally, it should in no way conflict with the co-operative bilateral and multilateral relations already existing in the region. This concept well reflected Japan's aim of pursuing a 'region-wide' co-operative relationship. The report contained few concrete proposals, confining itself mainly to the promotion of mutual understanding through the setting up of educational and research institutions. Japan's traditional reluctance to take the initiative was reflected in the report, intensified in this instance by a fear that, if Tokyo were perceived to be backing the concept too enthusiastically, other nations – particularly those of South-east Asia – would recoil, suspecting it of being merely a smokescreen for the peaceful establishment of a Japan-dominated Greater East Asia Co-prosperity Sphere.[16]

In the Canberra seminar, even the most ardent advocates of a Pacific Basin community agreed that caution was needed in pursuing the idea. The majority views in the meeting could be summarized as follows. First, as far as intra-regional trade and investment were concerned, a Pacific community already existed, but much remained to be done in the area of developing the economic potential of the countries of the region. Second, co-operative efforts through a consultative forum should be devoted to the economic and cultural areas, since attention at this stage to regional political and security issues would be liable to heighten rather than mitigate tensions. Third, in creating a body for orchestrating region-wide co-operation, due attention should be paid to the concerns and views of the member countries of ASEAN. Fourth, it was still premature to establish an intergovernmental body, and the most practical measure was to install a private-sector committee or informal forum responsible for the exchange of information concerning Pacific co-operation.[17] These limits on the scope of Pacific co-operation seem to be still valid today. But it seems equally true that the Canberra seminar laid down a precise political agenda which is still relevant for Japan: to redefine its role as that of initiator of region-wide co-operation, as will be discussed later.

Ohira's untimely death meant that the whole project was unfortunately suspended. But the next Prime Minister, Suzuki, energetically advocated Pacific Basin co-operation. He delivered a major speech entitled 'The coming of the Pacific Age' at the East–West Center in Hawaii in June 1982, during his last stop on a long journey including the economic summit at Versailles, the UN Special Session on Disarmament in New York, and state visits to Peru and Brazil. At the Versailles summit, Suzuki wanted to sound out Western leaders on his ideas for Pacific Basin co-operation before formally announcing them in Honolulu on his way home. He had already discussed the idea in Tokyo in April with the French President, Mitterrand, who was reported to have expressed strong interest.[18] How serious were the responses to Suzuki's ideas in Versailles was not clear. A rather cynical view was current among those tempted to dismiss Suzuki's proposal as something to distract his European and US critics from their trade dispute with Japan.[19]

The Suzuki speech at the East–West Center neatly defined five principles for Pacific solidarity: peace, freedom, diversity, reciprocity, and openness. On the basis of these five principles, Suzuki enumerated the major components of Pacific co-operation, referring to the coming Pacific Age. As for Japan's contributions in the political, security, and economic fields, he alluded to continued efforts for the early and peaceful resolution of the conflicts in the Indochinese and Korean peninsulas, and measures to open Japanese markets further for the benefit of the region and the revitalization of the world economy as a whole. He also emphasized development assistance, investment, and the transfer of technology to the Pacific region. There was no mention of a plan to establish a co-operative organization. With no blueprint for the future, this was at best an interlude between the low and high tides of Pacific regionalism. Still, the Japanese Prime Minister retained a conviction that the concept of Pacific solidarity could serve 'as a model for global co-operation'.

Shifting the centre of gravity of the world

Interest in Pacific co-operation rose once again on both sides of the ocean as the Nakasone government and the Reagan administration began to make successful policy combinations on international affairs. Before and after the May 1983 Williamsburg summit, the Reagan administration showed tremendous enthusiasm for opportunities and challenges in Pacific

Basin co-operation. In March 1983 Secretary of State Shultz testified
to the dynamism of the Pacific region, saying that the region had an
important future in which the United States should share. In May, just
before the summit, Norman Bailey, director of planning for the National
Security Council, made a notable speech in which he said, 'The economic
centre of gravity of the world is rapidly shifting to the Pacific Basin.'
In January 1984 Under-Secretary of State Lawrence S. Eagleburger
observed that US foreign policy was shifting its emphasis from Atlantic
affairs to those of the Pacific region. On the other side of the ocean a
new Japanese government began to move vigorously to reinforce Japan–
US relations, and Prime Minister Nakasone, by his Washington visit in
January 1983, demonstrated his firm intention to collaborate with the
Reagan administration in a wider range of security and economic issues
across the Pacific and beyond.

In Williamsburg the Japanese Prime Minister gave strong support to
President Reagan's position, and persuaded President Mitterrand to
endorse a firm statement on East–West relations, arms control, and a
new round of the GATT negotiations. Nakasone's pivotal role was no
mere accident but a result of the view of the 'Pacific Basin' group in
the Reagan administration. This saw Japan as holding a key position,
both filling the military vacuum in the Pacific through close US–Japanese
co-operation, and acting as an open economy to revitalize the Western
alliance. Nakasone's responses to these US overtures proved so satisfactory that Shultz admitted that the summit demonstrated how the
international agenda could be shaped in their common interests once the
two Pacific powers co-operated. Moreover, a White House official was
reported to have said, 'When historians look back on Williamsburg they
will record it as the political baptism of the Pacific Basin.'[20]

Whatever historians predict, relations between Japan and the United
States proved unprecedentedly close, with the Japanese Prime Minister
visiting the US twice within six months and the US President visiting
Japan in November and telling the Diet, 'Together, there is nothing our
two countries cannot do.' After Tokyo, Reagan also visited Seoul, and
in April the following year he went to China. These visits illustrated
US foreign policy's new emphasis on the Asian Pacific region, just as
the industrial and population centre of gravity within the United States
has shifted from Atlantic to Pacific in recent years. For Japan it is particularly significant that a security dimension was incorporated into its
Pacific policy under the Nakasone government, although this may or
may not be fortunate for the nation's future.

Meanwhile the 'Tokyo–Canberra' partnership for Pacific co-operation,
which emerged from Ohira's 1980 meeting with Malcolm Fraser, the
Australian Prime Minister, was consolidated, as illustrated by Prime
Minister Nakasone's trip to Fiji, Papua New Guinea, Australia, and New

Zealand in January 1985. Nakasone and his Australian counterpart, Bob Hawke, agreed on four principles of co-operation among the Pacific nations in the fields of economics, culture, and technology. In implementing such a plan, special attention should be paid to the initiatives of ASEAN countries, the two Prime Ministers agreed. Nakasone pointed out that an ASEAN Foreign Ministers' conference, also attended by external dialogue partners, would be a suitable forum in which to discuss the co-operation plan. Hawke, for his part, mentioned that Australia would make the utmost effort to promote economic and cultural co-operation with China. When Nakasone returned to Tokyo a delegation of the Federation of Economic Organizations (Keidanren) left on a tour of Malaysia, Indonesia, and Singapore, its first mission to the ASEAN countries. Then, in early March, the Japan Chamber of Commerce and Industry sent a large delegation of 100 members to China. These moves by the Japanese business community reaffirmed the private sector's role in leading economic co-operation.[21]

Meanwhile, the Canberra-born PECC proceeded with its rotational meetings for several years, elaborating a framework of task forces focusing on trade in manufactured goods, investment and technology transfer, and agriculture and renewable resources. However indecisive these PECC processes remained, the growing magnitude of Pacific economic co-operation could not fail to attract considerable attention, even from China and the Soviet Union. China sent its representative to the fifth PECC meeting in Vancouver in 1986, and gained formal membership of the forum alongside Taiwan. The Soviet Union also sent a member of its Canadian embassy as an observer for the first time in the history of the PECC.

Recent Chinese and Soviet attitudes to the concept of Pacific co-operation are a far cry from their positions in former years. Until 1984 China remained silent on the notion, inclined to scepticism of any proposal put forward by Japan. But it began to show serious interest in June 1984, when the director of the Centre for the Study of International Affairs, Huan Xiang, commented that there was one integrated world market of which today's China was also a part. In saying this, he acknowledged a basis for China's participation in the Pacific and world economy as a whole. The Soviet Union, on the other hand, had maintained an attitude of open opposition, as indicated by a 1982 Tass report whereby the community would be nothing more than a cover for the industrially developed Pacific countries to enslave the developing countries.[22] But a subtle change in this negative attitude occurred when Mikhail Gorbachev came to power. In a lengthy speech delivered in Vladivostok in July 1986, Gorbachev defined the Soviet Union as both an Asian and a Pacific nation, and emphasized the Soviet Union's understanding of and growing interest in the Asian Pacific region. This

127

heightened interest was reiterated in Gorbachev's September 1988 speech at Krasnoyarsk, in Siberia.

These shifts in policy towards the Asian Pacific, especially by the Soviet Union, have brought more complicated political and security factors into the general situation in the region. Japan will have to respond with a prudent strategy. The Soviet Union has intensified its political overtures to the countries of South-east Asia, as indicated by Foreign Minister Eduard Shevardnadze's visit to Thailand, Australia, Indonesia, and the Indochinese states in March 1987. Shevardnadze was anxious for opportunities to enter into closer relations with the main nations of ASEAN, to remedy the Soviet weakness of a lack of political influence in the region despite a strong military presence in the Pacific.

The Soviet Union has also in recent years made efforts to seek a foothold in the South Pacific through fishing agreements with financially troubled island states like Vanuatu and Kiribati.

The future of the South Pacific island region is affected also by the presence of Western Europe, especially France, which cannot be ignored as a factor in maintaining political stability and bearing responsibility for economic welfare in certain countries of the region. The European Community also has an institutional link with the South Pacific in the form of the Lomé Convention, which it has signed with African, Caribbean, and Pacific (ACP) countries, including eight small island states in the South Pacific. However, political tensions have been building up in countries such as New Caledonia, Fiji, Papua New Guinea, and Vanuatu, with dangerous splits reflecting ethnic and regional differences. The French policy of ruling out independence for New Caledonia causes great concern in the South Pacific region, already the scene of big-power rivalry.[23]

How to deal with such an intricate situation in the South Pacific is a serious problem for Japan and the other Western nations. The Japanese Foreign Minister, Kuranari Tadashi, toured the five countries of Australia, New Zealand, Fiji, Vanuatu, and Papua New Guinea in January 1987. In Canberra, Kuranari and his opposite number, Bill Hayden, agreed to move towards a new partnership transcending mere trade and commercial relations, and intensifying political dialogue over matters of mutual concern. In his speech in Fiji, Kuranari said that Japan would not allow new tensions in the area. He proposed a special fund for Pacific island countries, to administer foreign aid transferred from the West and, at the same time, to check Soviet influence. In addition, to assume a responsible role for Japan in maintaining peace and stability in the South Pacific, Kuranari proposed to invite leaders of the independent small states in the region to annual political consultations, as an extension of dialogue diplomacy.

The increasingly complex economic and security conditions affecting the political environment have now required participants in, and supporters of, Pacific co-operation to redefine its guiding principles. Since interference in political and security issues is liable to heighten tension in the region, it was stated in 'the 1980 Canberra context' that such issues should be avoided by the Pacific co-operation movement. But that does not alter the fact that the economic activities of the various countries are inextricably connected with their political and security interests. Furthermore, another critical question is whether the proposed Pacific co-operation can be translated into reality without the leadership of the major economic powers.[24] To answer that question, it is necessary to examine relations in the Pacific Basin in their economic, political, and strategic aspects.

Economic dynamism

The Asian Pacific economies can be grouped into three or four categories according to various different criteria: level of *per capita* income, growth performance, degree of external trade orientation, and relative import-ance of economic sectors (agriculture, manufacturing, and services). The first group comprises the developed economies – Japan, Australia, New Zealand – with high incomes, relatively low growth rates, and moderate orientation to external trade. The second comprises the newly industrial-ized countries (NICs) – South Korea, Taiwan, Hong Kong, Singapore – with a heavy orientation to external trade and rapid rates of growth. The third comprises the resource-rich ASEAN countries – Indonesia, the Philippines, Thailand – with relatively low levels of income, growth, and trade orientation, Malaysia, with an income level nearer the NICs', and Brunei, with an exceptionally high income. China belongs to the fourth group, together with the South Asian countries, with low levels of income and trade orientation but a significantly high rate of growth. A fifth group might possibly be discerned, comprising the three Indochinese economies, Burma, and North Korea, which, albeit geographically part of the region, are the least integrated into regional economic patterns and have the most stagnant growth rates. Despite the variation of growth performance, one salient pattern common to almost the whole region is a 'virtuous circle' expansion process – a cycle of exports–investment–exports which has gradually been developed since the mid-1960s.

After the impressive growth achieved in the 1960s and 1970s, in the 1980s most of the Asian Pacific economies have maintained a steady pace of expansion (see Table 5). The average *per capita* income of Japan, which is the premier economy in the region, has now reached a level no less than, or nominally even higher than, that of the United States (the recent surge of the yen against the dollar in a sense helped it to catch

Table 5: Population, GNP, and growth rates of Pacific Basin and EC countries

Country or group	Population (1986, million)	GNP (1986) (US$ billion)	GNP (1986) Per capita (US$)	Annual growth rate, 1980–5 (%)
Japan	121	1,955.6	16,162	4.0
United States	242	4,185.5	17,295	2.4
Canada	26	363.9	13,996	2.4
Australia	16	167.3	10,456	3.1
New Zealand	3	27.2	9,067	3.0
South Korea	42	98.1	2,336	7.6
Taiwan	19	71.4	3,758	6.0
Hong Kong	6	37.4	6,233	5.7
Singapore	3	17.3	5,767	6.1
NICs, total	70	224.2	3,200	–
Thailand	52	41.8	804	5.3
Malaysia	16	27.8	1,738	5.1
Indonesia	167	75.2	450	–1.1
Philippines	56	30.6	546	–0.6
ASEAN four, total	291	175.4	602	–
NICs and ASEAN total	361	399.6	1,100	–
China*	1,060	318.9	301	9.7
European Community	323	3,461.3	10,716	1.3

* Population and GNP, 1985.
Source: Ministry of International Trade and Industry, Tokyo, 1988.

up). As recently as 1965 Japan's average income was only a quarter that of the United States. The average income of Taiwan was less than one-fifth that of the United States in 1985. But if their respective average levels of growth over the past two decades were to be maintained at the same rate in future – 6.5 per cent in Taiwan and 2 per cent in the United States – the Taiwanese would be richer as early as 2023.[25] In the same way, the other NICs like Singapore and Hong Kong would stand on a level with the United States towards the first or second decades of the twenty-first century.

To make a further comparison of *per capita* GNPs based on recent trends, Singapore and Hong Kong will surpass Japan's 1980 level in 1991–3. Malaysia will reach Hong Kong's and Singapore's 1980 level in 2010. The Philippines, Thailand, and Indonesia will reach South Korea's 1980 level by 2010. If present trends continue, the region as a whole will have an aggregate economic size comparable to that of North America and Western Europe by the year 2000 (see Table 6). This is no more than speculation, because there are a number of variables, which could have major effects, such as fluctuations in exchange rates and political factors at home and abroad. Nevertheless, there is a strong possibility that between now and early next century all the developing regions in the Asian Pacific will be, or will virtually be, NICs.[26]

Table 6: Scale and growth potential of GNP: East Asia, North America, and European Community, 1987 and 2000 (US$ billion)

Region	1987	2000	Annual growth rate (%)
East Asia (ten countries)	2,844	5,308	4.9
North America (two countries)	4,844	6,940	2.8
European Community (twelve countries)	4,259	5,940	2.6

Note: East Asia includes Japan, three NICs, and six ASEAN countries.
Source: Kokumin Keizai Kenkyu Kyokai, Tokyo, August 1988.

What mechanisms have been, and will have to continue to be, functioning behind this region-wide trend? Japan's strong economic growth, especially between the two oil crises in the 1970s and in the subsequent period of oil glut, can now be seen to have provided the moving force for the developing regions to realize their export-oriented and investment-led patterns of growth. Japan's high rate of development functioned as a 'growth pole' for the surrounding countries in the Asian Pacific region, especially the NICs. In one respect, Japan's rapid growth triggered an active expansion in demand for exports from these countries. As a result, domestic investment activity in these countries rose significantly. However, their capital goods industries were still immature, and they had no choice but to import machinery and metal products from Japan. Thus Japan acted as a supply-base for capital goods. A 'virtuous circle' was thus created, promoting the cyclical process of exports–investment–exports.

The first oil crisis gave Japanese industries the incentive to upgrade their levels of technology in order to conserve energy and other natural resources. On the one hand, the rate of increase in energy imports was curbed and, on the other, the relative proportion of high-technology exports increased. The structure of foreign trade was greatly transformed in the process: imports of semi-processed goods have increasingly replaced raw materials, while export industries have concentrated on high-tech products, so strengthening their competitiveness. This structural change has enabled Japan's economic dynamism to be transmitted abroad, especially to the Asian NICs.[27]

Towards the beginning of the 1980s, the developing countries of Asia became relatively less dependent on capital goods imports from Japan as they became more industrialized themselves. At the same time, the share of high-technology goods in their total trade with Japan rose and the supply of Japanese capital and technology expanded. This has meant a significant increase in economic and industrial ties between Japan and Asian nations; in effect a 'horizontal international division of labour' is beginning to replace the 'vertical division', originally set up in the colonial age before the war, between primary goods producers and manufacturing industries. Evidence of this dynamic movement is that industrial goods account for an increasing proportion of trade between Japan, the Asian NICs, and ASEAN. A trade network which could be called an 'Asian economic sphere' based upon horizontal and intra-industrial co-operation is thus emerging in the vicinity of Japan for the first time in history.[28]

The foregoing is not the full story of this dynamic process. The picture of recent developments, in particular the Asian countries' progress towards NIC status, is incomplete without taking into account the important role of the US economy, which provides the principal market for exports from many East Asian countries. The Asian NIC–US trade has expanded tremendously in the past two decades, primarily as a result of the rapid inroads of Asian manufactured goods into the US market. The current market value of Taiwan's exports of industrial goods to the United States grew a hundredfold, from $6.3 million in 1965 to $6.6 billion in 1980; South Korea's grew ninetyfold, from $50 million to $4.5 billion in the same period; Hong Kong's grew sixteenfold, from $309 million to $5 billion; and Singapore's grew 250-fold, from $8 million to $2 billion.[29] Similarly rapid growth in industrial exports to the United States occurred in other developing Asian countries.

Since 1980 the Asian NICs have continued to expand their trade. They have accomplished the remarkable achievement of increasing their share of world trade from less than 2 per cent in the mid-1960s to 6.5 per cent in the mid-1980s. Between 1980 and 1986 the total exports of the four NICs grew from $76.4 billion to $131.2 billion; 55 per cent of this increase was absorbed by the United States (see Table 7). Indeed the US

Table 7: Asian NICs' trade with the United States, Japan, and the European Community, 1980–6 (US$ billion)

| | Exports | | | Imports | | |
	1980	1985	1986	1980	1985	1986
Total	76.4	114.0	131.2	88.5	107.2	116.1
United States	19.0	39.6	49.1	15.6	18.0	18.8
(% of total)	(24.9)	(34.7)	(37.4)	(17.6)	(16.8)	(16.2)
Japan	7.7	11.4	13.1	20.7	24.5	30.9
(% of total)	(10.1)	(10.0)	(10.0)	(23.4)	(22.9)	(26.6)
EC	12.7	12.3	17.3	8.8	11.5	14.1
(% of total)	(16.6)	(10.8)	(13.2)	(9.9)	(10.7)	(12.2)

Source: *World Financial Markets*, Morgan Guaranty Trust Company of New York, January 1987.

market has served as the principal outlet for Asian manufactured goods, providing an engine of growth for these smaller East Asian countries. With the foreign exchange received, the nations can import the capital goods, largely from Japan, which they need for their industrialization. The NIC–US economic relationship has been reinforced also by direct investment by US–affiliated companies, especially in the electronics sector. NIC–Japan economic relations have also been strengthened by Japanese activities in trade and investment, with the related transfer of technology. For most of the NICs Japan is the largest source of imports, just as the United States is the largest destination of exports.

Furthermore, US–Japan economic relations have been intensified by the Asian NICs' role as intermediary and indirect economic liaison between them. These interactions between the US, Japan, and the NICs, by acting as a mechanism of economic and trade integration, have provided a driving force in the formation of a 'Pacific triangle' which may generate a new momentum of growth. Problems still exist, of course, because of the large trade imbalances between the United States and both Japan and the NICs; if these continue they could lead to a rise in protectionism which would impede economic development in the Pacific. However, it is more likely that the growing economic relationship between Japan, the NICs, and ASEAN will create further opportunities for expanded trade across the Pacific.

While the United States and Japan have been the largest trading partners of the developing Asian Pacific countries, West European countries have also remained a major factor in the trade of the region. As Table 7 shows, the EC buys more exports from the Asian NICs than Japan does, but less than the United States. As after World War I, Europe's position as principal supplier of capital goods has been taken by Japan and the United States, but it remains indispensable as a major outlet for manufactures. In international capital flows, such as traditional commercial bank credits, direct investment, and concessional foreign aid, the Europeans maintain a significant role in the economic development of the Asian Pacific region.

The future of the 'Pacific growth triangle' is, nevertheless, threatened by the major economic dispute between Japan and the United States as well as by the growing protectionism of advanced Western countries. To halt protectionism in the developed countries, a new GATT round of trade negotiations – known as the Uruguay Round – was launched in 1987 on the initiative of the US and Japanese governments, and with the support of the Asian NICs and the countries of ASEAN. In order to maintain the health of the international trading system, Japan and the Asian NICs are being asked to open their domestic markets and realign currency exchange rates, and so help to establish more balanced trade relationships. As regards the US market, there is a growing awareness that its role as an engine of Asian growth in manufactured goods will reach its limit sooner or later, and may even diminish as the United States tries to rectify its trade and financial deficits. Opinion in Congress is hardening towards countries which run large surpluses with the United States; this is expressed most clearly in the omnibus trade bill discussions. East Asian developing countries will increasingly need to look to other large markets and to the diversification of exports to sustain further new growth. Certainly one of the most important alternative markets is Japan.[30]

One encouraging sign that the Japanese market is becoming more accessible is that the rise of the yen since autumn 1985 has effectively altered the trade flow within the Pacific triangle. Western Europe has also been affected. In 1986 the South-east Asian region enjoyed a boom in machinery sales to Japan, as a result of a rush by Japanese manufacturers to procure cheap components from the Asian NICs and offset the effects of the shift in exchange rates. In 1987 and 1988 consumer electronic goods from the four Asian NICs made significant inroads into the Japanese market. West European countries also made headway in the Japanese market, with products ranging from cars and chemicals to luxury goods, including clothes, leathers, and alcohol. Whereas the two regions – South-east Asia and Western Europe – positively exploited the yen's revaluation, the United States failed to penetrate the Japanese market to any significant degree. However, the rush to shift manufacturing production offshore, much of it to the United States, which was one of Japanese industry's main responses to the high yen, means that Japan should in the long run export less and import more.[31] The problem of resolving trade imbalances and restoring conditions for further economic growth is a formidable one, beyond the reach of a mere exchange-rate mechanism. There must be a more comprehensive approach.

As articulated in the two Maekawa Reports and proposed at the Tokyo and Venice summits as well as in dialogue within ASEAN, Japan's overall policy for tackling the economic and trade imbalances is based on a package of measures designed to expand domestic demand and improve access to the Japanese market for manufactured goods on the one hand, and, on the other, to reduce the trade surplus and increase economic co-operation.

Among these measures, the most effective has been to undertake extensive ODA-led investment programmes, recycling Japan's huge trade surplus. As noted in Chapter 7, an Asian Marshall Plan has long been in the air. Japan has by no means been solely responsible for taking this initiative or for putting it into effect. Although it is a welcome sign that Japan has started to put more effort into economic assistance to developing nations, some people in Japan are sceptical as to whether aid programmes can be effective, particularly since hitherto official aid policy has generally placed too much emphasis on merely raising the level of the finance disbursed, without giving sufficient attention to the specific projects under consideration. This means that aid is less effective than it should be.[32]

The Japanese government's efforts to raise the level of foreign aid (and increase defence expenditure) have hitherto been made partly under US pressure. They are also part of Japan's membership fee, as it were, for the Western club. However, if it wishes to become a truly responsible member, it cannot remain indifferent to the effective use of the club finances. While in the past ODA programmes have been undertaken on a bilateral basis, and Japan has followed the principle of non-interference in the recipient country's policy, it is coming to realize the importance of ensuring joint supervision of projects by the donor and recipient countries, through such international institutions as the OECD and the World Bank. Meanwhile it has become an established practice in recent years for Japan's ODA programmes to be studied at an annual Japan–US meeting, to improve the effectiveness of co-operation, especially in the South-east Asian region.[33] Compared with this and other Japan–US forums, collaboration between Western Europe and Japan is still inadequate in both quantity and quality.[34] However, the more broadly based demand created under the 'general untying' of Japanese ODA-cum-private funds can lead to increased procurements from the United States as well as from West European countries.

The political and security dimension

The economic flowering of the Asian Pacific region is a reflection of the relatively stable and peaceful political climate in the individual countries and the region as a whole. The political structure and regional order are still to some extent fragile, however, vulnerable to conflicts between the economic and security interests of the traditional powers themselves and of the post-colonial nation-states in the region. Broadly speaking, Asian Pacific politics represents two tiers: tripartite combinations – between the United States, China, and the Soviet Union as strong military powers and North America, Japan, and Oceania (of European origin) as capitalist powers – and locally divided, grouped, or associated nations, namely the two Koreas, the six members of ASEAN, and the three Indochinese states. Although the pattern of interaction between these major powers and groups is not a constant one, a persistent feature is competition between the great powers for influence over smaller countries in conflict- and tension-ridden areas. This competition stems from the different strategies and priorities of the nations concerned in the region. Their basic interests and roles must be examined in order to understand the regional order.

First, superpower relations in the Asian Pacific region are dominated by strategic military and security considerations related to the balance of power. The traditional theme of US policy towards East Asia and the Pacific has been to deny significant regional influence to any other single power. America's motivation in the Pacific war was to check Japan's ambitions in East Asia and the southern regions; even as far back as the late nineteenth century, the Open Door policy implied opposition to the division of China into spheres of imperialist influence. The policy of the Soviet Union is still rooted in Tsarist attempts to undertake a 'southern expansion'; this has been demonstrated by interventions rivalling those of its principal adversaries, as in Korea and Indochina. For China the guiding principle is 'anti-hegemonism'; in practice, this means opposing the penetration by the Soviet Union or Vietnam into the vicinity of the 'Middle Kingdom'.

At the risk of oversimplification, it can be shown that the great powers' competitive involvement in the region has deep historical roots, and that the experiences of the past three or four decades have proved that this involvement actually serves to shore up a relatively durable *status quo*, by inhibiting change in the international order. The United States uses its naval presence, military bases, and nuclear capability to stalemate the forces of the Soviet Union, which has established itself in the region in the past decade by a naval build-up and the siting of bases in Vietnam. The United States also provides political leadership to non-communist Asian nations, as exemplified in the UN debates on Kampuchea. Lacking a political influence commensurate with its military power, the Soviet Union has in recent years launched a peace offensive towards Japan and South-east Asia. But its involvement in Kampuchea remains a major stumbling-block to compromise with the ASEAN nations and, also, China. Bordering on Vietnam, Laos, and Burma, China has used military muscle to block Vietnam from expanding its sphere of influence over the Indochinese peninsula and beyond.

Both in spite and because of the stalemate in regional conflicts, the most likely prognosis for the Asian Pacific is that none of the Big Three, especially China, wants any border flare-up which might, perhaps, compel them to intervene. China, which views its economic modernization programme as its top priority, needs above all a quiet and stable frontier, with no significant conflicts for the rest of this century. The Soviet Union may vigorously continue to try to close the gap with the United States in terms of its military presence in the western Pacific. Yet it has sometimes been held that the true significance of the Soviet presence at Cam Ranh Bay in Vietnam lies in the political influence it gives Moscow in the region, rather than the military capability.[35] With a sluggish economy, and domestic reform much needed, the Soviets have been compelled to shift the focus of their foreign policy to the economic front; in the Asian Pacific context, this implies a trend to economic co-operation in the region.

Second, the US-led capitalist powers agree that a central balance of power is needed to offset the enhanced Soviet military presence in the Asian Pacific region. But their opinions appear to diverge on the scale of the Soviet threat and the responses that ought to be made to it. Canada, which is a neighbour of the United States and has traditional connections with Europe, considers that security against the Soviet military threat should be maintained through NATO, not by a Pacific alliance. Canada's primary concern in the Pacific is the security of communication lines mainly for commercial purposes in the northern Pacific crescent, extending to Japan and other Asian countries. While Canada has participated in the annual 'Rim of the Pacific' naval exercise, it has not reinforced efforts for Pacific defence.

Since 1983 Japan's conception of, and responses to, the Soviet nuclear and conventional military build-up have come much closer to those of the United States and Western Europe. While the Japanese do not feel they can usefully become involved in the negotiations for East–West arms control, they are concerned about how to reduce tension along the demarcation lines running from the northern islands off Hokkaido to the Korean and Indochinese peninsulas. There is little prospect of a Soviet–Japanese *rapprochement* unless a broader *détente* can be brought to the region first, with an end to the conflict in the two peninsulas. However, Japan is prepared to play some role in creating a climate in which these two conflicts can be settled.

For Australia and New Zealand, located in the southern hemisphere, the northern 'bear' is a distant animal and a minimal threat. Owing to New Zealanders' reluctance to grant US ships and aircraft carrying nuclear weapons access to their ports and air bases, Washington has had to abrogate the ANZUS treaty in its application to Wellington; but New Zealand can survive without it. Both Australia and New Zealand have maintained security ties with South-east Asian countries through the Five-Power Defence Arrangement, a regional defence co-operation agreement among British Commonwealth nations. The threat which this defence arrangement is directed against is more likely to come from local disputes than global confrontation.

Third, for the smaller nations of Asia which are peripheral to great-power competition, the Soviets and Americans no longer constitute an immediate danger. The direct threat to South Korea is North Korea, and vice versa. The countries of ASEAN vary in their perception of the potential threat from the communist big powers: for Malaysia and Indonesia, the more serious danger in the long run is China; for Thailand and Singapore, it is the Soviet Union. However, the most immediate threat for all the ASEAN nations is Vietnam. As a result, the ASEAN leaders are far more inclined to perceive threats in inter-regional political and economic terms, rather than in the context of external military security. It must be admitted that the North-east and South-east Asian nations' perception of internal threats differs radically from the American view-point, which is a corollary of US involvement in East Asia: the Korean war, the establishment of SEATO, the war in Vietnam, were all responses to threats from communist adversaries.[36]

Behind each newly independent East Asian nation's perception of its security and prosperity lies the fundamental change in national priorities that took place around the mid-1960s, a reorientation of national goals and strategy which rejects military confrontation to concentrate on domestic reforms, and stakes the regime's legitimacy and prestige on concrete economic achievements and outpacing its adversaries.[37] In South Korea, President Park quietly set aside national ambition by play-ing down Syngman Rhee's goal of unifying the divided Korean penin-sula. He thus paved the way for vigorous economic development, so enabling the South to overtake its adversary in the North in economic power and living standards. The eventual democratic reform under the successor Chun Doo Hwan and Roh Tae Woo regimes and the holding of the 1988 Olympic Games in Seoul symbolize a great enhancement of South Korea's international image and prestige. In his inaugural speech in February 1988 President Roh expressed the hope that (South) Korea, 'once a peripheral country in East Asia', would 'take a central position in the international community'. For South Korea 1988 was the date of the leap from the Third World to the First.[38]

In Indonesia, President Suharto reversed Sukarno's Konfrontasi, and organized 'development politics' by putting technocrats in the place of politicians. Indonesia's shift to a less antagonistic stance removed an obstacle to the formation of the ASEAN group to cope with the crises in Indochina and strengthen regional security. In Taiwan, after Chiang Kai-shek's death, the Kuomintang abandoned its historic mission of recovering the mainland, and took instead the promotion of Taiwan's export-led economy as a national objective. Chiang Ching-kuo's death in January 1988 and the succession of Lee Teng-hui, who is a native Taiwanese, will inevitably facilitate a further 'Taiwanization' of the country.

In mainland China, too, Deng Xiaoping has embarked on a cautious but determined new policy to ease the country out of the superpower strategic competition and concentrate on economic development. Behind this reversal lies Deng's drive to initiate a Chinese version of the Yoshida doctrine.[39] To renounce a 'national mission' based on military strength, and to concentrate on economic development as an essential means of restoring the nation's place in the forefront of world leadership – if that is the core of the Yoshida doctrine, then it can be said to have prevailed over the whole of East Asia. Japan is the unacclaimed pioneer of this grand strategy.

In summary, great-power involvement seems to have been challenged by economic dynamism in the peripheral region, and this can be a much more powerful factor for international change. Competition between the great powers in military and security terms has, in a sense, contributed to preserving the *status quo*, and preventing a drastic change of frontiers. But the existing international order could not repress regional conflicts or local contests. Yet economic development, however powerful as a factor of change, must be pursued without destroying the existing fabric of national and international security. How can we overcome this paradox in a new international order?

The international system for safeguarding peace and stability in the midst of great-power competition in the Asian Pacific region is constituted by bilateral security arrangements which combine, in the case of the non-communist camp, Japan, South Korea, the Philippines, and the countries of Oceania, under 'vertical' treaty networks ultimately guaranteed by the United States. But what has been lacking in the region is an international institution to combine and harmonize 'horizontally' all these individual nations' perceptions and responses, which do not necessarily coincide with those of the United States. No East Asian nations have any bilateral or collective security arrangements among themselves; this contrasts with their economic relationship, which is now at the beginning of a 'horizontal' collaboration.

The only existing institutional framework able to reflect broader perspectives on Asian Pacific affairs is the so-called ASEAN dialogue conference; this has been developed over the last decade as a meeting place for government representatives from the South-east Asian nations as well as from external partners such as Japan, the United States, Canada, Australia, New Zealand, and the European Community. ASEAN itself is neither an integrated political entity like the EC, nor a collective security system. It is a loosely organized regional association, but is capable of becoming the 'central political body' of the future with the objective of the integration of the Asian Pacific region in the fields of economics, science and technology, and cultural affairs.[40] This unique forum, then, can provide the parameters for the evolution of a new regional and international order through detailed discussions of different perceptions. The following chapters examine the character and achievement of the ASEAN dialogue in the 1980s and makes projections for the future.

Chapter nine

The ASEAN Dialogue: Regionalism at Work

In South-east Asia political geography forms a highway between oceans and a bridge between continents; in the extreme east are the Spice Islands, or Moluccas, and in the extreme west is a narrow channel, the Straits of Malacca, the shortest sea route from mainland China to continental India and Europe. For many centuries this channel seemed destined by nature to be a commercial route, with wealthy cities such as Shri-Vijaya (Palembang), Malayu (Jambi), Malacca, and Singapore successively holding sway over this gateway between east and west.[1]

The largest and most typical archipelagic nation is Indonesia, which employs the concept of *Wawasan Nusantara* (a theory of the between-islands), implying that the seas and straits must be utilized as economic and political bridges between the islands, regions, and numerous ethnic groups.[2] This concept is also embodied in the *Musyawarah* spirit, a practical aspect of indigenous political culture, which implies consensus-building through consultation. In this geopolitical and historical setting, the most recent attempt to realize a gateway between Asia and the West is ASEAN, a regional grouping of nations which constitutes a unique community in which all its members are connected by seas and straits. It holds frequent meetings of government, academic, and business leaders; the most notable is the so-called ASEAN dialogue, an annual discussion forum of the Foreign Ministers of the member countries and friendly nations. Occasional summit meetings at which ASEAN leaders meet their external partners who are visiting the region are another essential element of the dialogue.

Dialogue between the member nations of ASEAN and its external partners, built up and reinforced steadily over many years, constitutes the main forum in which different perceptions of the search for a new regional order are discussed and perhaps modified. In the early to mid-1970s a number of crucial international developments – the oil crisis, the communist victory in Indochina and the subsequent withdrawal of US military forces from mainland South-east Asia, the Sino-American and Sino-Japanese *rapprochements*, the Cultural Revolution in China –

spurred ASEAN to turn its attention to its external environment, a departure from the period in which its members were preoccupied by their own internal skirmishes. Countries outside ASEAN came to recognize its significance, and focused their attention on regional affairs through dialogue with it.

ASEAN's dialogue with extra-regional partners started as *ad hoc* negotiations on trade with Japan and the European Community, but since 1976 ASEAN has adopted a systematic approach based on the individual members' specific assignment to co-ordinate regular contacts with more countries and international organizations. Indonesia became the contact country for Japan and the European Community; Malaysia for Australia; Singapore for New Zealand; the Philippines for the United States and Canada; and Thailand for the United Nations Development Programme (UNDP) and the Economic and Social Commission for Asia and the Pacific (ESCAP).[3]

Until 1972 Japan–ASEAN relations had no formal multilateral diplomatic framework, because Japan's contacts with South-east Asian countries were organized on a bilateral basis or through its own wider forum, MEDSEA. Japan's explicit recognition of ASEAN came with the 1972 edition of the Foreign Ministry's *Diplomatic Blue Book* in which ASEAN was actually discussed as one of the main Asian regional organizations. But, ironically enough, the first contact at the policy level between Japan and the ASEAN countries was made after the 1973 ASEAN Foreign Ministers' meeting had strongly criticized the effect of Japan's synthetic rubber exports on South-east Asian natural rubber producers. Then the early years of Japan–ASEAN relations were clouded by economic tensions, as demonstrated during Prime Minister Tanaka's tour of ASEAN nations in 1974.

EC–ASEAN relations also became a matter of policy in 1972, when a Special Co-ordinating Committee of ASEAN nations (SCCAN) was set up to harmonize economic interests with the European Community; this reflected, in part, links from the colonial period. Then the two groups' formal relations were institutionalized with the establishment in 1974 of a Joint ASEAN–EC Study Group as an alternative to the commercial co-operation agreements which had been negotiated bilaterally between the Community and the Asian Commonwealth countries and others. Parallel with this, Australia established trade and economic relations with ASEAN on a multilateral basis in 1974. In 1975 New Zealand began a dialogue on development assistance projects, and Canada initiated dialogue mainly to enhance its lines of communication with ASEAN.[4]

Finally, ambiguities in US policy towards the region after 1975 delayed the setting up of formal relations between the United States and ASEAN until 1977, when the first US–ASEAN conference was held in Manila. The United States remained uncertain and unclear about its own role in Asia and the Pacific, and was reluctant to rely on a fragile ASEAN. It was suggested that formal US endorsement of the Association could prove to be the 'kiss of death', as it would justify Soviet and Vietnamese claims that ASEAN was a Western stooge.[5] ASEAN had argued that it should avoid formal links with any of the great powers, in consequence of the general desire for the creation of a 'zone of peace, freedom, and neutrality' (ZOPFAN). For both sides, the 1977 Manila meeting was a breakthrough, yet it proved a disappointment for the ASEAN countries, which obtained few economic commitments or concessions from the United States. Political discussions took place in an atmosphere of constraint.

As regards joint Japanese and Western approaches *vis-à-vis* ASEAN, it is noteworthy that, in the Fukuda–Carter communiqué in March 1977, Japan and the United States agreed to continue co-operation and assistance in support of the ASEAN countries' efforts towards regional cohesion and development.[6] This was the first time that the two countries had shown the high value they placed on activities which strengthened the self-reliance of the ASEAN countries. The tripartite relationship binding Japan, the United States, and South-east Asia was thereby reaffirmed. In June 1978 Sonoda became the first Japanese Foreign Minister to participate in the ASEAN Foreign Ministers' annual conference. One month later, Japan attempted to represent ASEAN's interests in economic co-operation with Western industrial countries at the Bonn summit. Afterwards a Japanese Cabinet Minister made a tour of the ASEAN region to report the outcome of the Bonn summit.[7]

Dialogue, phase one (1977–82)

Throughout the formative years of its contacts with external countries and organizations, the members of ASEAN demonstrated their mutual solidarity and cohesion, during policy dialogues with the main countries outside the region. By the time of ASEAN's first summit meeting in Bali in early 1976, it was mature enough to organize both the internal and the external machinery to ensure success. The ASEAN heads of governments signed two documents, the Declaration of Concord and the Treaty of Amity and Co-operation, and launched appropriate strategies for economic development, by endorsing functional arrangements for preferential trading and industrial complementation projects. These arrangements were bound to attract attention from the extra-regional industrial countries with which dialogue relationships began to be co-ordinated, each under the auspices of a different member country. Thus ASEAN's united approach to the main industrial powers became formal practice as a result of the Bali summit, which adopted a procedure for such joint action.[8]

The second summit meeting, in Kuala Lumpur in August 1977, which was held to commemorate the tenth anniversary of ASEAN's formation, ushered in a new form of external dialogue, with a series of top-level talks between the ASEAN leaders and the Prime Ministers of Japan, Australia, and New Zealand. The presence of visiting Prime Ministers on this occasion signified international recognition of, and support for, ASEAN's existence. The most notable single event was the promise, by Japanese Minister Fukuda, of US$1 billion for ASEAN industrial projects. The Kuala Lumpur summit led to an annual meeting with extra-regional countries in conjunction with the regular meeting of ASEAN Foreign Ministers; counterparts from Japan, Australia, New Zealand, the United States, Canada, and the European Community were invited in the following years. In addition to the Foreign Ministers' dialogue, meetings between ASEAN countries and Japan and other industrial nations have been held at finance or economic ministerial level on a more occasional basis.

The Kuala Lumpur summit took a conciliatory attitude towards the Indochinese states, issuing a joint statement calling for the reinforcement of peaceful and reciprocal relations with the communist countries and supporting Vietnamese admission to the United Nations. The final withdrawal of the United States from mainland South-east Asia left the situation in an extreme state of flux, and the ASEAN countries, influenced by the prevailing 'domino' theory, felt themselves to be at risk. In September and October 1978 Vietnamese Premier Pham Van Dong visited ASEAN capitals, and Chinese Vice-Premier Deng Xiaoping also toured the region in November. Premier Pham offered to sign treaties of friendship and non-aggression with neighbouring countries, but it was considered that his real aim was to divide, and so neutralize, ASEAN opinion in preparation for Vietnam's take-over of Kampuchea. But this attempt was defeated by ASEAN's solidarity.[9] By contrast, Deng's move was obviously part of a countervailing manoeuvre against Vietnamese influence over the region.

In this rapidly changing environment, the spectrum of the enlarged ASEAN dialogue broadened, with its emphasis shifting to controversial political issues as the organization began to play a role in regional affairs which could not be ignored. ASEAN's prospects of developing into a strong regional organization were enhanced by its growing political influence as it successfully co-ordinated a diplomatic campaign after Vietnam's attack on Kampuchea in December 1978 and marshalled international opinion in support of the ASEAN position. The (then) five ASEAN nations began to speak with one voice on international political issues when they took their first major diplomatic stand in condemning the Vietnamese invasion of Kampuchea in January 1979. The ASEAN point of view was taken up for the first time in the United Nations Security

Council, which adopted the ASEAN-sponsored resolution demanding the withdrawal of foreign troops from Kampuchea.

A special impetus to closer co-operation among the ASEAN nations came from Vietnam's expulsion of its ethnic Chinese community and the subsequent large exodus of 'boat people' into the South China Seas in the early summer of 1979. This posed a serious threat to the delicate racial balance in Muslim states like Malaysia and Indonesia. These states, and even Singapore, a city-state with an ethnic Chinese majority, did not allow boat people to stay long in their territories, for they regarded the refugees as a subversive element, on both economic and political grounds. The relentless policy of pushing the boat people back to the sea met with strong criticism from abroad. But the ASEAN nations succeeded in having the refugee problem accepted as one for which the international community should be responsible.

The Kampuchean issue: support for ASEAN policy

Held against the background of the tense situation in South-east Asia, the ASEAN Foreign Ministers' conference and post-meeting dialogue with Western partners in Bali in June 1979 accentuated the trend towards discussing urgent political matters and playing a greater role in resolving joint problems. At the Bali meeting, the ASEAN dialogue partners included representatives from the European Community for the first time. By inviting them to this particular meeting dealing with the Indochinese refugee problem, ASEAN hoped to encourage Western Europe to take a greater number of refugees. The Bali meeting was held just after the Western summit in Tokyo, which focused on the Indochina crisis, particularly the refugee problem. Japanese Foreign Minister Sonoda and US Secretary of State Vance flew straight to Bali from Tokyo. As noted in Chapter 5, this resulted from a Japanese initiative to implement a joint Japan–US 'support ASEAN policy'. Sonoda's intention here was to foster a more assertive role for Japan itself.[10]

In Bali, Sonoda called for an international conference to discuss how to secure peace and stability in Kampuchea. To further this plan, Japanese emissaries had already been sent to both Beijing and Hanoi. Sonoda wanted to sound out opinion about the proposed conference, to be attended by Vietnam, in discussions with his ASEAN counterparts, although conditions did not seem ready for convening it. In a positive manner calculated to attract ASEAN's interest, Sonoda announced Japan's plan to double its financial contribution to the United Nations High Commission for Refugees and to provide half the cost of Indonesia's proposed refugee reception centre. He also used the opportunity to introduce the concept of a pan-Pacific community; this was regarded as an improvised idea and provoked almost no reaction.

Vance cited the commitment of President Carter to double the number of refugees taken into the United States, and the Tokyo summit's pledge to increase aid significantly, as growing signs that the international community was coming to offer assistance. At the same time, Vance asked privately, but firmly, that leaders of the five South-east Asian nations reverse their stand and accept Indochinese refugees temporarily until they could be resettled elsewhere. The British Foreign Secretary, Lord Carrington, and the French Secretary of State for Foreign Affairs, Olivier Stirn, gave similar warnings when they stopped over in Kuala Lumpur on the way home from the Tokyo summit. Malaysia was prepared to soften its stand. The ASEAN Ministers in Bali finally adjusted their position in view of the major international efforts to resolve the refugee problem through a special conference in Geneva later in June.

The European Community's representative, Michael O'Kennedy (Ireland's Foreign Minister), was given a clear insight into ASEAN's view of the threat to stability presented by the refugees. The Community, like the United States, backed ASEAN's position on the Kampuchean crisis. The European Community even offended domestic public opinion, which was critical of the massacres by the disgraced Pol Pot regime, by supporting ASEAN's continuing recognition of it. In part, this reflected the West's growing economic interests in South-east Asia.[11] Not only the cautious EC, but all the dialogue partners endorsed ASEAN's position on the Kampuchean issue. Subsequently, an ASEAN resolution tabled before the UN General Assembly in November, demanding the continued admission of the 'Democratic Kampuchean Government' and Vietnam's withdrawal from Kampuchea, was adopted by an overwhelming majority, after an extensive campaign backed by Japan, Australia, New Zealand, Canada and the United States, and the nations of Western Europe. The 1979 Bali meeting thus witnessed an emerging 'support for ASEAN' policy by the West in the South-east Asian area.

In assessing this unique international political collaboration, it is important to recognize what sort of policy considerations were discernible behind the respective stands of the dialogue partners. Japan's initiative, aimed at convening an international conference for a political solution to the Kampuchean conflict, however premature, was viewed as an indication that Japan was assuming a new and more active role in regional political affairs. 'Whether or not the idea makes any headway, it may prove a watershed in Japanese post-war relations with South-east Asia. Hitherto, Japan has preferred to follow events, and particularly to follow US policy.'[12] It is, none the less, a fact that any political settlement of the Kampuchean problem – an issue overshadowed by intricate power politics between China, Vietnam, and the Soviet Union – has been far beyond the reach of any Japanese initiative. Moreover,

Japan's economic assistance to Hanoi had to be suspended in the face of ASEAN's objections.

The United States understood the Japanese initiative on Kampuchea, but maintained in public a position of interest without involvement.[13] America's role in South-east Asia remained ambivalent and noncommittal in political and security matters, as noted in the previous chapter. However, given the threat of a communist advance, Washington's political interest in the South-east Asian region was reawakened. Vance made clear the renewal of the US commitment to Thailand, specifying the provision of modern weaponry. But this was still a qualified commitment, for the United States continued to refuse any direct military assistance to the Democratic Kampuchea (DK) forces.

Australia joined in offering full diplomatic support to ASEAN, and denouncing Vietnam, a reversal of its previous conciliatory policy towards Hanoi. Adopting a strongly condemnatory posture on Vietnam, Australia cancelled its aid programme in January 1979. As to the political legitimacy of the DK, the Australian government argued for the ASEAN position of recognizing the Pol Pot regime, though this policy did not have unanimous support at home. (Australia eventually ceased to recognize the Pol Pot regime in 1981.)

Europeans were more sceptical about the disgraced Pol Pot regime: the British withdrew recognition of the regime after the Bali meeting in December 1979, and the French, sympathetic towards Vietnam for historical reasons, opposed any public EC condemnation of Hanoi. Obviously the French still intended to maintain their influence on the political future of the South-east Asian region, through their 'special relationship' with Hanoi. Nevertheless, it was clear that the European Community as a whole wished to keep close political contact with the ASEAN countries. Encouraged by West Germany, in March 1980 the Community decided to sign both an EC–ASEAN Co-operation Agreement, which was expected to usher in a new era of economic relations beween the two groups, and, more significantly, a 'Common Declaration on Political Questions', which called for a withdrawal of the invading Vietnamese troops from Kampuchea (in line with ASEAN's position). Prior to this declaration, Paris actually broke all ties with Phnom Penh, refusing to recognize the Heng Samrin government, as well as freezing all aid to Hanoi and severing diplomatic links.

The 1980 Kuala Lumpur dialogue also focused on the conflict in Kampuchea and the tension on the Thai–Kampuchean border, as well as on the situation in Afghanistan. On the eve of the ASEAN Foreign Ministers' conference in late June, an estimated 2,000 Vietnamese troops, backed by tanks and heavy artillery, crossed Thailand's eastern border with Kampuchea, and the refugees in their primitive border camps were caught in the crossfire. Vietnam's precipitate action was, in ASEAN's interpretation, calculated to disrupt the voluntary repatriation of Kampuchean civilians to their homeland as well as to cause confusion along the Thai–Kampuchean border. Although there was no doubt that it was timed to coincide with the Kuala Lumpur meeting, Vietnam's military adventure backfired and served to strengthen ASEAN's resolution on the Indochina crisis.

It also failed to exploit the split of opinion among the ASEAN partners in their approaches to the Kampuchean problem and the long-term regional threat.[14] While Indonesia and Malaysia believed that China, not Vietnam or the Soviet Union, was the greatest threat to peace and stability in South-East Asia, Thailand and Singapore took the opposite view. The Indonesian Foreign Minister, Dr Mochtar Kusumaatmadja, said in Kuala Lumpur that Indonesia's close relationship with Hanoi was itself part of ASEAN's strength, and he did not rule out a continued dialogue with Hanoi, in spite of the tense situation caused by the Vietnamese incursion. By contrast, the Thai Foreign Minister, Air Chief Marshal Siddhi Savetsila, when asked if he would respond to a Vietnamese invitation to visit Hanoi, replied, 'What do you expect me to do? They are killing my people and telling a different story.'

Despite these differing views and approaches towards the immediate threat, the Ministers of the ASEAN nations expressed their 'firm support and solidarity' with their Thai partners in the face of the border crisis. But there was no pledge of military collaboration to assist Thailand, only moral and political support. The Japanese Foreign Minister, Okita, who had attended the Western summit in Venice before participating in the ASEAN dialogue, threw Japan's support behind ASEAN as he denounced Vietnam for attacking the Thai frontier, and called for the establishment of a 'demilitarized peace zone' along the border to ensure the safe distribution of relief supplies to refugees. He also said that ASEAN had completed the foundations of a 'stable force' in Asia, and revealed that when Japan had actively intervened at the Venice summit it had kept fully in mind ASEAN's requests, especially on the North–South problem and trade protectionism.

Thai–Kampuchean border tension was linked with the situation in Afghanistan, the subject of serious discussion in Venice. The US Secretary of State, Edmund Muskie, who came to Kuala Lumpur from a NATO Foreign Ministers' conference in Ankara immediately after the Venice summit, hit out at Vietnamese aggression in Thailand as a threat to the peace, security, and stability of the South-east Asian region. He went on to say, 'The aggressors in Cambodia and Afghanistan are strategically connected and related. Russian expansionism and its implications can best be understood if one talks about the total effect.' Wrapping up the dialogue, the Malaysian Foreign Minister, Tengku Ahmad Rithauddeen, said there was a close parallel between the

Afghan and Kampuchean situations. Then the five visiting Foreign Ministers echoed ASEAN's position. (Roy Jenkins, President of the EC Commission, was silent.)

In their perceptions of the threat posed by the Indochina crisis, the differences among the ASEAN nations were not so great as to call into question the existence of the Association.[15] Indonesia and Malaysia adopted a flexible attitude towards Vietnam in their attempt to find a political solution to the Kampuchean problem; this resulted in the 'Kuantan doctrine' put forward at a meeting between President Suharto of Indonesia and Prime Minister Hussein Onn of Malaysia in March 1980. The Vietnamese military raid served to strengthen the position of the 'hard-liners' within ASEAN, Thailand and Singapore, and damaged the Kuantan doctrine. Yet the final result was not a split but renewed solidarity in ASEAN.

Economic challenge: growth amongst recession

The Kampuchean problem remained a key concern when the ASEAN Foreign Ministers and their Western partners resumed their dialogue in Manila in June 1981. However, to avoid the impression that this was a one-issue meeting, and to preserve ASEAN's original character as an economic group, the ASEAN Ministers reviewed their progress towards economic regionalism. They expressed satisfaction with co-operation in such fields as industrial projects, trade, food, energy, education, health, and science and technology. As one specific outcome of the Manila meeting, a basic agreement was signed on ASEAN industrial complementarity to open the way for greater participation by private business.

In contrast with their political cohesiveness, economic integration within ASEAN progressed more slowly than expected. Using the machinery of economic co-operation, such as preferential trading arrangements (PTA) and industrial complementation projects, ASEAN adopted a gradualist approach to the liberalization of trade and the implementation of industrial projects within the region, setting a pace acceptable to all members. By the time of the Manila meeting, the total number of commodity items under the PTA had reached 6,581, but its quantitative impact on intra-ASEAN trade remained negligible. As to the ASEAN industrial projects for joint ownership by the five members, with the host country taking 60 per cent of the equity and the other four subscribing the remaining 40 per cent, the original plans included urea projects in Indonesia and Malaysia, a rock salt–soda ash project in Thailand, a phosphate fertilizer project or a copper fabrication plant in the Philippines, and a diesel engine plant in Singapore. Of these projects, only the first two were definitely accepted as feasible by 1980 and implemented accordingly (the others had still not come into existence in 1988). The industrial complementation system proved difficult to organize. For example, the first such project was a scheme proposed by the ASEAN Automotive Federation at the initiative of the private sector. But this was actually a kind of patchwork scheme for assembling automobile parts from the various countries, without any real plan for the production of an 'ASEAN car' in the foreseeable future.

Despite the slow pace of the moves towards regional trade and industrial integration, the ASEAN economies were chalking up a faster growth than almost any other group of developing countries. Indonesia and Malaysia, the two major net oil exporters in the region, enjoyed the most favourable economic conditions in 1980, achieving rapid growth, with large current account surpluses, although these receded a little in subsequent years. Singapore's economic performance was also favourable, largely owing to the beneficial effects of buoyant economic activity in the two neighbouring countries. Although growth rates in the Philippines and Thailand slowed down in 1980–1, the ASEAN economies maintained better overall prospects than other developing regions, which were suffering from widespread inflation, sluggish growth and large balance of payments deficits.[16] Naturally, ASEAN's economic performance did not fail to attract the interest of Japan and Western industrial countries.

In early 1981 Japanese Prime Minister Suzuki made a round trip to the five ASEAN countries, his first overseas visit since coming to power, breaking the precedent of a first visit to the United States. This was also the first ASEAN tour by a Japanese Prime Minister since Fukuda's visit in 1977. During this tour, Suzuki renewed the continuing positive Japanese approach to the region, particularly in his assessment of the efforts made in what he termed 'the ASEAN challenge': he described ASEAN as a major factor enabling its member nations to maintain peace and stability in the region despite growing international tension, and to sustain high rates of economic growth amidst continuing global economic recession.[17]

In his policy speech in Bangkok, Suzuki outlined Japan's contributions to economic co-operation with the ASEAN countries in the fields of agriculture, energy, human development, and the promotion of small and medium-sized enterprises. Of those four areas, the main emphasis was placed on the third, the development of human resources – the task of training personnel to undertake the development of agriculture, rural communities, energy resources, and industries. The basic framework of this programme envisaged the opening of ASEAN human-resource development centres in each of the member nations, with another centre, the liaison office for the other five centres, to be established in Okinawa. Human-resource development had become Japan's main preoccupation since Ohira's pledge on *Hitozukuri* ('people building') at the 1979

UNCTAD V in Manila. Although it is not easy to produce an instant and tangible effect in this area, the subject proved to be capable of being tackled within a wider framework, and the 1984 ASEAN dialogue in Jakarta demonstrated a willingness to choose a human-resource development scheme in the context of Asian Pacific co-operation.

Following up his predecessors' diplomatic endeavours, Suzuki submitted his own message to the ASEAN people. He put it like this: 'A process of continuing dialogue and consultation – of constantly "thinking together and working together" – will always enable us to solve whatever problems may lie ahead of us.'[18] Against the background of this maturing relationship, Suzuki's visit accentuated the growing emphasis on the private sector to carry out the task of linking together diverse elements among peoples, as he described it. In a sense, Suzuki's stance may have been a response to the general feeling in the ASEAN countries that they did not expect the Japanese Prime Minister to be either a Santa Claus or a doctrine-maker. What ASEAN was really looking for was a willingness to import more manufactured goods from the region.[19] On the other hand, it had also been assumed that Japan would naturally be responsible for the defence of sea lanes under the US-led naval security network in the Pacific.[20]

Not only the Japanese but also the Americans were striving to boost trade with ASEAN.[21] The Americans lost trade opportunities in Southeast Asia when they were occupied in Vietnam, while the Japanese worked throughout the region, buying and selling at every opportunity. Realizing it had a lot of catching up to do, the United States started to look at ASEAN on its own merits in economic terms, and not merely as a piece on the geopolitical chessboard. The Reagan administration paid special attention to the role of private capital in the developing economies. The administration also encouraged US engineering companies to widen their participation in the ASEAN economies. To stimulate trade with ASEAN, the US government and businessmen attempted to persuade ASEAN to allow more foreign participation, especially in the banking sector. The Europeans were no exception, showing greater economic interest in the ASEAN region. After the signing of the EC–ASEAN Co-operation Agreement in 1980, all EC activities appeared to have the objective of promoting contacts between the private sectors of the two groups in order to strengthen the European presence within ASEAN, especially in investment.[22] For their part the ASEAN states were anxious to broaden their relationship with Europe to offset the dominance of their trade by the United States and Japan.[23]

The 1981 ASEAN Foreign Ministers' meeting in Manila adopted a basic agreement on industrial complementation projects, but difficulties remained in other fundamental areas such as the application of tariff preferences, monopoly rights, and protectionist measures for products manufactured under these schemes. Yet economic matters did not command as much attention in the ministerial meeting as political issues. The main item on the agenda was Kampuchea: a draft proposal for a comprehensive political solution of the conflict was presented to the Manila dialogue in June, in preparation for the international conference on Kampuchea to be held in New York in July and for the UN General Assembly in the autumn. The joint communiqué of the five ASEAN nations spelt out three initial steps towards a comprehensive solution: dispatch of United Nations peace-keeping forces; withdrawal of all foreign troops in the shortest time possible under the supervision of the UN forces; and then the disarming of all Khmer factions.

Sonoda, now Foreign Minister in the Suzuki government, listed the numerous steps which, in his view, covered the military, political, humanitarian, and even reconstructional aspects of a comprehensive settlement of the Indochinese conflict. While expressing appreciation of the Japanese effort, the ASEAN officials said it was premature to go into detail as to how the Vietnamese should withdraw before they had agreed to do so.[24] It was disappointing for Sonoda to receive this rather lukewarm reaction to his enthusiastic contribution, similar to the one which had met his 'premature' proposals in Bali two years before.

General Alexander Haig, the US Secretary of State, who came to Manila fresh from his talks with Chinese leaders in Beijing, revealed that the United States and China had agreed to bring pressure to bear on Vietnam over its relationship with the authorities in Phnom Penh. Speaking about the Reagan administration's Asian policy, General Haig stated, 'There is a new America that understands that it must once again bear the burdens that history has placed on its shoulders.' Given the American promise to 'defend Asia', the ASEAN Foreign Ministers welcomed Chinese efforts to construct an alliance by organizing various anti-Vietnamese forces in Kampuchea and the bases along the border with Thailand. Such a broad Khmer alliance or coalition was considered a strategically important step towards changing the image of the DK regime, and reinforcing ASEAN's position in the UN conference.

There was some anxiety among ASEAN countries that the Australian Labour government's decision to withdraw recognition from the DK government might undermine the unanimity of support for ASEAN from its dialogue partners. The Australian Foreign Minister, Anthony Street, was therefore questioned closely by his ASEAN counterparts on his approach to the UN conference and General Assembly. Perhaps reflecting their moral obligation to their dialogue partners, the Australians went no further than to abstain in the vote on DK representation in the UN. The Foreign Ministers of Canada and New Zealand reaffirmed that their governments would continue to vote for the DK representative, and assured their support for the next phase of ASEAN strategy on Kampuchea, while reaffirming their complete abhorrence of the Pol Pot regime. The Dutch Foreign Minister, Christopher van der Klaauw, representing the EC, said the European Community remained convinced that all foreign troops must be withdrawn and that the UN should supervise free elections in Kampuchea, in accordance with ASEAN's programme for a comprehensive political solution.

ASEAN had spent three years searching for a solution to the problem of Kampuchea and had gained the support of its dialogue partners for its initiatives. But, as regards any real solution to the crisis, ASEAN had done no more than speak fine words and make mutual pledges of support.[25] As a body, it still lacked the political power or military clout to persuade Vietnam. In that case, all that ASEAN could offer was economic competition, as suggested by Foreign Minister Dhanabalan of Singapore, who stated, 'ASEAN has shown how much more our economies have gained by forging close ties among the members, and by creating a climate of peace, stability, and commitment to growth. Vietnam can share in these benefits. The choice is Vietnam's.'

The Western economies: expectation and threat

The ASEAN dialogue in Singapore in June 1982 seemed to be downgraded by the Western partners, because, for the first time since 1978, the US Secretary of State could not come. General Haig decided to miss the Singapore meeting, as his summer agenda was extremely busy. His stand-in, Deputy Secretary of State Walter Stoessel, had made his career entirely in Europe, so was neither deeply involved in nor particularly knowledgeable about Asian affairs. The Belgian Foreign Minister, Leo Tindemans, who was president of the EC Council, had also chosen not to attend. The five ASEAN nations reacted with visible annoyance to this unhappy news, threatening to call off the talks with the Europeans, even though Wilhelm Haferkamp, the EC Commission vice-president, was ready to attend. Tindemans then altered his earlier decision and arrived just before the beginning of the enlarged dialogue meeting.

Although the impression of abrupt downgrading by the dialogue partners was avoided, enthusiasm for political discussion appeared to have passed its peak and was by then on a downturn as the Kampuchean situation had reached a stalemate. At any rate, apart from the meeting devoted solely to Kampuchea, it seemed more useful to re-examine the scope and range of the ASEAN dialogue. As indicated already at the previous Manila meeting, economic matters on not only an intra-regional but also a global scale had to be taken up more seriously. Through the irony of chance, the US and European attitude of detachment from ASEAN aggravated the Singapore meeting's apprehensions about the troubled Western economy.

The Prime Minister of Singapore, Lee Kuan Yew, set the course of the discussion by focusing on economic issues, not only in the intra-ASEAN context but in a global framework. 'Subtle measures will be used to divide ASEAN to make protectionism less blatant,' Lee warned in his opening address. He urged the ASEAN nations 'to stay together for greater collective strength to withstand external pressures and problems'. Pointing out the achievements of ASEAN's intra-regional co-operation, and contrasting them with those of the European Community, the Prime Minister observed that 'our progress towards regionalism has been less structured than that of the EC. It must be so because our histories in the colonial period before World War II were different. We have made progress in an Asian manner, not through rules and regulations, but through *Musyawarah* [the Indonesian for consultation] and consensus.'

Admittedly, however, there was a sense of apprehension over the difficulties of the Western economies, which were clinging to obsolete regulations and steadily degenerating into protectionism. Protectionism by the developed countries hurt ASEAN traders, and stymied ASEAN's efforts to secure fair terms of trade and economic growth. As economic growth in the industrial countries stagnated, ASEAN's exports of primary commodities suffered. A fall in demand, together with energy conservation in the West, also led to a weakening of crude oil prices for ASEAN exports throughout 1981. The Malaysian Foreign Minister, Tan Sri Ghazali Shafie, challenged the Versailles summit conclusions by saying that 'such a meeting would anyhow not achieve anything because the world's economic leaders lacked the crisis mentality necessary for solving present economic failure in the international arena'. The Philippines Foreign Minister, Carlos Romulo, criticized the US failure to ratify the Common Fund for Stabilization of Commodity Prices. The Indonesian Foreign Minister, Dr Mochtar, requested Japan to make special efforts to open its market further to ASEAN exports, including tropical products and manufactures. The Thai Foreign Minister, Marshal Siddhi, urged unity upon ASEAN: 'We stand united in our call for a more just and equitable international order. In our unity lies our strength. ASEAN can no longer be divided and bought off.'

Faced with this chorus of criticism by ASEAN, the Western dialogue partners and Japan were put on the defensive; they had to give assurances of positive co-operation in trade, investment, and development. For the United States, Dr Stoessel noted that the world slump highlighted the exposed situation of those underdeveloped countries which were too dependent on commodity exports that suffered from volatile prices, and he expressed US anxiety to overcome the growing protectionist trend. For the EC, Haferkamp assured ASEAN that the Europeans were determined to keep their markets open and would insist on others doing the same, even though they were faced with a practically stagnant economy and any increase in their imports would automatically be reflected in further job losses. Japan's Foreign Minister, Sakurauchi Yoshio, responded that his government was committed to working for trade liberalization through GATT, and had adopted across-the-board tariff reduction two years ahead of the schedule set in the Tokyo Round agreement.

The markets of the industrialized countries of the West and Japan are vital to the growth of any developing country, especially the export-oriented and raw-material-producing countries of ASEAN. But with the Western economies in difficulties, whatever fine promises the dialogue partners made, it became all the more important for ASEAN to look more to its own region to stimulate growth. As a former US high official argued, 'a re-dedication to the original economic and development pillars of ASEAN, without sacrificing what has been achieved in the political field, is already overdue. The Singapore meeting would be a good place to start.'[26]

In the ASEAN community itself, there were increasing indications that a real goal of a common market during the decade, say by 1990, should be set as a 'natural counterpart' to the unity exhibited by ASEAN during the previous fifteen years. ASEAN now had a voice in the community of nations, but it was heard predominantly on the Indochinese issue. However, if the motivation were sufficiently strong and the objective sufficiently well defined, ASEAN governments could co-operate and integrate policies. A task force was organized by the senior officials of the five nations to map a strategy which would help ASEAN achieve its objective of closer co-operation.

On the political front, ASEAN Ministers in Singapore continued their efforts to put pressure on Vietnam for a political solution for Kampuchea, while keeping the door open for it to come to the conference table. The Western dialogue partners also continued to support ASEAN on the Kampuchean problem. The highlight of this 1982 meeting was the strong expectation that a Kampuchean coalition government would be formed. A conference of the three anti-Vietnamese leaders, former head of state Prince Norodom Sihanouk, one-time Premier Son Sann, and the Khmer Rouge leader Khieu Samphan, was held in Singapore in September 1981, and a declaration of the establishment of a new government was signed in Kuala Lumpur in June 1982 just after the Singapore ASEAN meeting. The Coalition Government of Democratic Kampuchea (CGDK) was officially formed in July on Kampuchean territory. From ASEAN's point of view, the fact that the three patriotic factions were able to unite in a coalition government; that Prince Sihanouk, who was not only widely respected by the Khmer people but was also a man of standing in the international community, was nominated as the president of the coalition government; and that a person of integrity and experience such as Son Sann was appointed Prime Minister, could certainly be expected to increase international support for the right of the Khmer people to self-determination.[27] However, despite ASEAN's energetic efforts, this coalition was to look increasingly less credible, both because of the fragile ties between the three factions and because of the negligible progress in international negotiations with Vietnam.

To sum up the ASEAN dialogue in its first phase, persistent themes of discussion have revolved around two main issues: the problem of Kampuchea and regional economic co-operation. The focus of the annual meetings gradually shifted from the former to the latter, but discussions on both topics showed a broadening of perspective which defined policy approaches in terms of trans-regional, rather than local, concerns and interests. As for Kampuchea, the immediate concern with the refugees had to be extended to a longer-term interest in the formation of an anti-Vietnamese coalition government and, further, as a consequence of big-power rivalry, towards accommodation over regional conflicts. As to regional economic co-operation and development, *ad hoc* dealings over trade questions had to be transformed into serious attention to and collective pressure against protectionism in the Western advanced countries, and subsequently an involvement in trade liberalization through GATT.[28] These developments appeared to be reinforced in the second phase of the ASEAN dialogue, with the implication of a cross-linkage between the dialogue and the Western summits.

Chapter ten

The Broadening Agenda

At a time when the ASEAN economies had slumped and apparently needed more Japanese assistance, Prime Minister Nakasone Yasuhiro made his first visit to the six member nations (including Brunei) in April–May 1983. Immediately after becoming Prime Minister in November 1982, Nakasone had conveyed to the ASEAN leaders in a unique manner – over the telephone – the importance which he attached to Japan's relations with the region and his intention of making an early visit to the member countries. This trip was his third official overseas visit, after the visit to South Korea and the United States. His ASEAN tour was also timed to take place just before the Western economic summit meeting to be held in Williamsburg at the end of May; thus the problems troubling the ASEAN economies could be conveyed to the Western summit through the Japanese Prime Minister.

By the time of Nakasone's tour, Japan's relations with ASEAN had developed into a mixture of appreciation on the one hand and suspicion on the other. Appreciation of Japanese economic success was felt in several countries in search of a model for social and economic management. Lee Kuan Yew's Singapore had been 'learning from Japan' for some years. Inspired by the Japanese work ethic, which had first impressed Lee in Tokyo in October 1979, the Singapore government planted in the city-state a number of Japanese systems, ranging from a government styled on the Japanese Ministry of International Trade and Industry (MITI), Japanese–style house unions, a national productivity board, and an education curriculum to a network of *koban* (police posts). Dr Mahathir's Malaysia adopted a 'Look East' policy which identified Japan and South Korea as nations worthy to be followed. Dr Mahathir visited both countries in January 1983, and admired technological advances there which were no less outstanding than those of Western nations. *Sogo shosha*, the giant Japanese trading houses, offered useful examples to Malaysia, persuading Dr Mahathir to encourage his nation to be known as 'Malaysia, Inc.' in emulation of 'Japan, Inc.'.

Suspicions and apprehensions in South-east Asia, on the other hand, focused on proposals for Japan to defend sea lanes 1,000 nautical miles from Tokyo Bay, on Nakasone's hawkish description of Japan as 'an unsinkable aircraft carrier' in Washington, and on the rewriting of Japanese textbook accounts of World War II. All these could easily rekindle old memories of Japanese militarism, and revive antagonisms against the erstwhile conquerors of the region. Fears of a revival of Japanese militarism had been growing, especially in Indonesia and the Philippines, as shown by the reactions of those countries' leaders to Japan's defence build-up. Presidents Marcos and Suharto expressed their concern over Japan's increasing military capacity, particularly over the question of sea-lane defence, when they visited Washington in September and October 1982 respectively. During his overseas trip President Suharto also visited Japan, and showed even more serious concern over Japan's defence build-up.

Even on the economic front, there were many South-east Asian complaints about access to Japanese markets, concerning such items as high duties on Thai boneless chicken, discriminatory quotas on Indonesian plywoods, and high tariffs on Philippine bananas. South-east Asians felt that Japan's 'packages' of measures to open its markets were mainly a gesture to ease pressure from the Americans and Europeans, and that only secondary importance was attached to concessions to the South-east Asian region. It was in any case already obvious that the Tokyo government as such could not offer any dramatic measures on market opening, since these relied largely on initiatives by the private sector. Japanese officials had, therefore, to be very careful in their preparations for Nakasone's trip.

In response to this rather uneasy atmosphere, Nakasone tried to project a forceful impression, while keeping to 'soft' practical measures. In his major speech in Kuala Lumpur he declared, 'I have advocated the idea of "Japan open to the world" and have accordingly taken a series of market-opening measures at home. . . . I firmly believe that there can be no prosperity for Japan without prosperity for the ASEAN countries.' Concerning Japan's defence policy, Nakasone said, 'Japan is determined to commit itself solely and exclusively to self-defence and not to become a military power threatening neighbouring countries, as the Japanese government has repeatedly declared on numerous occasions. I, too, shall make every effort to adhere faithfully to this basic defence policy.'[1] These words were used, in substance, to plead for support from ASEAN for his present policies.

Fresh measures devised by Nakasone and his government in the pursuit of 'wider and deeper exchanges' between Japan and the ASEAN countries included, first, the transfer of technology, second, co-operation in the field of science and technology, and, third, personal exchanges. Regarding the transfer of industrial technology, the government of Japan intended to encourage co-operative relations at the private level, making full use of the initiative and vitality of the private sector. It also intended to hold consultations with the ASEAN countries on the creation of a climate likely to bring about a transfer of technology by means including the dispatch abroad of Japanese experts and the acceptance in Japan of foreign technical staff for training. Within this framework, Nakasone offered the specific concept of 'Co-operation in Plant Renovation', aimed at improving productivity and revitalizing existing industrial plant through technological transfer in such fields as plant operation, maintenance, and management.

In the field of scientific and technological co-operation, Nakasone proposed holding meetings of experts and a ministerial conference to study these important matters at a high level. Japan–ASEAN co-operation in science and technology was to be promoted in such fields as agricultural science, engineering, medical science, basic science, and new technologies. As part of a wider variety of personal exchanges and contacts Nakasone proposed to invite, over a five-year period, a total of 3,750 young people – the same people who would in future be responsible for ASEAN's nation-building – to Japan to study education and other fields. This was part of what he called the 'Friendship Programme for the Twenty-first Century', as a step towards realizing his long-cherished dream: 'Asia in the forefront of the future'.

All in all, what Nakasone submitted was a set of scintillating ideas, but mainly tending towards the 'softer' side of economic development,[2] concentrating on human resources such as technical manpower training and the promotion of personal relations. Trade, aid, and investment issues were dealt with merely by an increase in the ceiling quotas on the Generalized System of Preferences (GSP) for industrial products and by the expansion of the ODA soft loans; no major scheme like the 1977 Fukuda Fund was proposed.

Dialogue, phase two (1983–8)

The June 1983 Bangkok meeting of ASEAN Foreign Ministers reforged strong links with the Western dialogue nations. The United States and the European Community sent senior Ministers, including Secretary of State George Shultz, German Foreign Minister Hans-Dietrich Genscher, and two other European ministerial representatives. Against the background of ASEAN's fear that Vietnam might be moving towards the colonization of Kampuchea, political discussions tended to be depressing. The ASEAN Ministers voiced their serious concern over reports claiming that Hanoi was planning to resettle hundreds of thousands of Vietnamese in Kampuchea. Though the ASEAN Ministers reiterated their opposition to Vietnam's continued military presence there, the 'Vietnamized' *fait accompli* seemed irreversible. No progress had been made towards a political solution of the four-year conflict. Thailand's Foreign Minister Siddhi admitted that his latest proposal to Hanoi – that it should pull back its forces in Kampuchea 30 km from the Thai border – had not been acted upon. The Indonesian Foreign Minister acknowledged that the coalition of Kampuchean resistance groups had failed to live up to expectations.

Faced with this prolonged stalemate, the strategic perspectives among the dialogue countries diverged to a considerable degree. Genscher initiated the debate on the effectiveness of political, economic, and moral pressure on Vietnam by casting doubt on ASEAN's optimistic claim that 'time is on our side'. The Australian Foreign Minister, Bill Hayden, whose Labour Party had advocated a resumption of aid to Vietnam, actually told reporters that 'time is on Vietnam's side'.[3] Shultz, however, underscored the Reagan administration's disagreement with Australia over the move to resume 'humanitarian' aid to Vietnam. Following France's lead on the resumption of aid to Vietnam, Hayden planned to visit Hanoi for talks with Foreign Minister Nguyen Co Thach, immediately after the Bangkok meeting. The ASEAN five gave a polite but cool reception to Hayden's mission. Abe, the Japanese Foreign Minister, was criticized by his ASEAN counterparts over 'humanitarian' aid to Laos, but he indicated no change of direction. In the end, the Bangkok discussions wound up with renewed support for ASEAN's 'flexible approach' towards a comprehensive settlement of the Kampuchean conflict. It was only natural that discussions at a conference held in the front-line state of Thailand should centre mostly on the Vietnamese threat to Kampuchea.

The economic discussions took second place. Following on from the Singapore dialogue, which was regarded as an economically oriented meeting, the ASEAN Ministers did take up the problems of trade protectionism and the need for a fresh formula for economic aid to the Third World. However, the scope of the economic discussions was confined to the general terms of international trade and development issues, and was not fully geared to specific regional interests.

Changing old images

With the 1984 Jakarta meeting, a full rotation – of one ministerial meeting each year in each member country – had been completed since the new politically self-assertive ASEAN had emerged from the 1979 Bali meeting. Early in 1984 membership of ASEAN had been enlarged to six, when the Sultanate of Brunei joined. The enlargement implied a more integrated regional co-operation in South-east Asia. To mark Brunei's accession, a special meeting of ASEAN Foreign Ministers was held in

Jakarta in June, at which the Indonesian Foreign Minister, Dr Mochtar, in his capacity as chairman of the ASEAN Standing Committee and host of the regular conference in July, disclosed plans to make what was termed an 'image correction of the ASEAN dialogue'. Dr Mochtar referred to two economic issues, future co-operation in the Pacific and the outcome of the Western economic summit meeting in London, which, he said, should be put on the agenda of the ASEAN dialogue. 'If these economic topics are discussed in addition to the Cambodian problem,' he said, 'then a proper balance will be obtained.'[4]

At the Jakarta meeting, discussions were clouded by differences not merely over the political issue of Kampuchea but also over economic matters such as trade protectionism. On the thorny Kampuchean question, Hayden's unexpected proposal for a peace conference between the six ASEAN members and representatives of the Indochinese communist states of Vietnam and Laos gave rise to dissension among the participants. Dr Mochtar, the chairman of the meeting, rebuffed the Australian overture, and stated that there was no point in holding a conference if no prior agreement had been reached on the basic issue of Vietnamese troop withdrawal.[5] Despite disagreement over the Australian offer, diplomatic efforts continued in order to co-ordinate perceptions and policies among the dialogue partners. Japanese Foreign Minister Abe offered financial support for ASEAN's peace efforts and expressed a willingness to send personnel to supervise eventual free elections for self-determination. US Secretary of State Shultz, in one of the clearest enunciations of Washington's policy in the region, advocated a co-ordinated Japanese, South–east Asian, Australian, and US approach to Vietnam's occupation of Kampuchea.

In the economic discussions, the ASEAN Ministers complained about the increasing trade protectionism of the industrialized Western nations. They had for some time been feeling frustrated by the Western economic summits' failure to reflect ASEAN's interests, for example in talks on the new round of GATT trade negotiations. In response to ASEAN's complaints, Shultz pointed out that the US economic recovery had substantially helped ASEAN exports. However, agreement was much more readily achieved on the Indonesian-inspired proposal for wider Pacific co-operation, starting with a 'human resources development programme' that focused on training and education. This proposal was made at the first meeting between the six members of ASEAN and their five Pacific partners. The Six-plus-Five dialogue constituted the foundation-stone of a potential Pacific bloc, but the five external partners agreed with ASEAN's view that no institutional framework was needed. The best approach towards greater Pacific co-operation was, rather, a strengthening of the existing regional groups such as ASEAN and the South Pacific Forum.

The Europeans seemed to be left out of both Pacific co-operation and the co-ordinated approaches to the Kampuchean question. Having recovered from the shock of the Vietnam débâcle, the United States had come to redefine its politico-strategic and economic interests in one of the world's most dynamic regions. Japan, with its overwhelming economic involvement, was increasingly interested in searching for a political role in South-east Asia. By contrast, European perspectives towards the region remained less clear, although the Australians, to some extent, might be considered as representing Europe's views. Nevertheless, the human-resources development programme of Pacific co-operation was not meant to preclude EC involvement. More significantly, the ASEAN dialogue meeting could not be indifferent to the Western economic summits, as was shown by Dr Mochtar's special attention to the outcome of the London summit. (Mochtar thought it was quite in order to discuss the results of the London summit in view of the fact that the British Prime Minister, Mrs Thatcher, was going to send a special envoy to Jakarta to brief the chairman of the ASEAN Standing Committee on the outcome of the summit.[6]) The fact that the Western summits have become substantially linked to the ASEAN dialogue, not only via the Japanese route but also through the direct Asian–European route, is an encouraging sign of more European participation in the Asian Pacific arena.

A renewed bond of interest between the ASEAN nations and the former colonial metropolitan countries in Europe became evident when Mrs Thatcher toured the region in April 1985. She visited four ASEAN member nations – Malaysia, Singapore, Brunei, and Indonesia – as well as Sri Lanka and India, in what was seen as an attempt to boost Britain's diminishing position in the region, one which had been woefully neglected by British diplomacy since World War II. Whereas Nakasone's visit in 1983 was the seventh Japanese prime ministerial visit since ASEAN's formation in 1967, Mrs Thatcher's tour of ASEAN countries was the first official visit by a British Prime Minister to any ASEAN country during the same period, apart from Edward Heath's brief visit to Malaysia and Singapore for the 1971 Commonwealth Conference.

Mrs Thatcher described her feelings about the region before the trip by saying, 'it is a part of the world with a very important future, which matters to Britain, firstly because of historical connections, secondly for its interest in the defence of the free world, thirdly with trade and economic relations'.[7] At the beginning of the tour, Mrs Thatcher heard Malaysian Prime Minister Mahathir's speech of welcome, which included some hard-headed, even hostile, remarks: 'Malaysia had relegated the Commonwealth to the fourth place in order of priority in its foreign relations, because its ideals of sharing wealth had not been fulfilled.' At a banquet, however, Mrs Thatcher challenged Dr Mahathir's 'Look

East' policy, saying that if you looked further and further east, you eventually came to the west.

Anglo-Malaysian relations had been in a state of tension since 1981, when Dr Mahathir had strongly criticized Britain's decision to increase overseas students' tuition fees and negative reaction to Malaysia's policy of taking over foreign companies. In retaliation, Dr Mahathir had urged his compatriots to 'buy British last'. Despite such underlying strains, the period of tension appeared to be ending. Almost symbolically, the two Prime Ministers agreed in principle on a regular flight by MAS, the Malaysian airline, from Kuala Lumpur to London. In fact the Malaysian government was anxious for the British to increase their involvement in such sectors as rubber, machine tools, electrical equipment, and ceramics. Joint Anglo-Malaysian ventures in military and civil aircraft equipment, railway equipment, and high technology of various kinds were also welcomed.[8] Mrs Thatcher responded positively by emphasizing the keenness of many British companies to do more business with Malaysia.

In Malaysia and Singapore, Mrs Thatcher commented on the British government's victory over the miners' union. Singapore's Prime Minister Lee Kuan Yew expressed his great admiration for Mrs Thatcher's unbending political will. (The opposition in Britain accused Mrs Thatcher of breaking the unwritten rule that political leaders do not air domestic quarrels abroad, but her outspoken remarks were nevertheless appreciated by sections of British public opinion, which were reassured by her statement that industrial relations in Britain were a great deal better and more stable than they might think.[9])

The centrepiece of Mrs Thatcher's journey was Indonesia, where she made the first visit ever by a British Prime Minister. The highlight of her official appointments was a luncheon in the city of Bandung, where there is a technical university at which former President Sukarno studied engineering. In a speech there, Mrs Thatcher proposed closer collaboration between Britain and Indonesia in the new technologies and science. The field of communications, for example, is of particular importance to the economic development of Indonesia, a vast country with thousands of islands; Mrs Thatcher claimed that Britain was a leader in this field.

Mrs Thatcher's sales mission did not exclude the area of defence. Britain has defence links with Malaysia and Singapore under the Five-Power Defence Arrangement; with Indonesia, through arms sales; and with Brunei, since a British battalion of Gurkhas is stationed there. However, there were no proposals to enhance the British role in the regional defence arrangement. In Mrs Thatcher's view, what mattered more to Britain and its ASEAN partners was the future course of the world economy, the debt crisis, the price of commodities, and above all the prospects for an expansion of world trade. Though it lacked any spectacular successes, Mrs Thatcher's tour certainly consolidated the basis for dialogue between Britain and this part of the world.

A joint approach to the Western summit

The biggest political challenge confronting ASEAN was still the Kampuchean problem, when the six Foreign Ministers and their dialogue partners met in Kuala Lumpur in July 1985. The host, Dr Mahathir, called for patience combined with an active pursuit of every possible means to find a just, productive, and viable political solution. He also touched on the problem of drugs, making a specific proposal that the UN should take steps to establish a body to fight this menace, comparable with its approach to the refugee problem. On the economic front, Dr Mahathir urged entrepreneurs in the member countries to realize and exploit the vast ASEAN market, which, he claimed, was four times the size of the Chinese market. 'This can be done,' he stressed, 'by adopting a new direction and a new level in economic co-operation.'

The discussion of Kampuchea focused on 'indirect talks' aimed at a political settlement of the war on lines proposed by Malaysian Foreign Minister Rithauddeen and put forward by Thai Foreign Minister Siddhi when he visited Beijing. The proposed indirect talks would be conducted between the CGDK, on the one hand, and a Vietnamese delegation, including representatives of the Heng Samrin government, on the other; the two groups would converse through an intermediary. The ASEAN 'proximity talks' proposal stressed four basic elements: the withdrawal of Vietnamese troops from Kampuchea; an international control commission to supervise a cease-fire after their departure; national reconciliation of all warring parties; and a UN-organized election for Kampucheans to determine the future of their own country. The Foreign Ministers of ASEAN formally urged Vietnam to respond constructively to this new proposal from the Kuala Lumpur meeting.

The Western partners and Japan expressed their anxiety, in a closed meeting with ASEAN Foreign Ministers, about 'anything that has in it implicit recognition of the puppet arrangement the Vietnamese have in Cambodia'.[10] But US Secretary of State Shultz understood ASEAN's desire to keep the initiative in its political negotiations with Vietnam, and he informed the ASEAN Ministers that Washington would endorse their proposal. Abe, the Japanese Foreign Minister, supported ASEAN's proposal for indirect peace talks, in his statement on a four-point programme for Kampuchea (this called for withdrawal of the Vietnamese troops, Kampuchean self-determination, continued support for the DK government at the UN, and Japanese assistance to education and vocational training for Kampucheans who had fled to Thailand).[11] Hayden, Australia's Foreign Minister, also supported the ASEAN move, but with the reservation that the Khmer Rouge leader, Pol Pot, should be excluded from the peace talks.

The ASEAN initiative was once again rejected by Hanoi, which totally ruled out proximity talks with the so-called tripartite coalition government whose military bases along the Thai border had been swept away like 'rubbish' during the dry season. The harsh situation on the border and the response from Hanoi dismayed the ASEAN Ministers, who saw no prospect of breaking the deadlock. Shultz's comment in Bangkok that the question of Kampuchea was on the US list of topics for the talks in Geneva between Presiden Reagan and the Soviet leader Gorbachev later in 1985 gave some encouragement to a depressed ASEAN.[12] Shultz described Vietnam as the greatest threat to peace in East Asia. He disclosed a US plan to step up security assistance to Thailand, a front-line state where US military aid had already risen substantially from $39 million in 1980 to $107 million in 1984. The assistance for ASEAN as a whole increased from $173 million to $429 million.

Economic discussions at the Kuala Lumpur meeting centred on the international trade liberalization and GATT negotiations. Shultz stressed the urgent need for a new round of multilateral negotiations, in an important speech which unveiled a five-point programme of action by world governments to create a sustained period of global economic expansion. This included, first, the reduction of US federal spending and fiscal spending as well as reform of the tax system; second, West European economic expansion as noted in the statement at the Bonn summit; third, the opening of Japan's markets, with the high level of domestic saving being reduced and the trade surplus falling in consequence; fourth, structural adjustments being made to stabilize the economies of the developing nations, particularly debtor nations; and, finally, freer international trade that would benefit all nations.[13]

Tengku Rithauddeen of Malaysia, who spoke on behalf of ASEAN, expressed the group's full support for global negotiations as soon as possible to redress the international economic order, but he made it clear that the interests of ASEAN and other developing countries should be taken into consideration in the negotiations. For their part, following Dr Mahathir's appeal at the opening of the meeting, the ASEAN Foreign Ministers expressed their determination to step up intra-ASEAN trade by various liberalization measures. In additon, the ASEAN ministerial meeting identified thirty-two programmes for immediate implementation; these would be open to all member nations and other developing countries in the Pacific. Indonesia offered to train personnel in the shipping industry, but Malaysia was undecided as to which areas it could offer assistance in. Japan's Foreign Minister, Abe, attached special importance to the human-resource development programme, initiated by the previous ASEAN meeting as the primary field of Pacific co-operation.

He urged an early start to these projects, committing himself to fifteen of them, and offered to set up a joint study group to explore feasible links between vocational training and educational facilities at university level.

In the years 1985–6 the economic growth of the ASEAN countries declined sharply, after several consecutive years of high growth. The growth rate of the middle-income countries fell substantially, from between 5.8 per cent and 7.6 per cent in 1984 to between 1.9 and −1 per cent in 1985. The most drastic decline was by Singapore, which fell from 8.2 per cent growth to −1.8 per cent. (The Philippines were already in a poor state, with a minus growth rate in both years.) The reasons for the decline of these economies were threefold: the collapse in the prices of primary commodities; *de facto* devaluation of their currencies under the impact of this collapse and of the Japanese yen's appreciation; and rising protectionist tendencies in the United States and other industrialized countries, which were undermining ASEAN export, industries.

The most immediate threat to ASEAN economies was a consequence of the Japan–US trade war. Dr Mahathir gave a warning, at the Kuala Lumpur meeting, that economic tension between the United States and Japan must not be escalated, and any solution to their problems should not disadvantage ASEAN. Trade protectionism was a central theme in talks between Shultz and ASEAN Ministers, including Thai Marshal Siddhi, Indonesia's Dr Mochtar, and Malaysia's Tengku Rithauddeen, who were attending the UN General Assembly in New York in early October 1985. The ASEAN leaders voiced particular concern about the US textile Bill then before Congress which imposed strict limits on ASEAN exports to the United States.

In the same month, Singapore Prime Minister Lee, in a major speech before a joint session of the two houses of the US Congress, stated:

> Protectionism and retaliation will shrink trade and so reduce jobs. Is America willing to write off the peaceful and constructive development of the past forty years that it had made possible? Does America wish to abandon the contest between democracy and the free market on the one hand and communism and controlled economy on the other, when it has nearly won this contest for the hearts and minds of the Third World?

As to a trade war between the United States and Japan, Lee pointed out that US protectionist measures against Japan would hurt the rest of Asia twice over: first, the tariffs and barriers prevented it from selling to the United States; and, second, Asia could not sell to Japan because Japan could not sell to the United States. Lee did not expect that his small country could influence a powerful nation like the United States, but he appealed to the Americans to bear in mind the interests of their friends before taking any decision.[14] Very much moved by Lee's speech, US Congressmen had to postpone by one day their voting on the textile Bill.

The Reagan administration, which was also worried about protectionist feeling in Congress, appeared to be delighted with Lee's message. As a high-placed official said, 'The administration couldn't have a more credible Asian spokesman for free trade.' Singapore has in fact been undertaking a co-ordinating role for the ASEAN–US dialogue in recent years, and Lee proposed to explore new formulas for improving trade relations, saying that while much could be done to reduce the trade imbalances which the US had with its trading partners, particularly Japan, the measures taken should generate more trade, not less. (A new form of trade relations was to take shape under the 'ASEAN–US Initiative'.) The prospects for ASEAN economies would depend largely on improvements in the world economy sustained by the two pillars on either side of the Pacific, the United States and Japan.

President Reagan visited Bali in Indonesia, and attended the ASEAN conference from 29 April to 2 May 1986. This presidential trip marked the first time an American head of state had come to South-east Asia since the final withdrawal of US troops from the region exactly ten years before. Inviting the US President to a special conference of Foreign Ministers, the ASEAN leaders expected much US support as they dealt with political and economic issues. The ASEAN Foreign Ministers asked the United States to support Sihanouk's eight-point proposal for a Kampuchean settlement. But President Reagan did not mention it in the talks. As regards economic matters, he heard complaints about trade protectionism, but again made no specific commitment. All the ASEAN Ministers received was a promise by Reagan to convey their views to the Tokyo summit, which he was to attend after Bali.[15] Nevertheless, it is still significant that for the first time since the 1976 Bali summit, which launched the concept of enlarged dialogue, the ASEAN grouping gained 'symbolic' access to the Western economic summits through Washington as well as Tokyo and London.

When the Western economic summit convened in Tokyo in early May 1986, the ASEAN nations urged the leaders of the major industrial powers to pay more attention to the concerns and interests of developing countries. A fourteen-point memorandum to this effect was handed over to the summit leaders by the Philippines, which chaired the Standing Committee.[16] The memorandum expressed great concern at the accelerating protectionist pressures which were 'threatening to undermine the existing open market system'. It deplored the adverse repercussions on ASEAN and other developing countries resulting from attempts by certain developed countries to resolve bilateral trade problems; it also deplored the increasing trend among certain developed nations to invest in other developed nations, and the protectionist policies of developed countries which encouraged the establishment of manufacturing plant in captive markets behind tariff walls. These stern criticisms were apparently directed mainly at Japan and the United States, although no country was named. At the Western summit, which was being held in Asia for the second time, Japanese leaders were reminded of their responsibility to act for the developing countries of Asia. But a real admission that Japan had failed fully to live up to ASEAN's expectations would mean not merely conveying ASEAN's grievances to the summit, but hammering out its own policy measures on issues to be addressed directly in the coming ASEAN dialogue a month later.

Partnership with a global perspective

The June 1986 ASEAN Foreign Ministers's meeting in Manila opened in an atmosphere of renewal under the auspices of the newly inaugurated President Corazon Aquino, who took over the government after the February revolution in the Philippines. In her opening statement President Aquino bluntly told the ASEAN members to stop their endless talk and do something positive to promote economic success. Her speech found an echo as almost every Foreign Minister expressed disappointment at the record of economic co-operation and stressed the urgent need to restructure the Association. Then the main topic of the discussion was the proposed 1987 ASEAN summit in Manila and the immediate task to set up machinery to work out its agenda.

In spite of enthusiasm for an economic breakthrough, there remained some disagreement on how far the six nations would be able to integrate their economies. Whereas some countries like Singapore and Thailand were in favour of a quicker mechanism for decision-making on ASEAN joint-venture projects, making possible a 'quantum leap' in regional co-operation, Indonesia still cautioned against hastening the integration of ASEAN economies. Dr Mochtar said that a slow pace of integration was the price they had to pay for ASEAN's continued cohesion and success. However, at the end of the meeting, he also admitted the need to adapt to changing circumstances and new challenges. Eventually the ASEAN Ministers agreed to set up two high-level committees to prepare the machinery for the heads of government meeting, which would review ASEAN's achievements and shortcomings, and chart its future course.[17]

The enlarged dialogue meetings which followed the Ministers' sessions concentrated on trade and economic issues. The Ministers stressed to their Western and Japanese partners the need for easier access to their markets for ASEAN goods and better terms of trade. In the Japan–ASEAN dialogue, it was noted that while satisfactory progress had been made in the fields of culture, youth, and human-resource development, Japan should focus more attention on commodities and trade, investment,

167

and the transfer of technology. Foreign Minister Abe pledged a 'flexible and prompt' response to the true needs and changing circumstances of ASEAN countries in repaying yen debt. He also promised Japanese support for the promotion of ASEAN exports through increased investment in, and technological co-operation with, viable local industries.

US Secretary of State Shultz visited Singapore on his way to Manila, and met Prime Minister Lee. Shultz recalled that Lee's Congress speech had had a 'tremendous impact'. He thus demonstrated indirectly that the position of the Reagan administration on protectionism was almost equivalent to Lee's and ASEAN's. In the US–ASEAN dialogue in Manila, Shultz devoted his statement entirely to trade matters, emphasizing particularly that free trade should be a two-way affair and that ASEAN countries had to make sure their markets were accessible to US goods. He quoted trade figures which showed that ASEAN's exports to the United States had increased by $16 billion in the previous three years, though its exports to other areas of the world had decreased by $3.3 billion in the same period.

A bilateral Japan–US discussion between Abe and Shultz took place separately from the multilateral ASEAN dialogue. Noting the importance of the political and economic stability of the Philippines for the future of the region as a whole, Abe and Shultz agreed to reinforce the bilateral exchange of information about their economic assistance to that country, and to examine joint projects to help the recovery of the Philippine economy.

The European Community also showed a keen interest in the political situation in the Philippines, as evidenced by the prompt diplomatic recognition given to the new Aquino government by the various European governments. In the Manila dialogue, the EC delegation did not offer any specific economic measures to meet the immediate interest of the ASEAN countries. Nevertheless, taking their tone from the first-ever meeting of EC–ASEAN Economic Ministers in Bangkok in October 1985, the ASEAN Ministers made a strong bid for more EC investment and a new 'economic strategy' for their region by the European community. As Claude Cheysson, the Commissioner for North–South Relations, put it, the Community had a vital role as match-maker between private investors in member states and ASEAN. In the meantime it remained to be seen whether European investors could grasp the opportunities for reinforcing economic links with ASEAN on the one hand, and whether ASEAN would respond to the criticism by EC banks of its 'red tape and bureaucracy', which obstructed European investment plans on the other.[18]

The Kampuchean problem was relegated to second place after economic issues at the Manila meeting, but this did not mean that ASEAN had lost interest in it. On the contrary, the ASEAN leaders felt the urgency of putting forward some sort of concrete resolution to ensure that Kampuchea did not fade into the background of international politics, as seemed to be happening with Afghanistan.[19] They renewed their proposal, made at the previous Kuala Lumpur meeting, for indirect or proximity talks between the three-party CGDK and Vietnam. They also reiterated ASEAN's support for Prince Sihanouk's 'eight-point peace plan', which included immediate negotiations on the withdrawal of Vietnamese troops, a cease-fire, UN supervision of both the withdrawal and the cease-fire, and the setting up of a 'quadripartite' government by including the Heng Samrin regime together with the three-party coalition.

The Sihanouk plan was 'made in Beijing'. Even if the Hanoi-installed Heng Samrin regime were included in a possible coalition in Kampuchea, the Beijing-backed Khmer Rouge (Pol Pot faction) would never cease to be an obstacle to ASEAN's goal of inviting Vietnam to the negotiating table. While the Kampuchean issue has thus been deadlocked, ASEAN's efforts to keep its dialogue partners informed have helped to ensure that the issue was not forgotten by the rest of the world.

ASEAN's meeting in Singapore in June 1987 marked the twentieth anniversary of this experiment in regionalism through consensus, and the tenth anniversary of the system of dialogue with extra-regional partners. An inert political *status quo* combined with accelerating economic change had, however, proved too difficult to co-ordinate within the existing framework. The serious question facing ASEAN and its partners, therefore, was how to reinvigorate their relations in anticipation of the planned December 1987 summit.

As the host Prime Minister, Lee Kuan Yew, outlined it, major changes in the ASEAN countries were taking place against the backdrop of fundamental changes in the four big Pacific powers – the United States, Japan, China, and the Soviet Union. Both China and the Soviet Union had to implement fundamental institutional reforms if they were to breathe new dynamism into their economies. Facing the declining competitiveness of its exports, the United States had to conjure up the political will to attack its enormous budget and trade deficits at their roots. Japan needed to solve the problems its massive trade surplus had created for its trading partners, and needed to transform its economic impetus from export-led growth to domestic demand. But it could help revitalize the international economy, and could sustain its growth indefinitely if its trade were more in balance.[20]

This background shows that the ASEAN group has a stake in developments beyond South-east Asia, extending to the wider Asian Pacific region.[21] ASEAN's vital interest cannot be divorced from the economic tensions between Japan and the United States, the more active Chinese and Soviet involvement in the Pacific, or recent developments in the South Pacific islands. At the same time, the ASEAN dialogue meetings have for a decade provided a platform where the leading nations of the Pacific and European communities can gather to discuss substantive issues. There has also been a growing awareness among the ASEAN leaders that they should work towards a more institutionalized relationship through, for example, special trade and economic arrangements with countries such as the United States and Japan, or with the European Community.

At the Singapore meeting, trade protectionism in the developed countries and the lack of a global solution to problems such as unstable exchange rates and depressed commodity prices came under heavy criticism from the ASEAN Foreign Ministers. But Japan and the United States in particular were called on to play a wider role in the economic development of the region. ASEAN urged Japan to provide financial support for industrial development and to reduce the burden of debt; it called on the United States to launch an 'ASEAN–US initiative' that would allow broader trade and economic co-operation. For their own part, the six Foreign Ministers stressed the need to intensify efforts to ensure that the Manila summit resulted in 'qualitative improvements' in intra-ASEAN economic co-operation.

Japan's Foreign Minister, Kuranari Tadashi, in his major policy speech, defined the relationship between Japan and ASEAN as a 'partnership with a global perspective'.[22] The implication was that the partnership should contribute to finding a solution for world issues over a broad spectrum as well as for solving Japan–ASEAN bilateral issues. The objectives outlined by Kuranari included the establishment of a 'new ASEAN fund', which was to be linked with Japan's plan for recycling its trade surplus presented at the Venice summit of the industrial powers. The proposed new fund, to be worked out in detail by the December ASEAN summit, represented a major departure in that it transcended the limited framework of bilateral and vertical co-operation between Japan and ASEAN characteristic of the Fukuda Fund devised ten years earlier. The new fund would foster a broader approach, stressing multilateral and horizontal co-operation, with industrial ventures open to non-Japanese and even non-ASEAN participants.

Shultz also gave a new impetus to ASEAN-US relations by providing a better arrangement for dealing with trade and economic issues. The proposed 'ASEAN–US Initiative' would guarantee ASEAN special trading arrangements with the United States. Shultz also delivered a harsh message to his counterparts in ASEAN, stressing that 'aggressive, export-led growth' was becoming less effective and that the changes that were needed in world trade could cause a 'traumatic experience'.[23] This was a warning to ASEAN nations that they could not depend on US markets to absorb more exports.

The European Community seemed to be rather outshone by Japan and the United States in the ASEAN dialogue. The chairman of the EC Council of Ministers, Leo Tindemans, made a sad confession when he reported back on the Singapore dialogue to a meeting of EC Foreign Ministers in Luxembourg. He said that he had come home with a sense of disappointment because Europe had a very tarnished image in ASEAN.[24] It would continue to play a secondary role in Asia unless it raised its economic and political standing in the region. The Community could be used as a 'model and source of inspiration' for ASEAN's moves to boost regional co-operation, Tindemans said, but if Europe really wanted to make the most of the opportunities available, it needed to broaden and deepen the relationship.[25]

Political and security discussions covered a wider range of problems, for in addition to the eight-year Kampuchean crisis, East–West relations and arms control, human rights in the Soviet Union, the Soviet occupation of Afghanistan, and developments in the South Pacific were discussed. The main outcome of the discussions was expressed in the twelve dialogue partners' statements supporting 'the two non-communist factions' in the anti-Vietnamese CGDK, which, it stated, should work together to continue isolating Vietnam politically and economically, and respond positively to any sign of genuine willingness by Vietnam to withdraw its troops from Kampuchea. ASEAN's support for 'the two factions' was a result of the virtual dysfunction of the three-party coalition following Prince Sihanouk's decision in May to take a year's leave of absence as president of the coalition resistance government, in protest against the killing of soldiers loyal to him by forces of the Khmer Rouge.

A significant point made by Lee at the Singapore meeting was that, with Moscow and Hanoi both reassessing their positions and making the revival of their economies their first priority, an eventual negotiated settlement in Kampuchea was more likely than continuing Vietnamese intransigence. In other words, 'economic rationality' might be expected to induce the Soviet Union and Vietnam to consider a compromise that would 'lessen their military burdens, which are the principal cause of their existing economic woes'. Furthermore, as one of the leading ASEAN Foreign Ministers put it: 'the dynamics of the Cambodian conflict appears to have entered a new phase'.[26]

All the signs indicated a new stage in political and economic co-operation in Asian Pacific affairs. Symbolic of this 'Pacific-oriented' ASEAN dialogue, Papua New Guinea became the first non-ASEAN country to sign the Treaty of Amity and Co-operation in South-east Asia which had been concluded at the Bali summit in 1976. Stronger links between ASEAN and the South Pacific would help to bring about greater stability in that part of the world. A more active and more committed Pacific orientation had been needed for some years, but the

ASEAN nations had been too preoccupied with their own problems.

A new breakthrough?

The third meeting of the ASEAN heads of government in the Association's twenty-year history, also the first summit meeting in ten years, was held in Manila in mid-December 1987. It so happened that the Manila summit was to be overshadowed by major events such as the US-Soviet summit in Washington and the presidential election in South Korea. Furthermore, a heightened security problem around the city of Manila marred this historic meeting, limiting and shortening the itineraries of the participants. Nevertheless, the Manila summit represented a new breakthrough in the ASEAN movement, providing it with the political will to transcend the existing framework and form a cohesive power bloc.

The joint declaration – called the Manila Declaration of ASEAN Resolve – reads: 'ASEAN regionalism founded upon political, economic and cultural cohesion is more vital than ever for the future of South-east Asia.' Its main purposes and goals comprise the following points: first, regional cohesion for security, stability, and growth, especially if pressures and tensions of any kind challenge ASEAN; second, intra-regional economic co-operation to strengthen private-sector incentives and combat protectionism; and, third, intensified efforts to find a lasting solution to the Kampuchean problem and that of Indochinese refugees.

Despite its modest pretensions, the third summit marked the beginning of the next phase of ASEAN co-operation, with the firm resolve that 'the next twenty years will be even more productive than the last twenty'. If ASEAN regionalism was to be more vital to the future of South-east Asia, the group would have to identify itself as a viable political entity 'coping with the big powers' rivalry for influence and assuming a global role too to promote and preserve stability and world peace'.[27]

A practical incentive to intra-regional economic co-operation was the decision to apply preferential terms to no less than half the total value of intra-ASEAN trade in the next five years as against 5 per cent at the present time.[28] Trade was only expected to expand to a small extent as a result of the new scheme, but it would mean a marked improvement on the *status quo*, particularly in that it set a target date for trade liberalization. Hitherto, ASEAN had never set a real timetable for economic integration. Further improvements and concessions were made in the ASEAN industrial joint-venture scheme in order to provide more opportunities for the private sector inside and outside the region; and in the investment guarantee agreement, to make ASEAN more attractive to foreign investors.

In line with these new schemes, assistance of US$2 billion in soft loans to the ASEAN–Japan Development Fund was officially announced by Japanese Prime Minister Takeshita, the only non-ASEAN leader invited to the summit. The new fund differed from that previously offered by Japan, which had financed ill-planned and unprofitable projects (two fertilizer plants). The new one was to be used mainly for equity and loan financing of private-sector development projects. The aid package was part of a commitment by Japan to recycle some of its trade surplus of US$30 billion to developing countries in the Third World. How the money can be used effectively to help ASEAN will be a touchstone of whether Japan–ASEAN co-operation can achieve a new breakthrough; it will be a challenge for Japan in its role as the world's largest creditor nation.

How to combat protectionism in the advanced industrial countries has been another sensitive issue at the ASEAN meetings. As the Manila declaration states, regional cohesion is vital not only for security and political stability but also for economic growth, and this goal should be pursued when ASEAN faces pressures and tensions of any kind, including protectionism. In an extension of this logic, some scholars argue that some economic equivalent of Kampuchea, which threatens and thereby stimulates regional resilience, is needed if ASEAN is to be united economically. Such threats and pressures include the risks of economic recession in the industrial world, economic instability due to rapid fluctuation of exchange rates, increased protectionism in advanced industrialized countries, and the nagging problem of foreign debt. If ASEAN countries can join together to diversify markets, build up credibility in the dialogue countries, set up networks of automatic economic support stabilizers in ASEAN – all these in response to an 'Economic Kampuchea' – then there is a good chance that ASEAN will progress along the path towards greater economic integration.[29]

ASEAN's particular political and security concern with the Kampuchean conflict was addressed by the Manila declaration, but hardly in an exciting manner. By the time the Manila summit conferred on the problem ASEAN countries had been as much taken aback as other external parties by Khmer resistance leader Prince Sihanouk's unilateral decision to hold talks with Hun Sen, Prime Minister of the Phnom Penh regime, in France in early December. Thus, the Manila declaration reflected a wait-and-see attitude among ASEAN countries.[30] Several of the leaders stressed, in their speeches, that the summit agreed only to intensify all efforts for the early realization of a zone of peace, freedom, and neutrality. The idea of a South-east Asia nuclear-weapons-free zone (NWFZ) was shelved for further detailed study, although the leaders called for its early establishment.[31]

The Manila summit discussions showed that the concepts of ZOPFAN and NWFZ, which mainly reflected Indonesia's concern, could not be implemented because of continuing fighting in Kampuchea and the military presence of the US and the Soviet Union.[32] Indonesia and its regional partners were not in a position to translate those ideals into an orderly structure of regional relations. Indonesia has retained its vision of an exclusive pattern of relations between states in the region, perhaps under the term *Wawasan Nusantara*. But the gap between aspiration and achievement will remain until Indonesia and its ASEAN partners are able to play an effective role in the region.[33]

Peace prospects in Indochina, however, are increasingly fluid, perhaps not so much owing to ASEAN's efforts to find a solution to the Kampuchean problem as to Vietnam's and the Soviet Union's efforts to improve their impaired positions. Vietnam might pull its troops out in order to reduce its economic burden. The Soviets are trying to reinforce their political influence in South-east Asia; they may consequently respond to ASEAN's demand that they should persuade Vietnam to reach a settlement of the Kampuchean conflict. A Soviet attempt to woo ASEAN was apparent in Moscow's message of congratulation to the Manila summit.

How will a new breakthrough be achieved in the process of bringing peace to Kampuchea? An essential condition for a peaceful solution leading to the establishment of a neutral, independent Kampuchea is the withdrawal of the Vietnamese. All Khmers should be able to agree to this. Then, negotiations between Khmers, like the two meetings between Sihanouk and Hun Sen in December 1987 and January 1988, should be the next step in the peace process. Although only the Khmers can decide what they are ready to accept, and no solution can be imposed by the big powers, those negotiations could hardly have taken place without tacit Soviet–Vietnamese consent. Or it may be up to France, the most popular and best trusted outside power in the eyes of Khmers on both sides, to set the peace process rolling – down a path which may be difficult and tortuous, but not beset by insurmountable obstacles. Britain, which was co-chairman of the 1954 Geneva agreements and which still has significant interests in the area, and West Germany, which has excellent relations with China, should collaborate with France if Europe is to play its required role in resolving outstanding problems in Indochina.[34]

The United States still maintains a strong interest in South-east Asian security, as evidenced by its active participation in the annual ASEAN dialogue, but it has maintained a relatively low profile over Kampuchea. Its primary regional concern may be in US–Philippine relations. Nevertheless, US–Soviet co-operation on the Afghan problem has heightened interest in the more positive role the two superpowers could play in other regional disputes, such as Kampuchea.

Japan will continue to increase its economic presence, as shown by the latest example, the Takeshita Fund. Therefore its political and security stake in South-east Asia will rise and, however cautiously, it will have to take a part in regional power politics. The ASEAN nations may call on Japan to play a larger role to fill the vacuum left by the United States. As a prominent Asian statesman recently remarked, 'Politically, Japan is now qualified to play in international affairs; it can take initiatives and stake out positions like any other major West European power.'[35]

Japan's role in the ASEAN dialogue is to assume greater responsibility for maintaining a stable and dynamic economy in the region. This will give it greater political weight as a *summit power* both in Asia and in the West.

Funding for peace

There has been no better instance of Japanese 'twin-track' diplomacy than at the 1988 Toronto summit and Bangkok ASEAN dialogue. Asian concerns, ranging from Kampuchea and support for the Philippine government to the success of the Seoul Olympics, were a focus of attention for the Western leaders, and Japan's performance at the Toronto summit was much appreciated by the ASEAN leaders. This was evidence of Japan and East Asia's increasing global influence, their growing economic integration, and their common political and security interests.

A negotiated political settlement in Kampuchea looked possible for the first time since the Vietnamese invasion of December 1978. This greatly encouraged ASEAN Foreign Ministers gathered at the Bangkok meeting in July 1988. They wanted to take advantage of the new momentum to pave the way for the long-awaited peace talks with Vietnam. Although a solution was not yet in sight, there were clear signs that the main protagonists had begun to realize some fundamental truths.[36] First of all, there has been a striking change in Vietnam's position – from the previous 'irreversible' *fait accompli,* they have withdrawn some 50,000 of the estimated 120,000 troops stationed in Kampuchea. The Soviet Union under Gorbachev has abandoned its call for the total liquidation of the Pol Pot clique. China, for its part, has indicated that it does not feel that the Khmer Rouge should have a dominant role in a future Kampuchean government. On the ASEAN side, Thailand has accepted that the Vietnamese-backed Heng Samrin regime should participate in an interim government. Thus a new momentum, led by a sense of realism, may have prepared the way for a settlement in which all Khmer factions share power under the leadership of Prince Sihanouk.

It has taken a decade to reach the threshold of the negotiation phase in the Kampuchea question, and it may take another decade to settle it, with the Indochinese and ASEAN countries coming together in an exercise of tension reduction and confidence-building, and eventually forming a community based on peaceful and co-operative coexistence. In the meantime, in Bangkok the ASEAN Foreign Ministers agreed on a framework for preliminary contacts between the interested parties which took place in late July 1988 in a suburb of Jakarta. This meeting established a 'checklist' – rather than a 'peace plan' – of the key elements of a settlement. It included the withdrawal of the Vietnamese forces, the setting up of a four-party provisional Khmer government, disarmament, and peace-keeping during the interim period until free and internationally supervised elections can be held. Despite the optimistic mood of the Bangkok meeting, Indonesian Foreign Minister Ali Alatas, who had been active in promoting the proposed informal talks, would say only that the 'perception of some movement towards a solution presented opportunities'.[37]

The future of a Kampuchean solution will very much depend on Vietnam, particularly on its pledge on troop withdrawal, an issue which still arouses the other party's suspicions. Another key element is how to guarantee that Pol Pot's Khmer Rouge do not return to power. A new peace plan drawn up by the United Nations includes precise proposals for disarming the Khmer Rouge and pledges by all permanent members of the UN Security Council – including China, their main arms supplier – not to provide weapons or assistance to any faction. Then the peace-keeping force would ensure observance of these provisions, oversee the Vietnamese withdrawal, and for as long as necessary assist the new government that emerged from elections to maintain law and order.[38] How effective these international schemes will be in finding a way out of the stalemate remains to be seen. Continuing mutual distrust and guerrilla fighting among the Khmers can still cause serious setbacks – for example, the resignation of Prince Sihanouk as president of the coalition government immediately after the Bangkok meeting.

The plight of the Indochinese refugees has also remained high on ASEAN's agenda. Nearly a decade after the 1979 ASEAN meeting in Bali and the Geneva international conference on the Vietnamese 'boat people', there were still over 40,000 refugees in the region. The arrival of Vietnamese – mainly 'economic migrants' who escape for a better life abroad – threatened to undermine the existing orderly departure programme (ODP). Acknowledging that the decade-long strategy for dealing with the problem had ceased to work, US Secretary of State Shultz responded to ASEAN's proposal for a UN-sponsored international conference on refugees by suggesting an alternative, the possibility of voluntary repatriation of the Vietnamese refugees.[39]

Noting that the economic and political strength of each member was vital for regional security, the ASEAN Foreign Ministers discussed and gave support to an emergency package of aid to the Philippines.[40] Philippine Foreign Minister Raul Manglapus explained that his government was preparing a programme of projects to be funded by the aid package. The Philippines and the other ASEAN countries were ready to co-operate in a 'poly-sectoral programme', designed to help bring about Philippine economic recovery, broadly by tackling unemployment, the worsening foreign debt, and land reform. A positive response to this was made by the dialogue countries, which had already discussed a 'mini-Marshall Plan' for the Philippines at the Toronto summit in June. On the matter of US military bases in the Philippines, there was neither discussion nor a common stand among the ASEAN countries.

The ASEAN Foreign Ministers' economic discussion and subsequent meeting with their external partners revealed a convergence of agendas for inter-regional co-operation. The ASEAN side focused its attention on economic issues such as rising protectionism, exchange-rate volatility, trade in agricultural products, and commodity prices. It sought more positive co-operation from the industrialized countries in the fields of technology and industrial development. Japan announced a new plan, formally termed the 'Industrial Technology Transfer programme', under which Japanese private-sector experts could be sent to advise companies in the region on management and production techniques. Foreign Minister Uno Sosuke described this programme as further evidence of Japan's determination to enhance its role of promoting economic co-operation and strengthening the free-trade system.

The United States and the European Community were neither less enthusiastic nor less forthcoming than Japan, in the search for closer economic co-operation with ASEAN. On the eve of the ASEAN meeting the US Information Service broadcast a 'curtain-raiser' television programme by satellite which suggested that Secretary of State Shultz would do everything possible to strengthen relations with ASEAN. Shultz did not produce any specific eye-catching proposals beyond a firm endorsement of the Philippines aid plan, but in a comment on free trade he said that those with a modicum of intelligence in the United States knew that trade with the global economy could not be simply shut out. The European Community sent a strong delegation to Bangkok, including Commissioner Cheysson, German Foreign Minister Genscher, and Spanish Foreign Minister Francisco Ordonez. Cheysson pledged that the single market of West European countries to be created by 1992 would not lead to a fortress of protectionist measures. His assurances were designed not only to allay fears about a more inward-looking community but also to invite a positive view of this market of 320 million people. Furthermore, in line with the desire to open up greater two-way trade and investment with ASEAN, the EC saw opportunities for small and medium-sized European manufacturing firms to become involved in ASEAN industrial joint-venture projects.[41]

The 1988 Bangkok meeting provided a conspicuous illustration of the dialogue partners' 'support for ASEAN' policy, both in its economic and in its political and security dimensions. Especially for Japan, it was an occasion to establish a wider base for this policy, one which it has pursued ever since the beginning of the dialogue. It was now time to go beyond a mere 'supporting role'. Foreign Minister Uno offered to finance an international peace-keeping force in Kampuchea and to send civilians to join an international team to supervise elections there. This pledge, though it stayed close to Japan's traditional economic role, made Uno the first Japanese politician to define a political role for his country in a settlement in Kampuchea. The ASEAN member countries believe that such a peace-keeping force is crucial to prevent fighting and promote a legal settlement as Vietnam withdraws its troops. Secretary of State Shultz told Prince Sihanouk that the United States would support the creation of an international peace-keeping force to help guarantee an eventual settlement in Kampuchea.[42] The funding of a peace force can be identified as Japan's contribution to an international framework involving the United States and others.

As Japan comes to assume a political and security role, fears grow that it may also adopt an interventionist policy, using its potential military power. To allay such fears, Japan's defence chief, Kawara Tsutomu, visited Indonesia and Singapore a week before the Bangkok ASEAN dialogue. The first Director-General of the Japanese Defence Agency to visit South-east Asia since World War II, Kawara met President Suharto and Prime Minister Lee and repeated the usual Japanese pledges rejecting military power. But a new element appeared in his statement that:

> Japan needs the co-operation of the United States and countries in South-east Asia to protect sea lanes vital for its economic survival, but Tokyo cannot offer in return any form of bilateral defence co-operation with South-east Asian countries. . . . Japan channels non-military assistance for the purpose of safety and cleanliness in the Straits of Malacca.[43]

This illustrates Japan's view of security in its relations with the United States and South-east Asia. Whether in Kampuchea or in the Straits of Malacca, to guarantee peace and safety without using military or coercive means cannot be an easy task. But there is still no choice for Japan but to perfect its economic resources and its channels of political persuasion.

Chapter eleven

The Way Forward

This book has been devoted to examining the *interrelationship* between the two directions in Japan's foreign policy: towards the Western world and towards the Asian Pacific region. This interrelationship can be pictured as a tapestry, its horizontal threads to the West crossing its vertical threads to Asia. An overarching approach combining the two directions might lead to the best policy orientations from the various possibilities available in Japan's intricate circumstances. A central contention of this study is that a synthesis of Japan's traditionally dichotomized interests in Asia on the one hand and the West on the other is possible, and would serve not only Japan's own interests but also wider inter-regional co-operation.

The most viable formula, illustrated in the individual chapters of this book, is the emerging pattern of a new world power centre based upon rapid economic growth in the countries of the western rim of the Pacific. We should now consider how this market would relate to the international trading regime while realizing the aspiration to unity in Pacific Asia within a multi-centred structure in the twenty-first century.

Pacific co-operation

The institutional dimensions of Pacific co-operation present far more difficulties than, for example, those of the European Community. The geographical term 'Pacific Basin' suggests confluence into a great pool, rather than the fencing off of one continent or interest group, as 'Europe' does.[1] Given the variety of political and economic values and resources in the Pacific Basin, exclusive regional collaboration would be almost impossible. The Western Pacific nations and South Pacific countries, depend, no less than on their own region, on inter-regional co-operation and interdependence with the West (America and Europe) in trade, investment, legal and administrative practices, and general ethos. Under these circumstances, any attempt at organizational integration will have to be open-ended.

Pacific co-operation has so far resulted in no formal intergovernmental institution, nor will it for the foreseeable future. But there are two well established consultative bodies of like-minded nations: the PECC and the ASEAN dialogue meetings. Their membership of fifteen (thirteen countries and two 'regions') and twelve respectively is not exactly the same but contains some overlap. Both standing conferences have established a number of specific collaboration programmes such as manpower training, trade negotiations, energy, fisheries, and investment projects. An embryonic Pacific community can be perceived in these entities – the PECC foreshadowing a future 'parliament' and the ASEAN dialogue a 'cabinet'.[2] A constituent process between the two could transform them into a more organic commonwealth. In this creative endeavour, Japan is well placed to assume a mediating role.

The PECC, which had conducted its activities mainly through four task forces for investment, minerals and energy, fisheries, and livestock and grains, gained a new dimension when the November 1986 Vancouver General Meeting agreed to issue a regular report, *Pacific Economic Outlook*. A new task force under Japan's co-ordination was established for the purpose. Its first report was delivered at the May 1988 Osaka General Meeting. The *Pacific Economic Outlook* will have a significant role similar to the OECD's *Economic Outlook*, if it is recognized as the main co-operative economic policy indicator for the member countries. The research by and regular publication of *Outlook* are expected to provide material for discussions of economic policy co-ordination. When the *Pacific Economic Outlook* becomes as authoritative as the OECD's publication, then the PECC, the ASEAN Foreign Ministers' meeting, and its enlarged dialogue may embark on some kind of constituent process, analogous with the collaboration of the OECD, the EC, and the Western summits.

With the establishment of a US$1 million central fund linked to the eventual creation of a permanent secretariat and *ad hoc* task force on institutional development, the PECC reached the stage of political 'embryo', which may become a viable international organization.

Institutionalization of such a system remains a sticking-point, especially its leadership and membership aspects, as discussed in Chapter 8. Countries such as Japan and the United States have important leadership inputs to contribute to the broader Pacific co-operation. But the United States and Japan must avoid giving the Pacific Basin concept the 'kiss of death'. There has for some time been a consensus in ASEAN that a new, single, overarching institution would not serve the cause of greater pan-Pacific co-operation. Members prefer 'institutional co-operation without a central institution'.[3] However, recent years have shown a gradual modification of ASEAN's attitude, which now appears more inclined to favour some kind of organization in which views can be exchanged and policies co-ordinated on the key issues of trade and agriculture in the Pacific region.

A new perspective on membership was offered when the Soviet academician Yevgeny Primakov was an official guest at the Osaka meeting. Primakov, director of the USSR's Institute of World Economy, expressed a keen interest in *de facto* Soviet involvement in the 'system of international division of labour'. In such a system, he said, the Far Eastern region of the USSR would be treated as an autonomous part of a Pacific economic community.[4] He also disclosed, in a press interview, new experimental schemes, including the establishment of special economic zones around Vladivostok and elsewhere, as doorways to the Asian Pacific. Beside Moscow's bid, many countries in Latin America and the South Pacific region have shown an interest in the PECC. The rush for membership is a sign of the growing movement towards economic co-operation around the Pacific. But it makes institutional aspects more difficult. In view of the marked diversity of the region, any further development of the PECC is unlikely to be modelled on any existing international institution but will have to find its own unique form.

The Pacific co-operation movement has been linked with the search for appropriate responses to the collapse of the Bretton Woods system, since the Pacific nations have the most to gain from a stable world economic system and the most to lose from the world recession.[5] If the US uses protectionist measures to reduce its budget and trade deficits, grave consequences may ensue for the Pacific and the rest of the world, which have relied on access to the US market. Japan, the NICs, and near-NICs in South-east Asia, which have been shifting the world economic focus to the Pacific, must act now to show their willingness to make the international trading system work better, by agreeing to consultations with the industrialized nations in the OECD.[6] The limited success of the attempts to co-ordinate global economic policy so far achieved by bodies like the OECD or the Western economic summits underscores the importance and urgency of new initiatives. It is especially important that dialogue be established with the four Asian NICs, which can be considered the most successful economies and also the biggest threat to the stability of the system.

A conspicuous role in the economic and trade expansion in the Western Pacific region has been assumed by the East Asian NICs, which have become a new growth axis in recent years. With their remarkable economic growth and trade expansion, the four Asian NICs are playing an intermediary role in the Western Pacific economic system. In this region, Japan's market is the target of the Asian NICs, which are themselves the target of the ASEAN countries. In this process, the Asian NICs are expected to recognize their role as purchasers by liberalizing their import regulations and opening up their domestic markets, so providing scope for growth for latecomers. If the Asian NICs become a second growth pole in Asia comparable to Japan, then the Asian Pacific will become a region where growth in one country stimulates growth in another.[7] According to the OECD's annual analysis in December 1987, the manufactured exports of the four Asian NICs may be four-fifths of the size of Japan's by 1989. The surpluses of South Korea and Taiwan alone have already exceeded the combined surpluses of the main European member countries of the OECD.

As shown in Chapter 8, Japan's rapid development in the 1960s and 1970s, and continued, if slightly lower, growth in the 1980s, brought about a substantial increase in demand for exports from, and domestic investment activities in, the countries of the western Pacific region. A 'virtuous circle' was thus created in reinforcing a cyclical process of exports–investment–exports. Now we are witnessing the rise of the Asian NICs as new purchasers: they have gained productive capacity in the manufacturing sector in a short period of time, during which they have also generated demand for resources and input from neighbouring countries. According to one Japanese analysis, the ten countries of the western Pacific (the four Asian NICs, five ASEAN members and China) will account for 23.1 per cent of the real increase in world GNP and 41.9 per cent of the world expansion in trade in the period between 1986 and 1990. Certainly these countries are the most promising candidates to lead the expansion of the world economy in the 1990s.[8]

The changing international trade order

The international trading order will enter a new period of change at the beginning of the 1990s. At least three major developments are in train: first, the creation of the US–Canada Free Trade Area, in effect from January 1989; second, completion of the Uruguay Round of GATT negotiations by the end of 1990; and third, the removal of all internal barriers within the European Community by the end of 1992. These developments are asymmetrical and even contradictory, especially since the North American and European moves seem designed to establish regional trading blocs; this conflicts with GATT's aim of promoting world-wide free trade, although these countries argue that their agreements conform to overall GATT regulations. If the GATT negotiations end unsatisfactorily as regards a further expansion of world trade, new sets of regional trade agreements will surely proliferate.[9] Under such circumstances, the prospects for Pacific economic co-operation based upon 'open regionalism' may be seriously jeopardized.

Against the background of economic friction and consequent growing protectionism, the United States has proposed talks with a certain number of countries on free-trade agreements, on the lines of those leading to the agreements signed with Canada and Israel. An important new direction in US trade policy, such approaches are based on the assumption that if Washington cannot achieve the grander goal of 'comprehensive trade liberalization', it should move instead to establish free trade areas (FTA) in which the United States and certain other countries will, independent of the world-wide GATT, substantially reduce or even eliminate trade barriers against each other. The United States, for example, proposed talks on a US–ASEAN FTA in 1986, and this formula may well eventually be applied to the Asian NICs and ultimately to Japan.[10] In parallel with these moves, the United States continues to pressurize individual Asian NICs to adopt intellectual property protection legislation, adjust their currency exchange rates, and open up their markets. It has also taken steps to remove the four nations from the list of countries which will have duty-free entry to the US market for certain goods under the GSP from January 1989 onward. For the United States, these measures and the FTA approach represent a lever to make trade surplus countries correct imbalances. A particular target of the FTA formula is 'protectionist' countries that are recalcitrant in fully participating in multilateral negotiations. Its corollary, however, will be a proliferation of bilateral trade agreements outside the GATT regime.

In the early 1990s the European Community will attain its goal of a genuine common market in which people, goods, and capital will circulate freely. Besides opening internal borders, the creation of a single European currency and a new central bank may give momentum to the free exchange of resources and goods between the twelve economies. This prospect has motivated adjacent regions and countries, namely the European Free Trade Association (EFTA) and even Turkey on the southern flank of Europe, to seek a special relationship with the Community. If they succeed, the result will be a further enlarged market, far larger than the US–Canada one or the possible Western Pacific market grouping of Japan and its neighbours. If a more integrated internal market means more protectionism against non-members, the EC integration will unavoidably aggravate trade friction, especially with the United States. In the worst-case scenario, if either the European Community or the United States refuses to play by the multilateral GATT rules, or if either is seen to be seeking unilateral or bilateral solutions to its trade problems, then the entire world trading system will suffer.[11]

Japan's economic leadership

Whatever the future of the international trade order, the great potential growth sphere on the western rim of the Pacific will be involved in the changes. At this crucial stage for the world economy, when the existing international trading regime cannot bring about stable and efficient progress (mainly because of the relative decline of the US role in the maintenance of the system), the nations accumulating economic strength, like Japan and the Asian NICs, should be prepared to devote themselves to reforming the world economy. Their own economic future is at stake.

It is in the above context that Japan has to ensure the evolution of a more flexible trading system in the Western Pacific region. It has already committed itself openly to certain broad policy options but has not yet implemented them substantially.[12] The first priority is the adjustment of the macro-economic structure between Japan and the United States, which is now lopsided, as demonstrated by the persistent and serious trade imbalance. Japan should make continued efforts to stimulate its domestic demand in order to increase imports from the United States, and also to prevent Japan–US friction over trade from affecting neighbouring Asian countries. The United States, for its part should curtail its fiscal deficit to bring demand more into line with domestic supply capacity; it should also sharpen its competitiveness in order to improve its trade balance and the standing of the dollar.

Second, in the process of its structural adjustment with the United States, Japan should pay due attention to maintaining trade regimes which are free, multilateral, and non-discriminatory, thereby providing fair opportunities for developing countries. It can be counterproductive to insist on reciprocity and engage in bilateral negotiations which result in trade controls at the expense of third-party interests. Another imperative is to reduce the flow of funds from Japan to the United States, and devise a mechanism by which investment funds circulate to developing countries where economic growth potential remains uncultivated.

Third, in the process of restructuring its domestic industry, which has been stimulated especially by the dramatic appreciation of the yen, Japan should recognize an 'intra-industry' division of labour in the countries of the Western Pacific region. This new form of international industrial collaboration differs from the existing closed and integrated structure of Japanese industry; it entails a changed pattern of production-sharing for the manufacturing sector in which Japanese assembly firms, particularly those in the automobile and electric and electronics industries, would import parts and intermediate goods and also out-source through direct foreign investment.

Finally, combining all these policy programmes, the Western Pacific nations and Japan should work together to make the region a frontier of growth, using its dynamism to reorganize and balance Pacific triangular trade with the United States and Western Europe. Such creative endeavours would serve Japan's grand strategy for a synthesis of its relations with Asia and the West.

184

Japan's political role

'To fulfil an historic role it is uniquely qualified to perform: bridging and uniting the free systems of the Atlantic with those now growing fast in the western Pacific':[13] this would certainly be the best scenario for Japan. Yet there is also a worst-case scenario: 'the Japanese feel lost in the gap between conflicting goals, whether they belong to Asia or the West'.[14] Indeed, here the Japanese are faced with a geopolitical paradox. In a further paradox, Japan's very attainment of pre-eminence puts it in an extremely delicate and vulnerable position. Japan's way out of the impasse can only be through a symbiosis of the different contradictions.

Japan is faced with mounting pressure to play a more positive role, appropriate to its economic power. Reactions to its potential political leadership are mixed. On the positive side, the Japanese are reminded that they have graduated *magna cum laude*, and are advised to take what the Americans call affirmative action to support poorer and less fortunate groups.[15] In contrast to such calls on Japan for initiative, misgivings still linger over Japanese leadership. For example, some observers in China see Japanese long-term strategy as the establishment of a Pacific economic grouping centred on Japan which would stand, along with Europe and the United States, as one of the three major groupings of the twenty-first century. According to this Chinese view, the less developed Asian countries are unlikely to agree to a Japanese-led system of pan-Pacific co-operation. It affirms further that the United States is fundamentally opposed to the creation of a Pacific economic community centred on Japan.[16]

However, the time has certainly not come for the Americans to accept a secondary role in Pacific and global economic affairs. On the contrary, the United States has shown no sign of abandoning its leadership. According to European opinion, the Japanese vision is of a world system under US hegemony. Japan's policies towards its privileged zone of intervention, i.e. South-east Asia, are regarded by European observers as a form of 'economism'. The growing differential between incomes in Japan and in other nations is seen as a threat to these policies. Doubts have thus been raised about whether Japan alone, or even the two-headed hydra of Japan and California, would be strong enough to turn the situation in South-east Asia to their sole advantage.[17]

Be that as it may, to allay lingering misgivings overseas, to answer self-imposed dilemmas, and meet their hard assignment, it is important for the Japanese to make a distinction between 'leadership by initiative' and 'leadership by example'.[18] Americans are not ready to be followers; nor, for different reasons, are Asians. So Japan will not be able to assume leadership by a quick initiative. But it can and should strive for a position of leadership by example, opening its markets as a practical model of Pacific 'open regionalism', and extending the kind of economic assistance which the other nations are looking for. Another important distinction should be made between political 'leadership' and political 'influence'. Leadership requires the calibre to make others obey. Influence, however, needs the ability to impose one's beliefs through example. This latter is more appropriate for the Japanese political culture.

Accordingly, a new pattern tending towards an equilibrium of means and standards of living must be shaped through aid, finance, and technological assistance, the price Japan must pay for its economic presence in the Asian Pacific region. The final goal should be to raise the incomes of Japan's Asian neighbours to a level comparable with its own. Ironically, there seems to be an inevitable tendency whereby, despite prevailing suspicions about Japanese ambitions to dominate the region, other ambitious East Asian nations may, by emulating Japan, force it out of the area in which it was previously unchallenged and into a 'higher market' of industrial production. Japan may go the same way as the US, towards 'de-industrialization'.

However, as the EC case shows, no single nation can enjoy stable regional relations with its neighbours unless they are of similar economic capacity and at a more or less comparable level of industrial development. In the East Asian environment, if the other nations endeavoured to follow the Japanese example, then Japan's economic contribution could be translated most effectively into political influence.

As the countries of the Asian Pacific region, especially the four NICs, have become increasingly important and successful actors in the world economy, the Western countries within the OECD have begun to look for new partnerships with them. The Trilateral Commission of economists, business leaders, and politicians from the Western summit powers recommended, in its Tokyo report of April 1988, that South Korea and Singapore should be invited to join the Paris-based OECD. Neither South Korea nor Singapore seems ready to enter the 'rich-men's club', nor has the OECD officially invited them. But it has become quite obvious that the OECD mission to provide overall co-ordination of world economic policy cannot be fully carried out without including such fast-growing East Asian economies as dialogue partners.

When Japan was ready to join the OECD in the early 1960s, the then Prime Minister Ikeda envisioned that his country, in co-operation with other Asian countries, could be one of the three pillars of the free world. More than one generation later, this long-cherished expectation has been realized. For Japan, which has sought to reflect Asian Pacific interests at the Western summits for nearly three decades, it is an encouraging sign that the OECD seems to have realized the need to incorporate another East Asian growth pole into the international economic debate. If OECD membership for the Asian NICs were to be delayed, an alternative would be a Pacific OECD. This concept has been emerging from the intensified efforts at institution-building by members of the PECC, which the Atlantic-based OECD has been watching with interest and concern in recent years. How to find a meaningful link between the two provides a golden opportunity for Japan to synthesize its traditional dichotomy between Asia and the West.

Duties as a guarantor

Drawing together the threads of earlier arguments on Japan's role in the Western summits, the ASEAN dialogue, and the PECC discussions, it becomes clear that Japan has successfully begun to overcome its traditional conflict between two objectives – Asia and the West – in both the economic and the political dimensions. Throughout the 1975–88 period of Western summitry, especially since the late 1970s, Japan has tried to expand its role in Asia, and so enhance its status in the West. Japan has evolved into Asia's advocate; it has successfully focused the attention of world leaders on Asian Pacific affairs, using trade liberalization programmes, development aid, investment and financial flows, and many political initiatives. The 1978–88 ASEAN dialogues provided Japan with an opportunity to discard its reputation as a trespasser for a new role as a benefactor, also effacing its mixed image as either diffident or predatory. Finally, since 1980 the PECC movement has had the effect of drawing natural and human resources into the Pacific Basin from all directions, including the socialist countries.

Still, what remains to be solved by Japan, as a member of the West and at the same time a nation grounded in Asia, is its paradoxical role in both Asian Pacific and global security. Economic contributions through aid and investment have a political and security implication. According to a well-known principle, Japan uses diplomatic and economic means to play an important role in maintaining regional peace and stability in East Asia. A major role in economic assistance for developing countries is an integral part and outcome of what Japan terms a 'comprehensive security policy'. But there is still a considerable perception gap between the military-strategic aid policy of the United States and Japan's civilian welfare assistance policy. The Western allies seem not to be fully convinced by Japan's idea of maintaining security by non-military means only, in the face of adversaries determined to make their political and military weight felt in the Western Pacific region and elsewhere. On the other hand, increased aid and investment commitments may be more likely to commit Japan eventually to the burden-sharing role required by US strategic defence policy, instead of just maintaining a policy of economic aid alone.

Such a dilemma looms larger when Japan has to assume more of the costs of defending itself along the Western Pacific sea lanes and beyond, along the oil-supply route from the Persian Gulf. As the United States becomes a debtor nation it will, sooner or later, grow weary of defending Japan, the world's largest creditor nation and, in a sense, more prosperous than its protector. In the foreseeable future the Japan–US economic security relationship could become obsolete and untenable in the absence of large-scale adjustments implying Japan's commitment to a greater security role. Then the question will arise as to how Japan should redefine its general security role so as not to pose a military threat to its Asian neighbours or undermine stability and the balance of power in the Asian Pacific region.

To make this redefinition, a distinction should be maintained between the concepts of 'security' and 'guarantee'. In the broader sense, 'security' is the state of being secure, free from danger, protected or defended against attack and interference. In another sense 'security' means something given as a pledge to fulfil a promise. 'Guarantee' implies a positive assurance that something will be done in a specific manner to pay or a certain duty will be performed under certain circumstances. When these definitions are applied to Japan's policy, currently based on using co-operation to achieve peace, security in the sense of protection or defence against attack is not compatible with the limitations and constraints on military means. However, guarantee in the sense of performance of a duty could be more easily achieved through policies to 'fund' a peace force and foster a harmonious environment, and so resolve any major regional conflicts.

Bearing in mind these security connotations, the way to peace and stability must be sought through a multilateral framework involving not only Japan and the United States but also concerned parties in East Asia and the Western Pacific region. Japan's security commitment – lopsided towards the United States – is apt to provoke negative reactions from some of the Asian countries. At the same time, many Asian nations might find reassurance in Japanese military power incorporated into the US security system in the Pacific, which seems now to be less permanent. To steer a middle course between these opposing views, Japan must try to reconcile the conflicting perceptions of regional and global security. Such differences of opinion impede the prospects of a more stable order which could be achieved if burdens were shared more evenly among Asian and Western partners. In its role as linchpin Japan will have to act diplomatically, accurately predicting the consequences of its guarantor's role, and keep the correct balance between its economic and security commitments. Otherwise, the ambivalence between strength and vulnerability at the summit will remain.

Notes

1 Introduction

1 Robert Scalapino, *Asia and the Road Ahead: Issues for the Major Powers* (University of California Press, Berkeley, 1975), p. 50.
2 Richard Harris, 'Orient's inscrutable approach to power', originally printed in *The Times*, 10 August 1972, as quoted in Curt Gasteyger (ed.), *Japan and the Atlantic World*, Atlantic Papers 3 (AIIA, Paris, 1972), p. 7.
3 William J. Barnds, 'The United States in Asian affairs', in *Japan and the United States: Challenges and Opportunities* (Council on Foreign Relations, New York, 1979), p. 233.
4 Helmut Schmidt, 'Japan must chart global political course along with its new economic strategy', *Japan Economic Journal*, 28 June 1986.
5 Shibusawa Masahide, *Japan and the Asian Pacific Region* (Croom Helm, for the Royal Institute of International Affairs, London, 1984), p. 7.
6 Ohira Masayoshi, 'Diplomacy for peace: the aim of Japanese foreign policy', *International Affairs*, vol. 40, no. 3, July 1964, p. 394.

2 A departure from the old order

1 Marius B. Jansen, *Japan and its World: Two Centuries of Change* (Princeton University Press, Princeton, 1980), p. 112.
2 John W. Dower, *Empire and Aftermath: Yoshida Shigeru and the Japanese Experience, 1878–1954* (Harvard University Press, Cambridge, Mass., 1979), p. 419.
3 Roger Buckley, *Occupation Diplomacy: Britain, the United States and Japan, 1945–1952* (Cambridge University Press, Cambridge, 1982), p. 124.
4 Foreign Office Papers, Public Record Office, London. Anthony Eden to Malcolm MacDonald (Singapore), FO 371/92642, FJ 1127/17, 16 November 1951.
5 Esler Dening to Eden, FO 371/92642, FJ 1127/19, 20 December 1951. See Malcolm MacDonald Papers, University of Durham, 19/7/13. MacDonald visited Tokyo and issued a press statement there on 8 July

189

1952. It stated that 'in fact these territories in South-east Asia [Singapore and Malaya] are now buying more than twice as much from Japan as Japan is buying from them. We believe that there is ample room for a steady growth of two-way trade with Japan without any prejudice to those interests and that this will make a valuable contribution to prosperity, security and peace throughout the region.'

6   Dower, *Empire and Aftermath*, p. 421.
7   The concept of US economic aid to Europe exemplified by the Marshall Plan was applied to the non-European area, and was combined with a technical assistance and military defence programme in the Mutual Security Act of 10 October 1951.
8   This section is largely based on Dower, *Empire and Aftermath*, pp. 467–70.
9   See Kosaka Masataka, *Saisho Yoshida Shigeru* (Chuokoron-sha, Tokyo, 1968), and Nagai Yonosuke, *Gendai to Senryaku* (Bungeishunjyu, Tokyo, 1985), for discussion of Yoshida's belief that economic growth, not military strength, would restore both Japan's national power and its place as a world leader. This principle has been adopted by other Asian leaders, including Park Chung Hee, Suharto, and Deng Xiaoping. Richard Nations, 'The lure of a summit', *Far Eastern Economic Review*, 20 March 1986.
10 Yoshida Shigeru, *Kaiso Jyunen*, vol. I (Shincho-sha, Tokyo, 1957), p. 185.
11 Dower, *Empire and Aftermath*, p. 473.
12 *Economist*, 23 October 1954.
13 Foreign Office Papers, UK High Commissioner in Canada, FO 371/110467, 1 October 1954.
14 Japanese Ambassador's Memorandum, FO 371/110467, FJ 1931/67, October 1954. It stated: 'The recent creation of a regional security system by the free nations of South-east Asia (SEATO) is welcomed by the Japanese government, although at this stage it can offer no more than moral support because of limitations of its defence capability and the provisions of the Constitution. Security in South-east Asia depends primarily upon social stability and this in turn depends upon raising the standard of living of the countries in that region. In this connection, Japan is fully prepared to co-operate with free nations in such economic programmes as may be integrated with the collective security system.'
15 Crowe to Allen, FO 371/110467, 13 October 1954.
16 Foreign Office brief, FO 371/110467, October 1954.
17 Speech text in J 1731/90, FO 371/110498.
18 Yoshida's statement concluded as follows: 'The supply of capital through government or international banking institutions must be drastically enlarged. For the best result, investment aid should be distributed through an organization in which all the countries involved are represented. . . . We in Japan would do everything in our power to make it succeed. As the most industrially advanced of the nations in Asia – and as Asians – we know how to fit Western techniques of

human advancement into the patterns of living and local conditions of the East.' Yoshida, *Kaiso Jyunen* I, p. 239.

19 Dower, *Empire and Aftermath*, p. 477.
20 Makins to Eden, FO 371/110498, FJ 1631/107, 27 November 1954.
21 Ohira Masayoshi, *Brush Strokes: Moments from my Life* (Foreign Press Center, Japan, 1979), p. 94.

3 A twin-track diplomacy

1 Ohinata Ichiro, *Kishi Seiken 1241 Nichi* (Gyoseimondai Kenkyusho, Tokyo, 1985), p. 73.
2 ibid., pp. 205–7.
3 J.A.A. Stockwin, *Japan: Divided Politics in a Growth Economy*, second edition (Weidenfeld & Nicolson, London, 1982), p. 256.
4 Russell Braddon, *The Other 100 Years War: Japan's Bid for Supremacy, 1941–2041* (Collins, London, 1983), p. 175.
5 Ogata Sadako, 'The changing role of Japan in the United Nations', in Joshua D. Katz and Tilly C. Friedman-Lichtschein (eds), *Japan's New World Role* (Westview Press, London, 1985), p. 34.
6 Japan–US Joint Communiqué between Ikeda and Kennedy, 22 June 1961. Article II of the Treaty of Mutual Co-operation and Security provides that 'the Parties will contribute toward the further development of peaceful and friendly international relations by strengthening their free institutions, . . . by promoting conditions of stability and well-being they will seek to eliminate conflict in their international economic policies and will encourage economic collaboration between them'.
7 Yamamoto Mitsuru, *Nippon no Keizai Gaiko: Sono Kiseki to Tenkanten* (Nihon Keizai Shimbun, Tokyo, 1973), p. 131.
8 Problems relating to Communist China and Korea were mentioned explicitly in the 1961 joint communiqué, the first time in Japan–US summit talks.
9 Ohira Masayoshi, 'Diplomacy for peace: the aim of Japanese foreign policy', *International Affairs*, vol. 40, no. 3, July 1964, p. 396.
10 Hanabusa Masamichi, *Trade Problems between Japan and Western Europe* (Saxon House, for the Royal Institute of International Affairs, Westmead, 1979), p. 5.
11 *Times*, 31 October 1962.
12 ibid.
13 Ito Masaya, *Ikeda Hayato: Sono Sei to Shi* (Shiseido, Tokyo, 1966), p. 158.
14 Ikeda Hayato, 'Gaiko Zuitakoto' ('Awakening with diplomacy'), *Kokusai Mondai*, Tokyo, November 1963.
15 Robert Stephens, 'Seen from Whitehall: Japan's fear of trade blocs', *Observer Foreign News Service*, 14 November 1962.
16 Joint communiqué between Sato and Johnson, 13 January 1965.
17 ibid.
18 Kusuda Minoru, *Sato Seiken 2797 Nichi* (Gyoseimondai Kenkyusho, Tokyo, 1983), p. 254.

19 Joint communiqué between Sato and Johnson, 15 November 1967.
20 Aichi Kiichi, 'ASPAC still young and fluid', *Pacific Community*, vol. I, 1969, pp. 4–5.
21 Sato Eisaku, 'The Pursuit of Peace and Japan in the Nuclear Age', Nobel Lecture, 11 December 1974. Sato also referred, in this lecture, to the three non-nuclear principles, which were set down in his term of premiership, and gave concrete expression to the determination of the Japanese people not to have access to nuclear armaments. However, Sato was in favour of the peaceful utilization of nuclear energy.
22 Richard Nixon, *Real Peace* (Sidgwick & Jackson, London, 1984), p. 72.
23 Nakano Shiro, *Tanaka Seiken 886 Nichi* (Gyoseimondai Kenkyusho, Tokyo, 1982), p. 168.
24 Don Oberdorfer, 'Summit road is Japan's coming-out', *Guardian*, 27 September 1973.
25 William J. Barnds, 'The United States in Asian affairs', in *Japan and the United States: Challenges and Opportunities* (Council on Foreign Relations, New York, 1979), pp. 257–8.
26 Ogawa Masaru, 'Mr Tanaka in Europe', *Japan Times*, 7 October 1973.
27 Oka Takashi, 'Europe cool to Japan as partner', *Christian Science Monitor*, 30 April 1973. Henry Kissinger delivered his speech 'Year of Europe' to the Associated Press annual luncheon, New York, 23 April 1973.
28 Oka, 'Europe cool to Japan as partner'.
29 Dick Wilson, 'Europe takes the strain', *Financial Times*, 25 May 1973.
30 *New York Times*, 11 November 1973, quoting the words from the *Far East Economic Review*.

4 On the road to the summit

1 Eto Shinkichi, 'Evolving Sino-Japanese relations', in Joshua D. Katz and Tilly C. Friedman-Lichtschein (eds), *Japan's New World Role* (Westview Press, London, 1985), p. 57.
2 Yoshida Shigeru, *Japan's Decisive Century, 1867–1967* (Praeger, New York, 1967), p. 85.
3 ibid., p. 87.
4 ibid., p. 87. Yoshida argued further that 'if our co-operative relationship with South-east Asian countries is to proceed smoothly, it will be necessary not only to maintain good relations with the developing nations concerned, but also to draw upon the strength of the countries bordering the Pacific. The co-operation of such countries as Australia, New Zealand, Canada, and the Latin American nations will become vital.' ibid., p. 108.
5 Eto, 'Evolving Sino-Japanese relations', p. 58.
6 L'Observateur de l'OCDE, February 1969. The GNP of the United States and the Soviet Union exceeded Japan's, totalling respectively $843 billion and $359 billion (1966).

7 Endymion Wilkinson, *Japan versus Europe: a History of Misunderstanding* (Penguin Books, Harmondsworth, 1983), p. 158.
8 Brian Beedham, 'A special strength', *Economist*, 31 March 1973, p. 8.
9 Sakamoto Yoshikazu, 'Peaceful coexistence in Asia', *Guerre et Paix*, vol. 3 (Institut Français de Polémologie, Paris, 1968).
10 Tokuyama Jiro, paper presented to international symposium 'The Challenge of the Pacific', organized by the International Institute of Geopolitics, Paris, April 1984.
11 Beedham, 'A special strength', p. 64.
12 Brad Roberts, 'The enigmatic Trilateral Commission: boon or bane?', *Millennium: Journal of International Studies*, vol. 11, no. 3, 1984.
13 This episode was quoted by the Japanese ambassador to Paris, Kitahara Hideo. *21st Century Forum*, no. 29, Tokyo, December 1986.
14 Nakamura Keiichiro, *Miki Seiken 747 Nichi* (Gyoseimondai Kenkyusho, Tokyo, 1981), p. 141.
15 Kiyomiya Ryu, *Fukuda Seiken 714 Nichi* (Gyoseimondai Kenkyusho, Tokyo, 1984), p. 189.
16 Henry A. Kissinger, *American Foreign Policy* (Norton, New York, 1969), p. 11.
17 Beedham, 'A special strength', p. 47.
18 David MacEachron, 'New challenge to a successful relationship', in *Japan and the United States: Challenges and Opportunities* (Council on Foreign Relations, New York, 1979), p. 9.
19 Gerald L. Curtis, 'Domestic politics and Japanese foreign policy', in *Japan and the United States*, p. 59.
20 *Diplomatic Blue Book*, Ministry of Foreign Affairs (Foreign Press Center, Japan, 1980), p. 27.

5 A stage for the Western alliance

1 The most comprehensive study of this topic is the book by Robert D. Putnam and Nicholas Bayne, *Hanging Together: the Seven-power Summits* (Heinemann, for the Royal Institute of International Affairs, London 1984). See also Cesare Merlini (ed.), *Economic Summits and Western Decision-making* (Croom Helm, London, 1984).
2 *International Herald Tribune*, 5 January 1979.
3 *New York Times*, 7 January 1979.
4 *Sankei Shimbun* editorial, reprinted in *Japan Times*, 12 January 1979.
5 *Japan Times*, 16 January 1979.
6 Editorials of *Asahi Shimbun and Yomiuri Shimbun*, summarized by *Japan Times*, 16 January 1979.
7 *Japan Times*, 16 January 1979.
8 Takubo Tadae, 'Ottawa summit and Japan', *Asian Pacific Community*, spring 1981.
9 *Japan Times*, 16 January 1979.
10 Putnam and Bayne, *Hanging Together*, p. 112.
11 *Japan Times*, 10 January 1979.
12 Sonoda Sunao, *Sekai Nihon Ai* (Shinchosha, Tokyo, 1981), p. 128.

Sonoda's move to include the United States spurred a chain reaction in the ASEAN dialogue, which was enlarged by new participants such as Australia, New Zealand, and the European Community.

13 Hunabashi Yoichi, *Summit no Shiso* (Asahi Shimbun, Tokyo, 1980), p. 26.
14 Kawauchi Issei, *Ohira Seiken 554 Nichi* (Gyosei Mondai Kenkyusho, 1982), p. 114.
15 Merlini, *Economic Summits*, p. 21.
16 *Japan Times*, 25 June 1979.
17 *New York Times*, 3 August 1980.
18 ibid.
19 *Japan Times*, 22 June 1980.
20 *Japan Times*, 26 June 1980.
21 Merlini, *Economic Summits*, p. 24.
22 *Observer*, 15 June 1980.
23 James Reston, 'In defense of summits', *New York Times*, 25 June 1980. Reston pointed out that it was probably in their private talks that the leaders came to a closer understanding of their common problems.
24 ibid.
25 *Guardian*, 25 June 1981.
26 *Observer*, 26 July 1981.
27 *Financial Times*, 24 July 1981.
28 Ogawa Masaru, 'Our times: a successful summit', *Japan Times*, 26 July 1981.
29 *Observer News Service*, 17 July 1981.
30 *International Herald Tribune*, 28 July 1981.
31 *Japan Times*, 28 July 1981. At that time the Suzuki government remained under fiscal and political constraints in funding increased defence expenditures and updating a basic programme for forces modernization that was drafted as far back as in 1976.
32 *International Herald Tribune*, 29 and 30 May 1982.
33 *Financial Times*, 7 June 1982.
34 *Japan Times*, 5 June 1982.
35 Putnam and Bayne, *Hanging Together*, p. 164.
36 *Observer*, 29 May 1982.

6 Forging the political partnership

1 *Christian Science Monitor*, 6 June 1983. The decision to issue an *ad hoc* statement on security, as proposed by Reagan, matured in a relatively short space of time. See Cesare Merlini (ed.), *Economic Summits and Western Decision-making* (Croom Helm, London, 1984).
2 *Financial Times*, 27 May 1983.
3 *Financial Times*, 31 May 1983.
4 *Washington Post*, 2 June 1983.
5 Merlini, *Economic Summits*, p. 38.
6 *Economist*, 4 June 1983.
7 A senior Japanese diplomat confirmed the Nakasone episode in conversation with the author.

8 Putnam and Bayne, *Hanging Together: the Seven-power Summits* (Heinemann, for the Royal Institute of International Affairs, London, 1984), p. 191.
9 *Christian Science Monitor*, 6 June 1983.
10 David Owen, Zbigniew Brzezinski and Okita Saburo, *Democracy must Work* (New York University Press, New York, 1984), p. 73.
11 *Financial Times*, 11 June 1984.
12 Jurek Martin, 'Flying the free trade flag', *Financial Times*, 11 June 1984.
13 Henry Owen, 'High time for Europe to act in concert', *Financial Times*, 16 May 1984. This wise saying was made originally by US President Calvin Coolidge.
14 *International Herald Tribune*, 11 June 1984.
15 Trudeau's remarks, quoted in *International Herald Tribune*, 11 June 1984.
16 *Financial Times*, 24 April 1985.
17 A senior Japanese diplomat, who once served as 'sherpa', suggested this point in conversation with the author, Bonn, 1985.
18 *Financial Times*, 7 May 1985.
19 *Sunday Times*, 5 May 1985.
20 *Times*, 6 May 1985.
21 ibid.
22 *Japan Times*, 6 May 1986.
23 *Japan Times*, 5 May 1986.
24 *Asahi Shimbun*, 8 May 1986.
25 *Japan Times*, 5 May 1986.
26 *Japan Times*, 7 May 1986. A summit agreement to strengthen the mutual surveillance or close monitoring of economic policy co-ordination also carried the possibility that they would move to engineering a stronger yen to help correct Japan's trade surplus.
27 *Nihon Keizai Shimbun*, 7 May 1986.
28 US Trade Representative Clayton Yeutter's remarks in Washington, *Japan Times*, 7 May 1986.
29 Editorial of *Japan Times*, 7 May 1986.
30 *New York Times*, 10 June 1987.
31 *Asian Wall Street Journal*, 4 May 1987.
32 *Washington Post*, 10 June 1987.
33 *International Herald Tribune*, 11 June 1987. Wounded by the Iran-contra scandals, and defensive about the weak economic performance of the United States, President Reagan was subdued and unimpressive. It was a sharp contrast with his near-total control of the 1986 Tokyo meeting and its agenda.
34 *Japan Times*, 10 June 1987. Prime Minister Nakasone's spokesman claimed credit for this initiative by Japan.
35 *International Herald Tribune*, 11 June 1987.
36 Prime Minister Takeshita's statements on 4 May in London and on 1 June in New York. The New York statement mentioned the following five areas for 'co-operation to achieve peace': (1) Japan's diplomatic efforts for peaceful settlement over conflicts such as those between Iran and Iraq, and in Cambodia; (2) its assistance to the activities of the

United Nations in the field of preventing conflicts; (3) peace-keeping activities, including personnel despatch in fields such as the supervision of elections, transport, communication, and medical services; (4) assistance to refugees in various parts of the world; and (5) contributions towards reconstruction after the conflicts.

37 Reginald Dale, 'The Toronto summit: better than its billing', *International Herald Tribune*, 23 June 1988.
38 ibid.
39 Peter T. Kilborn, 'Japan asserts American-style clout in Toronto', *New York Times*, 20 June 1988.
40 Philip Stephens, 'Takeshita reflects Japan's search for higher profile', *Financial Times*, 21 June 1988.
41 *New York Times*, 20 June 1988.
42 Harald B. Malmfren, ' ''Follow the leader'' is not the game it was in the West', *Japan Times*, 29 June 1988.
43 *Financial Times*, 22 June 1988.
44 Kashiwagi Yusuke, 'Japan flexes new muscle in Toronto', *Japan Economic Journal*, 2 July 1988.

7 Agenda for the summit powers

1 Okita Saburo 'Japanese foreign policy in the 1980s', speech to the Foreign Correspondents' Club of Japan, 23 January 1980.
2 Wolf Mendl, 'Changing perspective of foreign policy', in Loukas Tsoukalis and Maureen White (eds), *Japan and Western Europe* (Pinter, for the Royal Institute of International Affairs, London, 1982), p. 87.
3 Okita Saburo, *Japan's Challenging Years: Reflections on my Lifetime*, adapted from the Japanese by Graeme Bruce with the assistance of Ann Nevile (Australia–Japan Research Centre, Canberra, 1983), p. 101.
4 ibid., p. 101.
5 *Diplomatic Blue Book*, Ministry of Foreign Affairs, (Foreign Press Center), Japan, 1981 p. 26.
6 Wolf Mendl, *Western Europe and Japan between the Superpowers*, (Croom Helm, London, 1984), p. 27.
7 Mendl, *Western Europe and Japan*, p. 94.
8 Reinhard Drifte, 'The European Community and Japan: beyond the economic dimension', *Journal of International Affairs*, vol. 37, no. 1, 1983, p. 156.
9 *Diplomatic Blue Book*, 1984 edition, p. 59.
10 Oka Takashi, 'Nakasone gathers Japan within the Western security net', *Christian Science Monitor*, 6 June 1983.
11 Nakasone Yasuhiro, 'Japan's Choice: a Strategy for World Peace and Prosperity', Alastair Buchan Memorial Lecture, International Institute for Strategic Studies, London, 11 June 1984.
12 Zbigniew Brzezinski, 'East Asia and global security: implications for Japan', *Journal of International Affairs*, vol. 37, no. 1, 1983, p. 12.
13 Kosaka Masataka, 'Japan's options – Japan's dilemmas', in *Atlantic Papers*, no. 3, pp. 17–18.

14 See Phil Williams, 'The limit of American power: from Nixon to Reagan', *International Affairs*, vol. 63, no. 4, autumn 1987.

15 Reginald Dale, 'Stock market crash spotlights the West's empty stage', *International Herald Tribune*, reprinted in *Straits Times*, 11 November 1987.

16 Lawrence Freedman, *The Troubled Alliance: Atlantic Relations in the 1980s*, Joint Studies in Public Policy 8 (Heinemann, for the Royal Institute of International Affairs, London, 1983), p. 22.

17 Paul Kennedy, 'How to decline as a power, gently', *Japan Times*, 25 January 1988.

18 Geoffrey Howe, speech at the Japan Press Centre, Tokyo, 12 January 1988.

19 William Wallace, 'What price independence? Sovereignty and interdependence in British politics', *International Affairs*, vol. 62, no. 3, summer 1986, p. 370. Wallace made this point in the context of British diplomacy with the United States, but it can also be applied to Western alliance politics involving Japan.

20 Satoh Yukio, 'Western security: a Japanese point of view', *Naval War College Review*, September–October 1983.

21 Nishihara Masashi, *East Asian Security and the Trilateral Countries*, Report to the Trilateral Commission: 30 (New York University Press, New York, 1985), p. 69.

22 William Wallace, 'Political issues at the summit', in Cesare Merlini (ed.), *Economic Summits and Western Decision-making*, (Croom Helm, London, 1984), pp. 148–9.

23 Laurens Jan Brinkhorst, 'Japan–EC ties are vital for world stability', *Japan Economic Journal*, 3 and 10 January 1987.

24 See Karel G. van Wolferen, 'The Japan problem', *Foreign Affairs*, winter 1986–7.

25 *New Economic Growth to Promote an Expanding Equilibrium*, Report of the Economic Council, Economic Planning Agency, Government of Japan, December 1985, pp. 48–9.

26 Motono Moriyuki, 'World trade issues require more than a piecemeal approach', *World Economy*, vol. 7, no. 3, September 1984, p. 234.

27 See Ronald A. Morse, 'Japan's drive to pre-eminence', *Foreign Policy*, winter 1987–8, and Ezra F. Vogel, 'Pax Nipponica?', *Foreign Affairs*, spring 1986.

28 E. Stuart Kirby, *Japan's Economic Future*, in the United Kingdom Paper no. 1, presented to the Institute of Pacific Relations, Tenth Conference, Stratford-upon-Avon, 1947, Royal Institute of International Affairs, September 1947, p. 3.

29 Robert D. Putnam and Nicholas Bayne, *Hanging Together: the Seven-power Summits* (Heinemann, for the Royal Institute of International Affairs, London, 1984), p. 163.

30 The Advisory Group on Economic Structural Adjustment for International Harmony (chairman: Maekawa Haruo) proposed a reduction of the surplus as a national policy goal to be achieved through: (1) expansion of domestic demand; (2) adjustment of the

industrial structure; (3) improved access to the Japanese market and expansion of manufactured goods; (4) stabilization of currencies and the internationalization of the yen; and (5) expansion of economic co-operation efforts.

31 *Economic Survey of Japan, 1986–7*, Economic Planning Agency, Government of Japan.
32 *Asahi Shimbun*, 4 January 1988.
33 Morse, 'Japan's drive to pre-eminence', p. 16.
34 Kondo Tetsuo, on the occasion of the announcement of the fiscal 1987 Annual Economic Report, 18 August 1987.
35 Motono, 'World trade issues', p. 236.
36 Vogel, 'Pax Nipponica?', p. 767.
37 Jean-Pierre Lehmann, 'Agenda for action on issues in Euro-Japanese relations', *World Economy*, vol. 7, no. 3, September 1984, pp. 273–4.
38 Morse, 'Japan's drive to pre-eminence', p. 21.
39 Wolf Mendl, *Western Europe and Japan between the Superpowers* (Croom Helm, London, 1984), p. 133.
40 *Times*, 20 June 1980; Guido Gravoglio, 'From Rambouillet to Williamsburg: A Historical Assessment', Cesare Merlini (ed.), in *Economic Summits and Western Decision-making* (Croom Helm, London, 1984), p. 23.
41 Satoh 'Western security', p. 82.
42 ibid., p. 88.
43 *Diplomatic Blue Book*, 1985 edition, p. 117.
44 C. Fred Bergsten, E. Davignon, and I. Miyazaki, *Conditions for Partnership in International Economic Management*, Report to the Trilateral Commission: 32 (New York, 1986), p. 46.
45 WIDER Study Group Series, no. 2, 7 May 1987. It consists of three parts: the rationale for substantial transfers, the scale and impact of a five-year plan of substantial transfers from Japan, and the mechanisms for implementing a programme of substantial transfer from Japan.
46 Lee Poh Ping 'Japan's aid programme comes under scrutiny', *Far Eastern Economic Review*, 3 September 1987.

8 The rise of a new power centre

1 C.R. Boxer, *The Christian Century in Japan* (Cambridge University Press, Cambridge, 1951), p. 14.
2 Arnold J. Toynbee, *Survey of International Affairs: 1920–1923* (Royal Institute of International Affairs, London, 1925), pp. 418–19. Toynbee pointed out that 'while Europe had been preoccupied with the War of 1914, the Pacific and its shores had become a theatre of world affairs, and, in the first scene played on this stage under the new conditions, the leading role had been assumed by Japan'.
3 R.D. Hill (ed.), *Southeast Asia: Systematic Geography* (Oxford University Press, Oxford, 1979), p. 154.
4 Goh Keng Swee, *The Economics of Modernization* (Asia Pacific Press, Singapore, 1972), p. 3.

5 Watanabe Akio, 'From the Old Triangle to a New Crescent? Southeast Asia in the US–Japanese Relations in the early post-war years', paper presented to a conference on Japan–US relations (Hawaii, January 1984), p. 7.

6 ibid., p. 8.

7 J.S. Furnival, *Netherlands India: a Study of Plural Economy* (Cambridge University Press, Cambridge, 1944), pp. 432–3.

8 Ian Nish, 'The Greater East Asian Co-prosperity Sphere', in Keith Nielson and Roy Prete, (eds), *Coalition Warfare: Uneasy Accord* (Wilfrid Laurier University Press, Waterloo, Ontario, 1983), p. 132.

9 John Bastin and Harry J. Benda, *A History of Modern Southeast Asia* (Prentice-Hall of Australia, Sydney, 1977), p. 109.

10 Endymion Wilkinson, *Japan versus Europe* (Penguin Books, Harmondsworth, 1983), p. 145.

11 John W. Dower, *Empire and Aftermath: Yoshida Shigeru and the Japanese Experience, 1878–1954* (Harvard University Press, Cambridge, Mass., 1979), p. 421.

12 Robert Hull, 'European Community–ASEAN relations: a model for international partnership?', *Asian Affairs*, February 1984, p. 25.

13 Nish, 'The Greater East Asian Co-prosperity Sphere', p. 131. Nish referred to a European analogy of a region-wide economic sphere: Napoleon used this in his Continental System, which had appealed to the self-interest of the merchant communities throughout Europe and had been one of the morale-boosting tactics he used to claim Europe for France during the Napoleonic wars.

14 Kojima Kiyoshi, *Japan and a New World Economic Order* (Croom Helm, London, 1977), p. 168.

15 ibid., p. 181.

16 Derek Davies, 'Exploiting the Pacific tide', *Far Eastern Economic Review*, 21 December 1979.

17 Saeki Kiichi, 'Outlook for a Pacific Era', speech delivered at the Pacific Energy Conference in Tokyo on 6 March 1987.

18 *International Herald Tribune*, 19 May 1982.

19 Dick Wilson, 'Is the Pacific community a sunken dream?', *Straits Times*, 20 May 1982.

20 Richard Nations, 'Pax Pacifica: the Reagasone Prosperity Plan', *Far Eastern Economic Review*, 14 July 1983.

21 *Daily Yomiuri*, 17 January 1985.

22 Robert Delfs, 'ASEAN is the key to Pacific progress, China believes', *Far Eastern Economic Review*, 14 July 1983.

23 *Asia-Pacific Report: Trends, Issues, Challenges* (East–West Center, Hawaii, 1987–8), p. 67.

24 Saeki, 'Outlook for a Pacific Era'.

25 *Economist*, 25 October 1986.

26 Shinohara Miyohei, 'Global Adjustment and the Future of the Asian-Pacific Economies', draft paper presented to IDE–APDC conference, Tokyo, May 1988.

27 Aoki Takeshi, 'Changes help Japan, Pacific-rim NICs', *Japan*

Economic Journal, 25 October 1986.

28 ibid.
29 *Asia-Pacific Report*, p. 38.
30 ibid., p. 40.
31 ibid., p. 40.
32 *Japan Times*, 26 October 1987.
33 Tanino Sakutaro, 'Japan and the United States: partnership in East Asian peace and progress', in *US–Japan Relations: New Attitudes for a New Era*, Annual Review 1983–84 (Harvard University), p. 196.
34 Murata Ryohei, 'Political relations between the United States and Western Europe: their implications for Japan', *International Affairs*, vol. 64, no. 1, winter 1987–8, p. 9.
35 *International Herald Tribune*, 11 March 1987.
36 See Robert C. Horn, 'US–ASEAN Relations in the 1980s', paper presented to the Seminar on South-east Asian Politics in the 1980s II, held at Universiti Kebangsaan Malaysia, 16–18 March 1984.
37 Richard Nations, 'Peace, pride and the rise to world power', *Far Eastern Economic Review*, 20 March 1986.
38 Brian Bridges, *Korea and the West*, Chatham House Papers 33 (Routledge & Kegan Paul for the Royal Institute of International Affairs, London, 1986), p. 89.
39 Nations, 'Peace, pride and the rise to world power'.
40 Prime Minister Nakasone's remarks quoted in 'Pacific Basin co-operation and the EC', *Press and Information Service*, Delegation of the Commission of the European Community in Japan, Tokyo, 3 December 1984.

9 The ASEAN dialogue: regionalism at work

1 J.S. Furnival, *Netherlands India: a Study of a Plural Economy* (Cambridge University Press, Cambridge, 1944), p. 2.
2 Chia Lin Sien and Colin MacAndrews, (eds), *Southeast Asian Seas: Frontier for Development* (McGraw-Hill International, Singapore, 1981), pp. 307–9. This concept is originally defined as one of national unity and security concern to Indonesia, in controlling 'internal waters' so as to inhibit external material support to the frequent separatist movements in the archipelago.
3 Alison Broinowski (ed.), *Understanding ASEAN* (Macmillan, London, 1983), p. 116.
4 ibid., p. 124.
5 ibid., p. 120.
6 It was in the joint communiqué between Fukuda and Carter that a Japan–US statement referred explicitly to ASEAN as a regional organization for the first time, and initiated the 'support for ASEAN' policy.
7 Minister of State for External Economic Affairs Ushiba Nobuhiko visited five ASEAN countries and Burma, for the purpose of briefing them on the results of the Bonn summit.

8 Declaration of ASEAN Concord (1976) provides, in its programme of action, for 'strengthening of political solidarity by promoting the harmonization of views, co-ordinating positions and, where possible and desirable, taking common actions'.

9 James P. Sterba, 'ASEAN's members start to speak with one voice', *New York Times*, 4 May 1979.

10 Sonoda Sunao, *Sekai Nihon Ai* (Shinchosha, Tokyo, 1981), p. 150.

11 David Housego, 'Asia's prosperous five forge unexpected unity', *Financial Times*, 14 November 1979.

12 *Financial Times*, 3 July 1979.

13 ibid.

14 *Straits Times*, 26 June 1980.

15 *Sunday Times* (Singapore), 30 March 1980.

16 Tun Thin, 'Asian economies are still tied firmly to West', *Asian Wall Street Journal*, 11 December 1981.

17 Address by Prime Minister Suzuki Zenko in Bangkok, 19 January 1981.

18 ibid.

19 Kunugi Teruo, 'Setting eyes on Japan, ASEAN '81', *Asahi Shimbun*, 1 January 1981.

20 Abe Yoshimasa, 'Expectations and fears in Southeast Asia', *Yomiuri Shimbun*, 13 January 1981.

21 *Asian Wall Street Journal*, 3 December 1981.

22 Housego, 'Asia's prosperous five'.

23 ibid.

24 *Straits Times*, 24 June 1981.

25 *Financial Times*, 24 June 1981.

26 Richard Holbrooke, 'United in spite of continuing differences', *Sunday Times*, 5 April 1982.

27 Tommy Koh, 'ASEAN – respected by friend and foe', *Sunday Times* (Singapore), 1 October 1982.

28 Saito Shiro, 'Agenda for ASEAN', *Nihon Keizai Shimbun*, 30 and 31 December 1982.

10 The broadening agenda

1 Address by Prime Minister Nakasone Yasuhiro in Kuala Lumpur, 9 May 1983.

2 *Asian Wall Street Journal*, 28 April 1983.

3 *International Herald Tribune*, 28 June 1983.

4 *Straits Times*, 5 July 1984.

5 *Straits Times*, 14 July 1984.

6 *Straits Times*, 5 July 1984.

7 *Financial Times*, 6 April 1985.

8 *Observer Verbatim Service*, 4 April 1985.

9 *Times*, 16 April 1985.

10 Don Oberdorfer, 'ASEAN sways Shultz on Cambodian peace talks', *Washington Post*, 12 July 1985.

11 *Nihon Keizai Shimbun*, 11 July 1985.
12 *Times*, 10 July 1985.
13 *Times*, 13 July 1985.
14 *Straits Times*, 10 October 1985.
15 *Asahi Shimbun*, 3 May 1986.
16 Tara Chin, 'Concern for developing nations urged', *Japan Times*, 6 May 1986.
17 *Straits Times*, 23 June 1986.
18 Shada Islam, 'EC keen to invest more in ASEAN', *Straits Times*, 5 October 1986.
19 *Straits Times*, 23 June 1986.
20 *Straits Times*, 16 June 1987.
21 *Straits Times*, 12 June 1987.
22 *Japan Times*, 19 June 1987.
23 *Japan Times* 19 June 1987.
24 *Straits Times*, 24 June 1987.
25 Stuart Harris and Brian Bridges, *European Interests in ASEAN*, Chatham House Papers 19 (Routledge & Kegan Paul for the Royal Institute of International Affairs, London, 1983), pp. 80–1.
26 *International Herald Tribune*, 13 June 1987.
27 Quotations are from the remarks made respectively by Lee Kuan Yew and Suharto, *Straits Times*, 15 December 1987.
28 The number of items covered under Preferential Trade Agreement increased from 12,647 in June 1986 to 18,922 by October 1987. The estimated trade increases due to the new scheme would be the highest at 4.05 per cent for Indonesia and the lowest at 0.05 per cent for Singapore. Adapted from Thamavit Terdudomtham, '*The Effects of Intra-ASEAN Tariff Preference: 1978–1985*', Thamasat University, Bangkok, January 1988.
29 Snoh Unakl, address at the 1987 Annual Conference of Thai Economists held in Bangkok, 19–20 December 1987.
30 Rodney Tasker, 'Eighteen-minute solidarity', *Far Eastern Economic Review*, 24 December 1987.
31 *Straits Times*, 19 December 1987.
32 *Far Eastern Economic Review*, 24 December 1987.
33 Michael Leifer, *Indonesia's Foreign Policy* (Allen & Unwin, for the Royal Institute of International Affairs, London, 1983), pp. 180–1.
34 John Pedler, 'Kampuchea and peace prospects in Indochina', *The World Today*, vol. 43, no. 10, October 1987, p. 176.
35 Remarks made by Lee Kuan Yew in the exclusive interview with *Nihon Keizai Shimbun*, 12 January 1988. As to the observations on ASEAN's attitude to Japan, see Nishihara Masashi, 'Southeast Asia beyond Cambodia', paper presented in a conference of the Japan Institute of International Affairs, 3–4 March 1988.
36 Singapore Foreign Minister Dhanabalan's remark, *Straits Times*, 4 July 1988.
37 *Straits Times*, 5 July 1988.
38 *Times*, 5 July 1988.

39 *New York Times*, 10 July 1988.
40 *Asian Wall Street Journal*, 6 July 1988.
41 *Straits Times*, 9 July 1988.
42 *New York Times*, 9 July 1988.
43 *Straits Times*, 2 July 1988.

11 The way forward

 1 Stuart Kirby, 'Toward economic co-operation in the Pacific Basin',
    Asian Affairs, February 1985.
 2 *South China Morning Post*, 25 May 1985.
 3 Matsumoto Hiroshi and Noordin Sopiee (eds), *Into the Pacific Era:*
    Southeast Asia and its Place in the Pacific (Association for Promotion
    of International Co-operation, Japan, and Institute of Strategic and
    International Studies, Malaysia, 1984), p. 4.
 4 *SOVNAPEC Newsletter*, vol. 1, no. 1, Moscow, May 1988, p. 6.
 5 Summary Statement of the Standing Committee of the Sixth Pacific Co-
    operation Conference, Osaka, 17–20 May 1988.
 6 ibid.
 7 The policy recommendations on 'The Structural Adjustment of the
    Economies of Japan, US and Asian NICs', Japan Forum on
    International Relations Inc., March 1988, p. 31.
 8 ibid., p. 24.
 9 Murray Seeger, 'A new trading order is slowly taking shape', *Straits*
    Times, 3 March 1988.
10 Bernard K. Gordon, 'Truth in trading', *Foreign Policy*, no. 61, winter
    1985–6.
11 Willy De Clercq, 'The United States and the European Community:
    brothers yet foes?', *European Affairs*, no. 1, spring 1987.
12 This scenario is partly based on the policy recommendations made by
    the Japan Forum on International Relations, op. cit. Authors include
    Okita Saburo, Amaya Naohiro, Iida Tsuneo, and Watanabe Toshio.
13 'Beyond VJ Day', *Times*, 15 August 1985.
14 Dick Wilson, *The Sun at Noon: an Anatomy of Modern Japan* (Hamish
    Hamilton, London, 1986), p. 209.
15 Lee Kuan Yew's remarks at the various occasions of press conferences
    at the National Press Club in Washington in October 1985 and Nihon
    Kisha Club in Tokyo in October 1986.
16 *Far Eastern Economic Review*, 14 July 1983.
17 Pierre-Noel Giraud, 'Japan at the turning point', *Futures*, February
    1987.
18 Richard Cooper, 'Nation's role foreign aid, free trade leader', *Japan*
    Economic Journal, 17 January 1987.

Bibliography

Allen, Charles (ed.). *Tales from the South China Seas: Images of the British in Southeast Asia in the Twentieth Century*, Futura, London, 1983.

Allen, Louis. *The End of the War in Asia*, Beekman/Esanu, New York, 1979.

Amaya Naohiro. 'Nation must back up values, Constitution', *Japan Economic Journal*, 31 January 1987.

Aoki Takeshi. *Taiheiyo Seicho no Toraianguru* ('The Growth Triangle in the Pacific: Structural Adjustment between Japan, the United States and Asian NICs'), Nihon Hyoron-sha, Tokyo, 1987.

Barnds, William (ed.). *Japan and the United States: Challenges and Opportunities*, Macmillan, London, 1980.

Barnett, R.W. *Beyond War: Japan's Concept of Comprehensive National Security*, Pergamon-Brassey, Washington, 1984.

Baylis, John. *Anglo-American Defence Relations, 1939–1984*, Macmillan, London, 1984; in Japanese translation, *Domei no Rikigaku*, Toyo Keizai Shinpo-sha, Tokyo, 1988.

Beedham, Brian. 'A Special Strength: Survey of Japan', *Economist*, 31 March 1973.

Braddon, Russell. *The Other 100 Years War: Japan's Bid for Supremacy, 1941–2041*, Collins, London, 1983.

Bridges, Brian. *Korea and the West*, Chatham House Papers 33, Routledge & Kegan Paul, for the Royal Institute of International Affairs, London, 1986.

Broinowski, Alison (ed.). *Understanding ASEAN*, Macmillan, London, 1982.

Buckley, Roger. *Occupation Diplomacy: Britain, the United States and Japan, 1945–1952*, Cambridge University Press, Cambridge, 1982.

Chapman, J.W.M., Drifte, R., and Gow, I.T.M. *Japan's Quest for Comprehensive Security*, Pinter, London, 1983.

Chen Qimao. *Taiheiyo Kyodotai to Higashi-Ajia* ('The Pacific Community and East Asia'), presented to a symposium of Waseda University, Tokyo, October 1985.

Chia Lin Sien and MacAndrews, Colin. *Southeast Asia Seas: Frontiers for Development*, Institute of Southeast Asian Studies, Singapore, 1981.

Chin Kin Wah. *The Defence of Malaysia and Singapore: the Transformation of a Security System, 1957–1971*, Cambridge University Press, Cambridge, 1983.

Cortazzi, Hugh. *Higashi no Shimaguni Nishi no Shimaguni* ('The Island Countries in East and West'), Chuo Koronsha, Tokyo, 1984.

Curtis, Gerald. *The Japanese Way of Politics*; in Japanese translation, *Nihongata Seiji no Honshitsu*, TBS Buritanica, Tokyo, 1987.

Darby, Phillip. *Three Faces of Imperialism: British and American Approaches to Asia and Africa, 1870–1970*, Yale University Press, New Haven, 1987.

Dore, Ronald. *Taking Japan Seriously: a Confucian Perspective on Leading Economic Issues*, Athlone, London, 1987.

—— 'Neo-mercantilism clouds trade issue', *Japan Economic Journal*, 11 April 1987.

Dower, J.W. *Empire and Aftermath: Yoshida Shigeru and the Japanese Experience, 1878–1954*, Harvard University Press, Cambridge, Mass., 1979.

Downen, R.L., and Dickson, B.J. *The Emerging Pacific Community: a Regional Perspective*, Westview Press, London, 1984.

Drifte, Reinhard. 'The European Community and Japan: beyond the economic dimension', *Journal of International Affairs*, vol. 37, no. 1, 1983.

Drucker, Peter F. 'Japan's choices', *Foreign Affairs*, summer 1987.

Eguchi Yujiro and Usui Tsutomu. *Kan Taiheiyoken no Jidai* ('An Age of Pacific Basin'), Aki Shobo, Tokyo, 1988.

Eto Shinkichi, 'Evolving Sino-Japanese relations', in Joshua Katz and Tilly Friedman-Lichtschein (eds), *Japan's New World Role*, Westview Press, London, 1985.

Freedman, Lawrence (ed.). *The Troubled Alliance: Atlantic Relations in the 1980s*, Heinemann, for the Royal Institute of International Affairs, London, 1983.

Funabashi, Yoichi. *Managing the Dollar: from the Plaza to the Louvre*, Institute of International Economics, Washington, 1988.

—— *Sumitto no Shiso* ('A Thought of the Summits'), Asahi Shimbun-sha, Tokyo, 1980.

Furnivall, J.S. *Netherlands India: a Study of Plural Economy*, Cambridge University Press, Cambridge, 1944.

Giraud, Pierre-Noel, and Godet, Michel. *Radioscope du Japon*, Economica, Paris, 1987.

Goh Keng Swee. *The Economics of Development*, Asia Pacific Press, Singapore, 1972.

Gorbachev, Mikhail. *Perestroika: New Thinking for our Country and the World*, Collins, London, 1987.

Hanabusa Masamichi. *Trade Problems between Japan and Western Europe*, Saxon House, for the Royal Institute of International Affairs, Westmead, 1979.

Harris, Stuart, and Bridges, Brian. *European Interests in ASEAN*, Chatham House Papers 19, Routledge & Kegan Paul, for the Royal Institute of

International Affairs, London 1983.

Higgott, Richard, and Robison, Richard (eds). *Southeast Asia: Essays in the Political Economy of Structural Change*, Routledge & Kegan Paul, Melbourne, 1985.

Hooper, Paul F. *Building a Pacific Community*, East–West Center, Honolulu, 1982.

Hosoya Chihiro (ed.). *Nichi-ei Kankei-shi 1917–1949* ('A History of Anglo-Japanese Relations'), Tokyo University Press, Tokyo, 1982.

Howe, Geoffrey. *East–West Relations: Realism, Vigilance and Open Mind*, prepared for the Foreign and Commonwealth Office by the Central Office of Information, 1987.

Inoguchi Takashi. *Kokusai kankei no Seiji Keizai-gaku*, ('The Political Economy of International Relations'), Tokyo University Press, Tokyo, 1985.

Institut du Pacifique, *Le Pacifique, 'Nouveau Centre du Monde'*, Berger-Levrault, Paris, 1983.

Institute of Strategic and International Studies (ISIS), Malaysia. *ASEAN at the Crossroads: Obstacles, Options and Opportunities in Economic Co-operation*, Kuala Lumpur, 1987.

—— *Crisis and Response: the Challenge to South–South Economic Co-operation*, Kuala Lumpur, 1988.

Jansen, Marius B. *Japan and its World: Two Centuries of Change*, Princeton University Press, Princeton, 1980.

Japan Center for International Exchange and Japan Society. *Report of the Seventh Shimoda Conference*, Oiso, 1987.

Japan, International Development Co-operation Study Group. *Toward a New Perspective for International Co-operation*, Tokyo, July 1987.

Japan National Committee for Pacific Economic Co-operation Conference. *Nijyuisseiki no Taiheiyo Kyoryoku* ('Pacific Co-operation towards the 21st Century'), Jiji Press, Tokyo, 1988.

Kennedy, Paul. *The Rise and Fall of the Great Powers: Economic Change and Military Conflict from 1500 to 2000*, Random House, New York, 1987.

—— *The Realities behind Diplomacy: Background Influences on British External Policy, 1865–1980*, Fontana, London, 1981.

Kissinger, Henry A. *American Foreign Policy: Three Essays*, Norton, New York, 1969.

Kosaka Masataka. *Kokusai Masatsu: Taikoku Nihon no Yowatari Gaku* ('International Friction: Japan's Worldly Wisdom'), Toyo Keizai Shinpo-sha, Tokyo, 1987.

—— *Saisho Yoshida Shigeru* ('Premier Yoshida Shigeru'), Chuo Koron-sha, Tokyo, 1968.

Lau Teik Soon. 'Defence expenditure of ASEAN states: the regional strategic context', in *Defence Spending in Southeast Asia*, Institute of Southeast Asian Studies, Singpore, 1987.

Lehmann, Jean-Pierre. 'Agenda for action on issues in Euro-Japanese relations', *World Economy*, vol. 7, no. 3, September 1984, pp. 257–76.

Leifer, Michael. *Indonesia's Foreign Policy*, Allen & Unwin for the Royal

Institute of International Affairs, London, 1983.

—— *Conflict and Regional Order in Southeast Asia*, Adelphi Paper no. 162, International Institute for Strategic Studies, London, 1980.

Lim Chong-Yah (ed.). *Learning from the Japanese Experience*, Maruzen Asia, Singapore, 1982.

Maekawa Report. *Economic Structural Adjustment for International Harmony*, submitted to Prime Minister Nakasone, April 1986.

Matsumoto Hiroshi and Noordin Sopiee (eds). *Into the Pacific Era: Southeast Asia and its Place in the Pacific*, Institute of Strategic and International Studies, Malaysia, Kuala Lumpur, 1984.

Mendl, Wolf. *Western Europe and Japan between the Superpowers*, Croom Helm, London, 1984.

Merlini, Cesare (ed.). *Economic Summits and Western Decision-making*, Croom Helm, with European Institute of Public Administration, London, 1984.

Mori Kazuko. 'Ajia-Taiheiyo ni Mukau Chugoku no Me' ('China Looks Asian-Pacific'), *Kokusai Mondai*, February 1986.

Morris, James. *Pax Britannica: the Climax of an Empire*, Penguin Books, London, 1979.

Morrison, Charles E., and Suhrke, Astri. *Strategies of Survival: the Foreign Policy Dilemma of Smaller Asian States*, University of Queensland Press, Queensland, 1978.

Morse, Ronald A. 'Japan's drive to pre-eminence', *Foreign Policy*, winter 1987–8.

Motono Moriyuki. 'World trade issues require more than a piecemeal approach', *World Economy*, vol. 7, no. 3, September 1984.

Murata Ryohei. 'Political relations between the United States and Western Europe: their implication for Japan', *International Affairs*, winter 1987–8.

Nagai Yonosuke. *Reisen no Kigen: Sengo Ajia no Kokusai Kankyo* ('Origins of the Cold War: the International Environment of Post-war Asia'), Chuo Koron-sha, Tokyo, 1978.

—— *Gendai to Senryaku* ('Our Times and Strategy'), Bungei Shunjyu, 1985.

Nakatani Iwao. *Bodaresu Economi: Sakoku Kokka Nihon eno Keisho* ('The Borderless Economy: Alarm for Japan's National Isolation'), Nihon Keizai Shimbun-sha, Tokyo, 1987.

Naya Seiji. 'The Private Sector as a new Engine of Growth: Implications for the Asia-Pacific', unpublished paper presented to the Japan Institute of International Affairs Conference, Tokyo, March 1988.

Nish, Ian (ed.). *Anglo-Japanese Alienation, 1919–1952: Papers of the Anglo-Japanese Conference on the History of the Second World War*, Cambridge University Press, Cambridge, 1982.

Nishihara Masashi. *East Asian Security and Trilateral Countries*, Report to the Trilateral Commission: 30, New York University Press, New York 1985.

Nixon, Richard. *Real Peace*, Sidgwick & Jackson, London, 1983.

Ohmae Kenichi. *Toriado Pawa: Nijyuisseiki no Kokusai Kigyo Senryaku* ('Triad Power: International Business Strategy towards the 21st Century'), Kodansha, Tokyo, 1985.

Okawara Yoshio. *Koritsuka wo Sakerutameni* ('To Keep Clear of Isolation'), Sekai no Ugoki-sha, Tokyo, 1985.

Okazaki Hisahiko. *Kokka to Joho: Nihon no Gaiko Senryaku wo Motomete* ('The State and Information: in Search of Japan's Strategy'), Bungei Shunju, Tokyo, 1980.

—— 'Magarikado no Nichibei Domei' ('A Turning Point of the Japan-US Alliance'), *Chuo Koron*, July 1988.

Okita Saburo. *Japan's Challenging Years: Reflections on my Lifetime*, Australia–Japan Research Centre, Australia National University, Canberra, 1983.

—— *Economisuto Gaisho no 252 Nichi* ('252 days of the "Economist" Foreign Minister'), Toyo Keizai Shinpo-sha, Tokyo, 1980.

Owen, David, Brzezinski, Zbigniew, and Okita Saburo. *Democracy must Work*, A Task Force Report to the Trilateral Commission, New York University Press, New York, 1984.

Ozaki, Robert S., and Arnold, Walter (eds.). *Japan's Foreign Relations: a Global Search for Economic Security*, Westview Press, London, 1985.

Pacific Economic Co-operation Conference. *Pacific Economic Outlook: Dynamism and Adjustment*, summary statement of the Standing Committee of the Sixth Pacific Economic Co-operation Conference, Osaka, May 1988.

Patrick, Hugh, and Rosovsky, Henry (eds.). *Asia's New Giant: How the Japanese Economy Works*, Brookings Institution, Washington DC, 1976.

Peterson, Peter G. 'A New Pacific Compact', paper prepared for the joint meeting of Keidanren and Atlantic Institute, Tokyo, April 1987.

Prasert Chittiwatanapong. 'Japan's Role in the Asia-Pacific Region: The Political Dimension', unpublished paper presented to the Japan Institute of International Affairs Conference, Tokyo, March 1988.

Putnam, Robert D., and Bayne, Nicholas. *Hanging Together: the Seven-power Summits*, Heinemann, for the Royal Institute of International Affairs, London, 1984.

Randolph, R. Sean. 'Pacific overtures', *Foreign Policy*, winter 1984–5.

Rosovsky, Henry (ed.). *Discord in the Pacific: Challenges to the Japanese-American Alliance*, Columbia Books, Washington, 1972.

Saeki Kiichi. 'Outlook for a Pacific Era', unpublished paper delivered at the Pacific Energy Co-operation Conference, Tokyo, March 1987.

Saito Shiro. *Tenkanki no Sekai-zo* ('The World Image in Transition'), Asahi Shobo, Tokyo, 1972.

Sakamoto Masahiro. *Pakkusu Americana no Kokusai Shisutemu* ('The International System of Pax Americana'), Yuhikaku, Tokyo, 1986.

Sato Seizaburo. 'Japan's Politico-military Role in the Asian Pacific Region', unpublished paper presented to Japan Institute of International Affairs Conference, Tokyo, March 1988.

Satoh Yukio. 'Western security: a Japanese point of view', *Naval War College Review*, September-October 1983.

Scalapino, Robert A. *Asia and the Road Ahead: Issues for the Major Powers*, University of California Press, Berkeley, 1975.

Schmidt, Helmut. *A Grand Strategy for the West*, Yale University Press, New Haven, 1985.

Segal, Gerald (ed.). *The Soviet Union in East Asia: Predicaments of Power*, Heinemann, for the Royal Institute of International Affairs, London, 1983.

Shibusawa Masahide. *Japan and the Asian Pacific Region: Profile of Change*, Croom Helm, for the Royal Institute of International Affairs, London, 1984; in Japanese translation, *Nihon wa Ajia Ka*, Simul Press, Tokyo, 1985.

Sinha, Radha. *Japan's Options for the 1980s*, Croom Helm, London, 1982.

Sonoda Sunao. *Sekai Nihon Ai* ('The World, Japan and Affection'), Shincho-sha, Tokyo, 1986.

Sopiee, Noordin. 'Kampuchea: the Way Forward', unpublished paper presented to the Third Malaysia-Japan Colloquium, Kuala Lumpur, June 1988.

Soviet National Committee for Asia-Pacific Economic Co-operation. *SOVNAPEC Newsletter*, vol. 1, no. 1, May 1988.

Spero, Joan, E. *The Politics of International Economic Relations*, St Martin's Press, New York, 1985; in Japanese translation, *Kokusai Keizai Kankeiron*, Toyo Keizai Shinpo-sha, Tokyo, 1988.

Steel, Ronald. *The End of Alliance: America and the Future of Europe*, Viking Press, New York, 1964.

Stockwin, J.A.A. *Japan: Divided Politics in a Growth Economy*, Weidenfeld & Nicolson, London, 1982.

Tanaka Toshiro. 'Oshu Giteisho to Ekinai Shijo' ('The Single European Act and the internal market'), *Kokusai Mondai*, July 1988.

Tanino Sakutaro. 'Japan and the United States: Partnership in East Asia', in *Annual Review 1983–84*, Center for International Relations, Harvard University.

Thorne, Christopher. *The Issue of War, States, Societies, and the Far Eastern Conflict of 1941–1945*, Hamish Hamilton, London, 1985.

Tokuyama Jiro. *Taiheiyo no Seiki* ('The Pacific Century'), Diamond, Tokyo, 1978.

Turner, Louis. *Industrial Collaboration with Japan*, Chatham House Papers: 34, Routledge & Kegan Paul, for the Royal Institute of International Affairs, London, 1987.

United States–Japan Advisory Commission. *Challenges and Opportunities in United States–Japan Relations*, report submitted to the President of the United States and the Prime Minister of Japan, September 1984.

Urata Masutaro. 'Japan's Market Structure and Industrial Policy in International Trade', in *Annual Review 1983–84*, Center for International Relations, Harvard University.

Vasil, Raj K. *Governing Singapore*, Eastern Universities Press, Singapore, 1984.

Vogel, Ezra F. 'Pax Nipponica?', *Foreign Affairs*, spring 1986.

Wallace, William. 'What price independence? Sovereignty and interdependence in British politics', *International Affairs*, summer 1986.

Watanabe Akio. 'From the Old Triangle to a New Great Crescent?

Southeast Asia in US-Japanese Relations in the Early Post-war Years', unpublished paper prepared for the US-Japanese Relations from 1950 to 1980 Conference, Hawaii, January 1984.

—— (ed.). *Sengo Nihon no Taigai Seisaki* ('Postwar Japan's External Policy'), Yuhikaku, Tokyo, 1985.

Watanabe Toshio (ed.). *The Policy Recommendations on the Structural Adjustment of Economies of Japan, US, and Asian NICs*, Japan Forum on International Relations, Tokyo, March 1988.

Wilkinson, Endymion. *Japan versus Europe: a History of Misunderstanding*, Penguin Books, London, 1983.

Williams, Phil. 'The limits of American power: from Nixon to Reagan', *International Affairs*, autumn 1987.

Wilson, Dick. *The Sun at Noon: an Anatomy of Modern Japan*, Hamish Hamilton, London, 1986.

Wolferen, Karel G. van. 'The Japan problem', *Foreign Affairs*, winter 1986–7.

Wong, John. *ASEAN Economy in Perspective: a Comparative Study of Indonesia, Malaysia, the Philippines, Singapore and Thailand*, Macmillan, London, 1979.

—— *The Political Economy of China's Changing Relations with Southeast Asia*, Macmillan, London, 1984.

Yano Toru. *Nihon no Nanshin to Tonan-Ajia* ('Japan's Southern Advance and South-east Asia'), Nihon Keizai Shimbun-sha, Tokyo, 1975.

—— *Reisen to Tonan-Ajia* ('The Cold War and South-east Asia'), Chuo Koron-sha, Tokyo, 1986.

Yoshida Shigeru. *Kaiso Jyunen* ('Reflections on the Ten Years'), Shincho-sha, Tokyo, 1957.

—— *Japan's Decisive Century 1867–1967*, Frederick A. Praeger, for Encyclopaedia Britannica, New York, 1967.

Zakaria Haji Ahmad. 'Obstacles to Greater pan-Pacific Cooperation: a View from ASEAN', in *Into the Pacific Era*, ISIS Malaysia, Kuala Lumpur, 1986.

Index